YOUTH AND THE ETHERIC HEART

RUDOLF STEINER (1923)

YOUTH AND THE ETHERIC HEART

Rudolf Steiner Speaks to the Younger Generation

Addresses, Essays, Discussions, and Reports
1920–1924

TRANSLATED BY CATHERINE E. CREEGER

INTRODUCTION BY CHRISTOPHER BAMFORD

RUDOLF STEINER

SteinerBooks

CW 217a

SteinerBooks
Anthropososophic Press

402 Main Street No. 58
Hudson, New York 12534
www.steinerbooks.org

Original translation from the German by Catherine E. Creeger.

This book is volume 179 in the Collected Works (CW) of Rudolf Steiner, published by SteinerBooks, 2007. This translation has been updated by Marsha Post according to the German *Geschichtliche Notwendigkeit und Freiheit: Schicksalseinwirkungen aus der Welt der Toten* published by Rudolf Steiner Verlag, Dornach, Switzerland, 1993.

ISBN: 978-0-88010-614-6

Printed in the United States

CONTENTS

Addresses Given in 1923

Essays on the Youth Section of the Independent School of Spiritual Science

Addresses Given in 1924

Appendix

INTRODUCTION

CHRISTOPHER BAMFORD

Youth and the Etheric Heart, which comes to twenty-first-century readers in the somewhat deceptive wrapping of a historical documentation of Rudolf Steiner's addresses to young people during the years 1920–1924, is, at least for those concerned with the future of Anthroposophy or with the future of spiritual life generally, one of the more extraordinary and prophetic volumes in his collected works.

In it, readers will find the mission, the task, and even the path of Anthroposophy expressed in a very different way than they are used to. Addressing passionately committed, socially active young people who were on fire with the ideal of service and of transforming human consciousness into something whole, healthy, and spiritually oriented in a profoundly universal way, Rudolf Steiner was able—perhaps for the first time—to state in the clearest, most accessible, ordinary language the new way of knowing and being that he was trying to bring into the world in service to the Archangel Michael. What we have here, then, are nothing less than new "seeds"—a second planting. To understand them, however, some background is in order.

The First World War ended on November 11, 1918. Less than four months later, on March 5, 1919, Rudolf Steiner's "Appeal to the German People and Culture" appeared in newspapers all over Germany and was widely distributed in booklet form. In it, Steiner voiced what many others felt: to rebuild society would take a completely new kind of thinking. Old thinking and old institutions simply would not do: the carnage and devastation of the last four years had showed how bankrupt they were.

The new approach that Steiner proposed was "threefolding" the social organism. By this, he meant separating on the basis of their own, specific natures the three fundamental elements of social life—the economic, the judicial-political, and the cultural—and making each independent, so that they could then interact, obviously interdependently, but with each performing its own particular function, just as the various organs of the body do. Steiner would dedicate the rest of his life to attempting to realize social-cultural renewal of this kind.

At the same time, he understood that such an initiative could not come out of Anthroposophy unless it, too, changed in radical ways. His last five years were dedicated to these two projects, the one outer and cultural, the other inner, esoteric, and related to the Anthroposophical Society, with which he would ultimately unite his karma. Separating them in this way, however, may be artificial—or worse, regressive. After all, in a real sense, for Steiner, the distinction between exoteric and esoteric activity no longer held any validity. To him, both projects were a spiritual necessity, called for by the spiritual world.

Practically speaking, "threefolding," as Steiner himself said, was the only viable alternative to the kind of communistic social order proposed by the Bolshevik Revolution of 1917. At the same time, it was also clear that behind the scenes Fascism (National Socialism) was already in preparation. Meanwhile Anthroposophy itself—and the Anthroposophical Society—would naturally have to change to meet these challenges. It would have to become a new kind of spiritual organization, much more open to all seekers of good intention: a contemporary mystery center from which spiritual insight and research could radiate into the culture.

With typical energy and dedication Steiner therefore worked intensely on all these fronts. Tirelessly, he spoke and wrote on the general idea of a "threefold commonwealth." He traveled the country, addressing both workers' groups and business people on the possibility of a new associative economic life. Putting theory into practice, he started businesses himself, all the while thinking about how to reorganize the Anthroposophical Society itself on threefold lines. Simultaneously, he addressed the cultural sphere by taking up in a public and practical way issues of education and religion. All these activities attracted many young people, who resonated especially with Anthroposophy's cultural mission, for they were mostly university students. Education for them was primary: without transforming it, there would be no social transformation. They knew that education builds the future.

The spiritual world clearly agreed. Within days of the war's end, as the German Revolution (which led to the Weimar Republic) was taking place, Emil Molt, a Stuttgart industrialist, was in Dornach and heard Steiner lecture on Marxism and threefolding as polar alternatives for the future. A week later, talking to someone about the problem of educating workers' children, Molt had the idea of founding a school for the children of the workers in his cigarette factory. He spoke to Rudolf Steiner about it and asked him whether he would be the adviser. Steiner agreed. Nine months later, in September 1919, the first Waldorf School opened its doors.

As important a deed as educating children for the future was, it was still only a beginning. Higher education was equally if not more important. It was there, finally, that the scientific, epistemological, and cultural paradigms were established and where any new paradigm would emerge. Not surprisingly, then, in 1920 Steiner turned toward the universities and the professions.

That year the first "Medical Course" was held. Steiner lectured on the "boundaries of modern science" and "Anthroposophy and the different branches of learning." A "Union for Anthroposophical College Work" was founded, and in the autumn the first Anthroposophical "College Course" was held. These new activities began to draw a new, different group of people: college students. Aspirant student philosophers, doctors, scientists, theologians, and so on began to appear at Steiner's lectures and at the Goetheanum. In the universities and colleges in Germany, Switzerland, and Austria, Anthroposophical student groups came into being.

During this time, Steiner also worked to transform Anthroposophy and the Anthroposophical Society to meet what was coming toward it. The "needs of the time" called for change. In a sense, of course, all depended on Anthroposophy's ability to meet the new challenge. During this whole period, then, as a continual background to all that was going on, a profound metamorphosis in the life of Anthroposophy and the Anthroposophical Society was also constantly in process.

This process, too, was a struggle—as great a struggle perhaps as the outer one to bring the Threefold Social Order into the world. One cannot underestimate the demands that going public involved:

Anthroposophy, for the first time, was being called upon to truly open its doors to the world.

The effect was twofold: Anthroposophy not only had to go out into the world, but it had to meet the world at home in the form of seeking young people, who were coming toward it in increasing numbers.[†] Almost without warning, what had been more or less an "esoteric school" with its roots in nineteenth-century esotericism and Theosophy was transformed into a broader movement for spiritual, social, and cultural change. Older members found themselves being asked to change: to become representatives of Anthroposophy and to translate what they had thought of as their spiritual path into public, accessible discourse. Not only was this difficult in itself, it was psychologically difficult—and often impossible—for them. After all, they were comfortable and happy with the old model—they had grown up with it. It fitted them. Thus, from the beginning a tension arose between the old and the new, a new that came above all in the form of a new generation.

Born around the turn of the century, these young people came of age as the war ended. They were the first post-Kali Yuga (post-1900) generation. They were true "Michaelites"—for the Michael Age had begun in 1879—and they brought something new. They came to Anthroposophy innocently, out of their hearts' needs, without any connection to traditional esotericism. They did not think of themselves as aspirant "occultists." Rather, they were spiritually open *activists*, practical philosophers. They wanted to be spiritual, social, scientific, cultural, and philosophical *pioneers*. They wanted to change the world and change themselves. They knew that if the old world were allowed to continue unchecked, "life as usual" would only result in further catastrophe.

Steiner welcomed them. He had been waiting for this moment, for these young people, all his life. Whatever and whoever else he was, Steiner always possessed a radical, even revolutionary side. Like those who came to him, he had no patience for conventional values and conventional thinking. Conventionality, in fact, was one of the few things that irritated him. He saw it as a symptom of a potentially fatal disease whose unthinking espousal of egotism, utility, and comfort dominated not only social and cultural life but also academic, artistic, scientific, and even religious life. And here were educated, seeking, young people who agreed with him, and who wished to make a difference with their lives. They wanted to develop spiritually *and* intellectually. They yearned to overcome the separation between everyday life and the disciplines of science, art, history, psychology, religion, and so on. They wanted learning to be *real*. They wanted spiritual, professional, and personal life to be one, a continuum, lived from the same source. Above all, they wanted life to be *whole* and saw Anthroposophy as just that: as a *holistic* way of life—self- and world-transformation in one.

In other words, they were a gift. They understood and responded to Rudolf Steiner's call. But they were also demanding. Prizing freedom and independence, they wanted to pursue the "free spiritual life" offered by Anthroposophy, but as it seemed to demand, they wanted to do it in their own way. They were not satisfied—or happy—with the mood, tenor, and spirit of the Anthroposophical Society as they found it. Very early, then, they sought to organize their own society.

The documents printed here give little indication as to what precisely was occurring behind the scenes, and unfortunately, the history of the Youth Movement in Anthroposophy still remains to be written. What is clear, however, is that the young people came with certain expectations and Rudolf Steiner was determined to meet them. For instance, during the first members' meeting of the Society after the war—held on September 4, 1921, in Stuttgart—following the vote by a student from Tübingen University, he exclaimed:

> A representative of the Youth Movement has spoken! Here sit a whole number of student representatives! My dear friends: That members of such a movement or organization have come to our Anthroposophical Society is something that we must look on as *epoch-making* in the history of our Anthroposophical Movement. We must do everything that may rightly be expected from the Anthroposophical Society.

In fact, the youth expected a great deal. They wanted to appropriate Anthroposophy *in their own way*. Already in March 1920, they had circulated a "Call for the Foundation of a Youth Branch." And in April of the same year, one of their members, Otto Palmer, made their case at the Goetheanum:

> If you want to understand this movement rightly, you must see it above all as a protest that has come alive among the youth against the old life of the branches… In fact, something in the youth feels the need not to see Anthroposophy as a mere Sunday afternoon decoration. Rather, it wants to lead what we are given in Anthroposophy into life and translate it into practice.

He concluded, directly addressing the concerns of the older members:

> [The Youth Movement and its call for its own branch] really has to do with making the attempt to realize the freedom of spiritual life insofar as this can be done within such a limited framework. For this it is worth overcoming a certain fear that still rules in this regard that a free spiritual life of this kind will awaken counterforces, which could and would make for difficulties. One can undertake such a task only if one believes that one has something living in oneself from which the powers can come that are in a position to overcome the counterforces.

This was just the beginning. In April, Ehrenfried Pfeiffer wrote:

> The work in the Youth Branch should proceed above all so that the youth can become the bearers of Anthroposophically oriented spiritual science.... If we can make our action follow our will, then the struggle against the old thinking can be taken up everywhere. If the work of the Youth Branch occurs in this way, then its outer form will come about by itself.

For the next two years (1920–1922), the struggle to establish a true working forum for the younger generation continued against rising and increasingly strident opposition from the older generation. By

1922 a turning point in orientation seemed to be called for. The fate and future of Anthroposophy appeared to hang in the balance.

That year Steiner's theme was "the Being of Anthroposophy." He undertook two major lecture tours through twelve German cities. It was exhausting. Besides the tours, he gave countless other lectures, including for the first time since the war lectures to large audiences in England and Holland. It was the last time he would do anything comparable. After 1922, he turned inward to focus more on the Society and the movement. The reason was not so much the rising chaos in Germany as that his intentions were not being actively taken up by the Society. It was, he said, "asleep." Institutions were failing; difficulties were everywhere. Even the Goetheanum had financial problems. At the same time, there was much that was positive. The Whitsun East-West Congress in Vienna was a great success. The Christian Community was founded, after a year of preparation.

And above all, there were the young people.

For them, the turning point came following the East-West Congress (June 1922) when a group came to Dornach to speak to Rudolf Steiner. He agreed to hold a large meeting for them in October. Ernst Lehrs, who wrote to Steiner to report on his travels among the youth in preparation for the meeting, said that he found everywhere a new, shared impulse. He wrote: "The insight has arisen universally and is confirmed in our circles that any attempt to work together in the consciousness-soul epoch must become a 'working alongside one another.'" Scientists, artists, philosophers, and teachers must work together to build community. Learning and teaching, education and self-education, must become one. In Berlin a group had been studying *Mystics after Modernism*. They had been struck by the chapter on the Friend of God from the Highlands and his circle of twelve. Just such a circle, Lehrs stressed, represented the deepest desire of the young.

The October meeting—the so-called Pedagogical Youth Course (*Becoming the Archangel Michael's Companions*) brought together about eighty young people between the ages of eighteen and twenty-five in Stuttgart. There were a few older people. Older members were generally not invited, which naturally increased their pain and alienation. Asked about this, Steiner replied that he did not know what the young people wanted. A few had come to see him; they had talked about everything imaginable. He had agreed to meet with them for a lecture course. What it was to be about, he had no idea. Again, older members were shocked. How could he agree to do such a thing? Steiner explained that the young people thought a rigid program was somewhat antiquated, and he completely agreed with them!

Following this course, in 1923 the reality of an independent Anthroposophical Society arose. In 1924, a section for youth was inscribed within it.

The talks and conversations surrounding these events are contained in this volume. Their implications are far-reaching and deserve the serious consideration of every thoughtful Anthroposophist.

Such, then, is the background to this extraordinary volume, which is, as stated, a volume of documentation. As such, it is intended by its editors to be supplementary to the central turning point of the movement, the 1922 Pedagogical Youth Course, published as *Becoming the Archangel Michael's Companions* (CW 217). This course can therefore be read in tandem with *Youth and the Etheric Heart.* Together, they present Steiner's vision for Anthroposophy as he hoped it would permeate culture through young people able to take it up as a spiritual, intellectual, and socially transforming path. From this point of view, it is as relevant today as it was eighty years ago. What we have before us, therefore, is a prophetic document.

It opens without fanfare, but with deep implications. Steiner begins by addressing academic work and the sorry condition of the universities. These have been taken over by materialism. They no longer recognize the true purpose of education—namely, the search for knowledge and truth. But by their nature, truth and knowledge are individual and those seeking them should be given freedom. Then as now, however, the universities were monolithically and homogenously materialist. Enthusiasm, idealism, and any kind of originality or spiritual objective were forbidden. Nevertheless, the universities and their intellectual work are fundamental. Therefore, they must be transformed. Not only real social change depends upon them, but also and above all the possibility of the spiritualizing of culture: the returning of humanity to a spiritual perspective. But this can only happen—and this is why Steiner is addressing young people—if those students who are spiritually motivated or are Anthroposophists *engage* their spiritual longings with their academic disciplines. All too often in the past, as happens still today, Anthroposophists (or Theosophists) have separated their spiritual disciple from their academic discipline. They have kept them in separate compartments. The new generation must not be Anthroposophists on the weekends and scientists or philosophers during the week. They must integrate their spiritual and their academic disciplines.

Above all, of course, academic activity must be humanized. Abstraction must be overcome. As Steiner says: "We must work toward bringing the human being to the fore in so-called objective scholarship, which must be grounded in life and in human beings...It must not become dry and shriveled."

Freedom is essential for this grounding in life—freedom in thinking, freedom from authority and the past, and freedom from sectarianism. Anthroposophists must now be willing to engage everyone. Therefore Steiner concludes the first "Higher Education" course with a plea: "Let me simply ask you not to be selective or sectarian in your actions. You must work on the largest possible scale. Exclude no one; include everyone who wants to work with you... We must be open-minded and welcome anyone who honestly wants to work with us...."

However logical this sounds to us today, it is important to understand how different a Steiner this is than we are used to. A glance at the wide-ranging and fascinating 1921 question-and-answer sessions that follow the two addresses on academic work make this clear. In these far-ranging comments, Rudolf Steiner covers many different, still-relevant topics—from the history of the Youth Movement, building community, and exploring nature to questions of social reform, education, and the spiritualist, Theosophical ambiance of Anthroposophy's beginnings and how this relates to today. He is astonishingly direct and at ease. One senses how at home he feels with these young people and how broad, deep, and inclusive his view of Anthroposophy is. At one point he tells them:

> Anthroposophy is not simply a matter of assuming a worldview. Being an Anthroposophist involves participating with your whole

> being… There are many different routes to Anthroposophy. We must move beyond collisions with individual Anthroposophists to attempting to experience Anthroposophy as such. At present, Anthroposophy is actually the only nondogmatic worldview, the only one that is not set on very specific ways of doing things and makes an effort to take a variety of perspectives. Anthroposophy's main concern is life, not the forms things assume…
>
> I see Anthroposophy as something living, something capable of transforming individuals into beings different from what they were before. Through the substance of Anthroposophy, we become free. After a brief period of development, we become really free human beings. A question that has passed through life cannot be resolved by thinking about it. If tackled from the perspective of freedom, however, it will be solved through real life….

But what does this really mean? What is involved in the process? By the end of the volume, it becomes clear what is at stake.

As the documents unfold, of course, the situation changes, for reality is never static, especially not in these years. Thus, as the Youth Movement becomes a fact of Anthroposophical life, with its ups and downs, history is also irresistibly moving forward into the decisive events of the twentieth century and beyond to our own time. Outer events, both in the political world—where Adolf Hitler has moved from the shadows into the half-light—and in the world of Anthroposophy, are moving very fast. The sense of urgency increases, and in the last year-and-a-half of his life Rudolf Steiner's way of talking deepens, becomes even more intimate, and the task becomes ever clearer.

The task, which underlies the whole volume, and to which we too are called by service to the Archangel Michael, is to open to the etheric heart in humanity. This becomes clear in Rudolf Steiner's final addresses, first that of June 17, 1924, when he is talking to the young people who attended the "Agriculture Course." The question here is the rediscovery of the spirit in nature in an appropriately contemporary form—the creation of a Michaelic approach to nature. Youthful souls "long to remember and connect with the divine source of everything on Earth and in the starry heavens." They long to know nature in a new way. How?

> In our hearts we must learn to transform artificially thought-out spirit, which remains estranged from nature, into developed spirit, which finds its way out into the world of natural objects... Today, the only way to find spirit is to clothe it in words provided by nature, so that our perceptions can grow strong again. Now, in the Age of Michael, you are on the right path if you manage to develop real reverence out of what is already knowable but appears to dwell exclusively in the realm of ideas. Transforming such knowledge into reverence is the best path of all. Meditation means transforming what we know—specifically what we know about individual concrete things—into reverence, and the results are sometimes surprising....

About a month later, on 20 July 1924, Steiner again, and for the last time, had the opportunity to address the young people attending a teacher's conference. Without referring to what he had said before, he now explained:

> What is needed is not thinking about what should happen. People should feel that the spirit outside of us speaks in the flames of nature. The sunrise has changed.
>
> But also our heart has changed: we no longer bear the same heart in our chest. Our physical heart has grown harder, and our etheric heart more mobile. We must find access to our supersensible hearts. This is the way we must understand spiritual science.... In this respect, young people have hearts ideally suited to this, to feel when something is right. It simply requires courage to really think it.

It is in the light of "our supersensible heart" that this whole volume—and indeed Anthroposophy today—should be read. May we develop it.

YOUTH AND
THE ETHERIC HEART

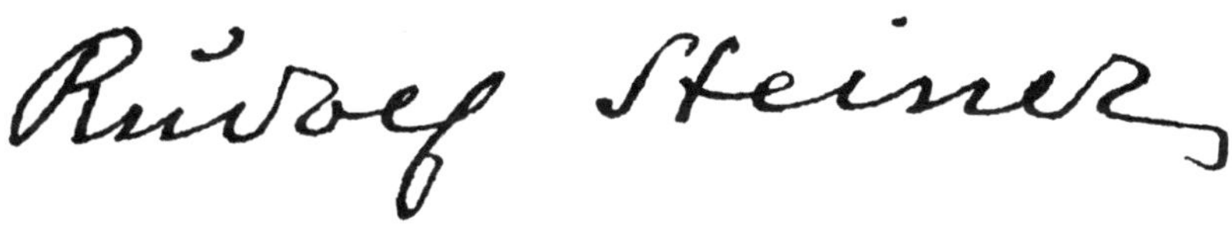

ADDRESSES GIVEN IN 1920/1921

"Exclude no one; include everyone
who wants to work with you."†
—Dornach, October 16, 1920

Toward Independent Scholarly Work

Address on the Recently Issued Appeal to Academic Youth†
Given during the First Anthroposophical Higher-Education Course
at the Goetheanum

DORNACH, OCTOBER 1, 1920

I am sure you will understand that because the contents of the recently issued "Appeal to Academic Youth"† are so closely associated with me personally, I cannot really speak to them in any way. Instead, let me speak to you today about the impulse emerging among today's students to work toward new goals for academia and for society and culture in general. This appeal reminds me of another one that also originated in Stuttgart not long ago and called for the establishment of a cultural council.† When our work in Stuttgart began in 1919, it was initially based on the "Appeal to the German People and Culture,"† which I had formulated and released in March of the previous year, and on my attempts to provide guidelines for restructuring society in *Toward Social Renewal* (CW 23). A number of individuals supported this book's perspective and social goals. Their intention was to show the world the real need for a renewal of cultural affairs, the need to imbue cultural activity with new impulses, and they saw the establishment of a cultural council as one of the most pressing issues.

As you know, *Toward Social Renewal* points out that the highest aspiration of our time must be to raise a subconscious goal of modern humanity to the level of conscious activity. I refer to the threefold reordering of the body social. Anyone with a bit of insight into the undercurrents of human aspirations will sense that this book is not utopian in the least. As the product of thirty to thirty-five years of observation, it essentially presents nothing more than what most individuals want (or, more accurately, *would* want if they followed their instincts and feelings) but have not yet confessed to wanting because they somehow fear raising it to consciousness.

We can see the need for new directions in all three domains of human activity—culture, politics and law, and economics. In my book, *Toward Social Renewal,* I attempted to demonstrate that the main obstacle to discovering these new directions is the idea that a monolithic state has to do everything. Over the past three or four centuries, this idea has become firmly implanted in our minds, and the state has gradually appropriated the system of higher education. But we must not forget that our education system actually developed directly out of cultural activity. Not all that long ago the reputation of higher education was based on the productivity of individual universities. Just recall how people spoke of the law school in Bologna, the medical school in Salerno, or any of the other important universities. The international reputation of the higher-education system was based on the unique accomplishments of individual universities. But through recent annexation by governments that have assumed more and more power, our system of higher education has been totally transformed to serve the outer needs of individual nation-states.

Originally, the universities themselves determined the extent and character of their relationship to the state. A historical recollection of that time should still be alive in anyone who feels connected to the spiritual striving for knowledge or to cultural aspirations in general. During the Age of Enlightenment in the late eighteenth and early nineteenth centuries, it was emphasized repeatedly that in the Middle Ages, scholarship existed to serve theological and ecclesiastical activity. You know I am no follower of Kant,[†] but this statement of his is worth mentioning: The time of academic disciplines serving as the trainbearers of theology is over.

Kant held that scholarly activity had become independent and was called upon to be the standard-bearer for all other aspects of culture. But it was only after such statements became popular (out of legitimate resistance to religious activity in academic fields) that the trend emerged that has now transformed our system of higher education into the servant of politics, the state, and the legal system. I ask you, is it better to carry the train of theology, which is at least a spiritual and cultural element, or to carry the train of the political system? This judgment will be left to times still to come. Roughly a century after

Kant's statement, the famous physiologist Emil DuBois-Reymond, then the president of the Berlin Academy of Science, said that the members of the academy felt very honored to be called the scientific security squad of the Hohenzollerns.† This statement is indicative of what I call "state occupation" of the higher-education system.

It goes without saying that the state's first concern is for its civil servants, not for scholarship. Recently the president of the University of Halle published an essay that sheds a very strange light on changes during his tenure.† He seemed to be somewhat informed about important events behind the scenes, because his very concerned and exhaustive editorial alerts us to a state plan to close a large number of German universities and replace them with training schools for civil servants. Such issues account for the rather pointed language of the Stuttgart call for a cultural council. State influence on the universities has not been limited to imposing unpleasant exams and deciding on the hiring of professors. It has even taken hold of academic disciplines themselves. It has taken hold of knowledge, of spirit itself. To rectify this situation, we issued this appeal to everyone we thought might have some sense or feeling for how to support and promote cultural affairs in general and the educational system in particular.

Initially, the well-meaning and warmhearted people who responded to this call hoped for insight and collaboration from the representatives of cultural activity, specifically, university instructors. This collaboration was not actively forthcoming, and what the instructors said instead was quite surprising. They said that if the threefold organizing of the body social was accomplished and the independence of cultural affairs guaranteed, university instructors would have to replace the minister of education and his civil servants in the administration of the entire educational system. They said they preferred to be subject to ministry oversight than to the decisions and actions of their own colleagues, about whom they had very strange things to say. While exploring the opinions of university instructors, we had plenty of opportunity to hear what A had to say about B and B about A. In the end, there were very few people left who would have been trusted with the administration of an independent cultural body. This experience was quite depressing. As you may know, the entire appeal, in spite of its good intentions, turned out to be just a waste of paper, because we found virtually no cultural workers willing to advocate for the independence of cultural activity.

Even externalities reveal the changes in recent decades, though many people still have not recognized them for what they are. Let me simply emphasize that the result of an academic education was once an expression of the striving for scholarship and knowledge itself. The degrees granted by various schools and departments had something to do with striving for knowledge. But now it is evident that the system of state exams has infiltrated the process of getting a degree to such an extent that the scholarly content has been reduced to mere decoration.

Initially, of course, such issues are merely symptomatic. As symptoms, however, they clearly demonstrate that cultural affairs have been largely subsumed by external political activity. You can be quite sure that our present state system will kill off the universities because it does not need them as such, as havens of scholarship and knowledge. They will all be transformed into training schools for civil servants because that is all the state needs. That is the current trend. Such statements are always taken for doomsaying or false prophesy, but it is important to see where we are heading. Law schools are becoming schools for civil servants, and medical schools are attempting to turn healers into mere cogs in the state machinery. And what about philosophy departments? What are they good for if not to prepare people to be "instructional civil servants" rather than teachers? In democratic Germany, that model country, we do not even call our instructors teachers or professors anymore. These are superficial details, but they reflect the intrinsic spirit of academia. It is truly disheartening to discover that our teachers have absolutely no feeling for the importance of independent cultural activity.

When I hear the appeal coming toward us from students, I experience this state of affairs as a reproach. To put it bluntly, if old people are not going to make changes, then the young must feel it as their sacred duty to advocate for independent cultural activity, because if no one insists on a renewal of knowledge based on original sources, the situation will certainly be very bad by the time our civilization's next generation grows up. It is indeed significant that Oswald Spengler,[†] a highly intelligent man, applied a great deal of energy and disciplined scholarly methods to proving that Western civilization is heading toward barbarism.

Needless to say, all this is a tremendous burden on you young people, who cannot be allowed to become adults with blind faith in authority. You must have your eyes wide open to see what is going on in the institutions you attend to prepare yourselves for life. Apart from the portions of the appeal that relate to me personally, it made a good impression that followers, rather than old leaders, were taking a stand and making concrete statements about what they want. Tirades and rhetoric will not make cultural activity independent. Taking back what the state has absorbed is imperative, but it will happen only if our cultural activity possesses real energy. In the age of materialism, academia was impotent to resist being sucked in by the state. Similarly, sciences that remain materialistic will also remain impotent to resist being dragged into barbarism by the state ambition to absorb them. Only some positive force will succeed in extricating the spirit of science, the spirit of knowledge, from the quagmire of politics. Material science has fallen prey to unscientific forces, but it can be rescued by the intrinsic strength and character of spiritual science. Only spiritual science is in a position to establish an independent cultural life within the body social.

Of course, those of you who signed this appeal must realize that others will experience it as a breaking storm, especially since it comes from you. But it takes a storm to accomplish anything today. Without the will and the courage to make transformation happen where it is needed, we will not be able to move forward. Instead, we will fall into decline and barbarism. You must not expect your appeal to be accepted with good grace in all quarters. But surely you realize—all of you who signed it with full hearts and courageous souls—that an appeal received with goodwill would accomplish nothing. You must be prepared to fight for what you must want, for what is right.

Strange things have been known to happen when young, aspiring minds are drawn into the machinery of cultural affairs. I could think of many examples but will tell you only one—a little scene that took place at a university when a young philosophy instructor went to the department chair, who thought well of him, to apply for promotion to a professorship. He suggested a subject for his inaugural lecture, but the department chair, who really did want to see him become an assistant professor, said to him, "That really won't do! I can't recommend you to my colleagues; they'd have my neck. You've written only about nineteenth-century events and personalities in philosophy. We can't make you an assistant professor until you've written about much older topics." "Well," said the young Ph.D., "what should I do now? I thought what I've written about Schopenhauer [born in 1788] and the development of aesthetics in the nineteenth century would be suitable. Surely the Viennese in the department will know whom I'm talking about?" "But you know," said the department chair, "what you write about isn't important; it just has to be something old and unfamiliar. Let's see if we can find some old, unknown Italian aesthetician." So they opened the encyclopedia to the letter G and found the name Gravina.† Neither of them knew anything about him, but the department chair thought he would be just the right subject for a professorial dissertation. So the young Ph.D. wrote on the very interesting subject of a totally unknown and insignificant Italian aesthetician [who was born in 1807], and then the department chair approved his assistant professorship. This all took some time, however—a year and a half, I believe—because it was no easy matter to show the accomplishments of this unknown aesthetician in the right light. This is an extreme example, but it is only one among many.

Let us consider the gradual disappearance of all freedom of choice with regard to dissertation topics. In the field of modern languages, for example, Wilhelm Scherer† systematized the entire topic-selection process. A student requesting a topic is simply assigned one regardless of his particular expertise or interest. The topic is chosen purely on the basis of its usefulness to some professor or other who wants to draw on individual dissertations for an exhaustive book on the subject. To a greater extent than we might believe, this outer practice is indicative of the inner process of our cultural life. I believe I am not mistaken when I say that the best thing you could do would be to counteract this mindset with a fresh new approach to scholarly work. You could form study circles that would do real, basic, original research using all the aids and sources available to you. My advice to you, should you want it, would be to form local groups of students who want to work out of this spirit. If scholarship and knowledge are to flourish again, interdisciplinary efforts will be needed. Chemists, physicists, philosophers, law students, historians, and philologists will all have to contribute to work on common themes. If you wish, those of us involved in the higher-education courses in Dornach will help establish an independent committee of people who have lectured on various branches of knowledge enriched by Anthroposophically oriented spiritual science. This committee would suggest topics to be addressed next, not in the way that dissertation topics are now assigned but simply on the basis of what is needed in the general cultural life of humanity. The ultimate choice, of course, would always be up to the individual. Committee members with some experience would suggest what is needed, and individuals would be free to choose topics they feel especially suited to address. This arrangement would permit ongoing collaboration and independent cultural and scholarly exchange between the pioneers of an independent higher-education system here in Dornach and students who are interested in and enthusiastic about the impacts of spiritual science on Western cultural life and civilization.

This is a rough description of an initial positive way of using academic work to transform the words of your appeal into a reality. It is not yet time for more detailed advice. But you can rest assured that those who are already working out of Anthroposophically oriented spiritual science, both here and in Stuttgart, will be ready at any moment to put all their energy into promoting, supporting, advising, and collaborating. In short, they will do whatever is necessary to help enthusiastic students everywhere to contribute to our monumental ideal, to the great, intense, and comprehensive task of using renewed spiritual research based on original sources to guide human spiritual life—and thus human culture and civilization in general—toward an ascent or dawn, not the decline or dusk that many believe to be inevitable.

Having promised you that I will do everything in my power to encourage intense yet harmonious scholarly collaboration, let me now answer the question that was addressed to me: What is the first positive step that I would advise you to accomplish? If we truly work together in this way, students themselves will accomplish what their supposed leaders unfortunately cannot. If these leaders do not prove to be such leaders, then a good training in freeing yourself from all faith in authority is what you must go through, if you want to have as your foundation free scientific work. If you stand on this foundation, I can predict that you will work very well together with spiritual science and with the intentions of those in Dornach and Stuttgart. I speak to you today out of this conviction.

Humanizing Academic Life

Address on the Last Day of the First Anthroposophical Higher-Education Course

DORNACH, OCTOBER 16, 1920

As this event draws to a close, it is evident how heavily Anthroposophically oriented spiritual science is counting on you. We are counting on you because academia, which has placed us in our current situation, is the only institution capable of counteracting the impending demise of Western civilization. I do not want to spend much time demonstrating that the destructive anticultural institutions of modern times are essentially products of scholarly activity, because this connection is already obvious enough. We do not need to talk about it here, but there is something else we should consider.

It is also self-evident that the proletariat must be included in any restructuring of society today. In a public lecture in Stuttgart, I once said something that caused considerable offense, both locally and in broader circles. I said that the bourgeoisie is suffering from brain decadence† and is therefore absolutely dependent on replacing physical brain work with the spiritualized work of the etheric brain. This is as obvious as anything can possibly be. In contrast, the brains of the upwardly mobile proletariat have not yet become decadent. If we can convert them to brain work, proletarians are still capable of working out of the physical brain. Of course, these statements caused offense in bourgeois circles, but the point nowadays is not to avoid giving offense but to bring the truth to light.

The modern proletariat, however, is Janus-faced, to use a rather grotesque expression. How does this two-sided character manifest? On the one hand, proletarians always tend to say, "We don't want to know anything about what you academics are trying to tell us. It's too difficult for us, and we're just not interested." On the other hand, these proletarians have been fed exclusively on the waste products of nineteenth- and early-twentieth-century scholarship.† Waste products are all they have to work with. We must make every effort to see their situation in this light. It will not be easy to make the results of our serious scholarship accessible to the proletariat. But if we do not allow ourselves to be scared off, if we persist in the social action of winning the proletariat over to intellectual activity, we will be able to introduce them to this healthy element just as surely as they were introduced to Marxism and Bolshevism. We must simply not give up prematurely; we must persist in doing what we have recognized as right. Because this has always been my precept in Anthroposophical work, I have never compromised. I am fully aware that my rejection of dilettantism has made enemies, but there was no way around it. If someone felt it worth the effort, it would be very easy to prove that the bulk of our current enemies are people I once rebuffed because of excessive dilettantism. That is what you would find if you looked into the details. Admittedly, that would require some compensation for memory, which is no longer so highly developed, as you realize when you tackle spiritual-scientific training. You learn how to assess your enemies, who often appear out of nowhere years later.

If you are not afraid to persist in doing what you know to be right, you will also have success with the proletariat. Proletarians are simply suffering from an exaggerated feeling of authority. As soon as you get them on their own, you will be able to win them over. At present, the biggest hurdle is convincing these people that their leaders, big and small, are their greatest enemies—parasites, in fact. Once we succeed in convincing them, we will probably be able to interest the proletariat in our healthy scholarship. In fact, they will be an exceptionally good audience. Of course, the proletarian masses will have to be the "audience" for a long time to come.[†]

But now I want to draw your attention to a different issue. You see, in my years of activity in the Anthroposophical Movement, I have always attempted to bring Anthroposophy together with specialized academic disciplines, but I have always encountered difficulties. Let me give you a few specifics. Many years ago, an expert in the field of Oriental and Assyrian studies[†] became enthusiastic about Anthroposophy. It goes without saying that we expected him to make some connection between his field of expertise and his newfound enthusiasm, but he could not bring himself to do it. He could not be persuaded to bridge the gap between these two areas of study. He forged ahead in both fields but was unable to bridge the gap. Nonetheless, it is absolutely necessary to attempt to find or to build this bridge, and we will find it. It must be possible to gain access to every academic discipline through Anthroposophy.

In a similar instance, I once knew a very famous professor of botany who was also an ardent Theosophist.† This man wrote books on botany in addition to writing about theosophy. He belonged to the Theosophical Society, not the Anthroposophical Society, so he wrote about Theosophy after the manner of Annie Besant. As soon as he closed his books on theosophy, he was a botanist through and through, but when he lectured or wrote about theosophy, he was the consummate Theosophist, and no one could tell that he was also a botanist. I sometimes brought up the subject of botany as a prelude to bridging the gap, but he was actively averse to talking about it with me.

You see, this "double-entry bookkeeping," as I always call it, is a consequence of the culture of a century ago. People want to read about everything related to their professional life in professional journals and everything related to feeling, to the "inner person," in the Sunday supplements to the newspaper. Politics falls somewhere in between; in keeping with the current version of the "threefold" ordering of society, they want to get their politics from the newspaper itself. It is most important to see through these things. In a certain sense, though the issue will not always be so cut and dried, you yourselves may be best qualified to find the bridge.

As early as the turn of the eighteenth to the nineteenth century, poor Hölderlin† put it very beautifully. He said that when he looked around at his Germany, he saw civil servants everywhere, along with factory owners, cabinetmakers, and tailors—but no human beings. He saw scholars, artists, teachers, and so forth, but no human beings.

Today we might say that this is especially true of the academic professions—there are no human beings there! We have academic disciplines and scholars drifting around as if they were real, but to the extent that we feel human, we live almost entirely outside our academic knowledge. Just think about what people do today when they sum up all of their scholarly knowledge to write a paper or apply for promotion to a professorship. What do they do? They cannot just sit down and write about whatever flows out of their souls, because there is no place for that in an academic work. They would soon be accused of writing off the cuff, and you are not allowed to write off the cuff. To write your dissertation, you must study books you would not bother opening otherwise. Even for your dissertation, you might simply look for quotations and note the pages instead of actually reading the books. Your relationship to your subject is supposed to remain as superficial as possible. You are not supposed to develop an intimate relationship to it!

When people engaged in this type of work get together after hours—well, I could tell you stories about strange encounters I had in Weimar while working in the Goethe and Schiller archives. As soon as anyone mentioned anything related to Goethe or any scholarly subject whatsoever, someone would say, "Here we go again, talking shop. Cut it out!" The whole purpose of getting together seemed to be to avoid getting a reputation for talking shop. This attitude, however, is in large part responsible for our current situation. In the seven years I spent in Weimar, I found very little difference between nationalities in this respect. When Mr. Thomas,[†] who came from the far West, from an American university, wrote about Goethe's *Faust*, his work and thinking were essentially international; there was no way to distinguish them from those of any student of Schmidt or Scherer. The only thing that distinguished him as an American was the fact that he sat cross-legged on the floor to get to the books on the bottom shelf. In all other respects, he did his work just like everyone else. The only exception was a Russian privy councilor. No one was sure what he was researching. Whenever he came into a bar in the evening, people said to each other, "Don't turn around, the privy councilor's here!" People avoided sitting with him because he always started talking about what he knew about *Faust*.

Now these seemingly trivial incidents are actually more important than we might imagine. If we considered many more such examples, they would explain many gradual developments in academic life. But this is exactly what we want to get away from! We certainly do not want to become pedants or people who talk shop all the time, but we must realize that human beings take precedence over all academic disciplines. As human beings, we must not allow ourselves to be tyrannized by academic knowledge. In our efforts to emancipate cultural activity, we are combating the abstract character of academia as such and placing human beings first. Our academic knowledge will develop beyond what Bölsche[†] described as "immortal" knowledge. He proposed a spiritual science of sorts, but he went looking for it in libraries, where the actual spirits are hidden behind paper and printer's ink.

Humanizing academic activity is our goal. We must work toward bringing the human being to the fore in so-called objective scholarship, which must be grounded in life and in human beings. Those of us who engage in it must not become dry and shriveled. On the contrary, by "combating abstract existence," as I call it, we become useful contributors to the very necessary process of counteracting the barbarization of Western civilization.

This is what is most essential for those entering academic professions or occupations supported by academic disciplines. It is also why I believe it will be such a great blessing if you form groups in your individual universities and independently tackle themes as we attempt to do in Anthroposophical groups, especially in the Waldorf School. I imagine these study circles as something very different from being like a school. We will attempt to bring together different threads from the fabric of the necessities of our time. We will draw from the total context of our culture in suggesting topics. Certain members of our Waldorf School faculty will stay in contact with those who have lectured here and will collaborate with them to discover topics that need to be addressed today.[†] They will then suggest to you, our student members, certain tasks that seem necessary from the perspective of insights available in our circles. What happens next will not be like getting assignments; it will be an attempt to get to the bottom of issues that are especially critical today. There will be real opportunities for scholarly work. But I want to emphasize that establishing little scholarly circles that are—or at least claim to be—working on these topics is not enough. Of course they must happen; they can and will be very useful, but alongside them we need a large-scale movement of student groups, a movement that is truly aware that young people simply cannot continue to abide by the intentions of people who come out of older times and old traditions, the people who are now sitting in academic offices. I mentioned that the Social Democrats need to get rid of their leaders. It is equally necessary for young people today to get rid of their old leaders, and that will be more difficult to accomplish than it actually should be.

You see, I cannot avoid mentioning the crucial point. Please understand that I am telling you this in complete honesty and sincerity. You can rest assured that it would be easy to advance our Anthroposophically oriented spiritual movement if we were free to work only for spirit and if spirit were all that spurred us on. Meanwhile, we are not the people who are assigning posts, granting degrees, and allowing students to fail their state exams. Other people are doing that. This is an important factor that we certainly do not underestimate. We know very well how much courage and audacity it takes for prospective academicians and intellectual workers to join us and stay with us, because we still have very little to offer. The situation will improve as our individual initiatives really begin to pull their own weight. When the Waldorf School was founded, I commented that its founding was all well and good, but it would be meaningless if we did not open at least ten additional schools in the next quarter year. Only then would the Waldorf School be truly established.

The need is clear, and that is why you must find the courage to ally yourselves in some way with our intentions. But on the other hand—I am thinking in practical terms about how the Waldorf School was founded—once we are really in a position to emancipate cultural activity, there will be more and more Waldorf Schools, and then we will be able to offer our young graduate friends a future. I am not being at all unidealistic when I say this. Until then, reciprocal support is essential. Our work to establish independent schools, up to and including institutions of higher learning, will be successful only if we meet with understanding on the part of students. For that, we need not just small groups but a large-scale student movement to support our intentions.

Since I always pursue practical ideas, not just ideas that one can simply hand down, I have considered the possibility of our schools' employing people who tackled their studies as Dr. Stein did.† As he tells it, he registered for courses, attended the first few lectures to see what was going on, and then spent the rest of his time studying my lecture cycles and works quoted in them and managed to complete his academic course of study in that way. Of course, his approach is not universally applicable, because probably only three-quarters of the professors would tolerate it if all their students were like Dr. Stein, showing up only for the first three lectures and then taking a hike.†This approach is not realistic for the general public, and so I will not recommend it. Nonetheless, I want to suggest to you that the spirit now occupying lecterns in our university lecture halls has no future if it is transferred to elementary and secondary classrooms.

During this conference, I told you about the World School Association. I want you to know that I take its founding very seriously. I imagine this association as international in scope, arising out of people's thoughts and feelings about cultural activity. In reality, there are only two competing movements in the world today. One is Bolshevism, which is leading the world into a morass; the other is the threefold organizing of the body social. If we can convince the world of this dichotomy, people will be forced to make a choice as soon as they realize that old impulses are going nowhere. Those who want to advance culture in any sensible way must gradually get used to the idea of a threefold social order. If they do not—if they are too lazy to do that—then Bolshevism will inundate Europe and barbarize European culture. Once people understand this, it will be easier to win them over than it is now.

In this connection, there are three things we really must consider. When we speak to the international community about a project such as our building in Dornach and the fact that we need money for it, their reaction is, "We mustn't be so petty as to donate money for undertakings based on pure idealism. Money is much too filthy to be used for such an idealistic project!" In other words, without lengthy preparation, people are not prepared to contribute. Given the currency situation in Central Europe, we cannot raise sufficient funds here to complete our building, so we are dependent on other parts of the modern civilized world, where people are tightfisted and not prepared to donate. In contrast, it is relatively easy to solicit donations for sanatoriums, for example. If you are building a sanatorium, you can get as much money as you want. The middle way is what I am hoping for with the World School Association. That association, if rightly understood, will be able to finance all sorts of cultural facilities. Because people understand schools better than they understand something like our building, we must agitate on behalf of the middle ground. That is why advance preparation or drumming up support for the founding of this World School Association† is so important.

I believe that the best thing you students could do would be to become enthusiastic and convince everyone you meet of the need for an international World School Association and of the importance of its task, which is to emancipate cultural activity and to finance as many independent schools as possible all over the world. The emancipation of cultural activity must happen on the largest possible scale. We must succeed in liberating ourselves from cultural subjugation, but we can do so only by actively drumming up support for the idea. The tyranny is greater than we think.

I myself will initiate the founding of the World School Association here, but this effort must be preceded by mustering support. Nothing can be achieved today by working in groups of a dozen or fifteen people. Everything depends on the broadest possible dissemination of the idea that a World School Association must come about. Of course, I realize students do not have very deep pockets, and I am not asking you to donate. That is what other people are there for. But even if you cannot open your wallets, you can open your mouths. If you talk up the World School Association wherever you go, our request will not fall on deaf ears. When we approach people in the near future about founding the association, they will be primed and receptive. This is what has to happen.

You see, we have plenty to do. We need nothing more than real courage and an independent view of the world. Why should we not use youthful energies to overcome the obstacles that threaten to bring us to our knees, especially when those obstacles bear the imprint of times past? We cannot allow ourselves to be brought to our knees. We must realize that we are dancing on a razor's edge today—or on a volcano, if you prefer. It is not true that things can continue as they are now. We are facing very, very depressing times, but with courage and energy we will get through them. I believe the spiritual science of Anthroposophy can be a support to you, or to anyone, in this process.

In conclusion, let me simply ask you not to be selective or sectarian in your actions. You must work on the largest possible scale. Exclude no one; include everyone who wants to work with you. The only determining factor should be whether someone honestly wants to work in the same direction in preparing for scholarly vocations that have been so abused. We must be open-minded and welcome anyone who honestly wants to work with us. We must not draw distinctions among individuals. We must allow anyone of goodwill to work with us. In essence, this is how it has always been in the Anthroposophical Society. We have never asked people to abandon anything they stand for in the world. We simply ask that they accept what comes to them from the Anthroposophical Movement.

Let me inject a personal note here. You know I have been repeatedly reproached for my former association with the Theosophical Movement. But the reality of the situation is that the Theosophical Movement approached me. The Theosophists joined forces with me for a while until they abandoned what I represented. In my first meeting with them in London, I told them that we were all bringing our gifts to the common altar. There was no question of simply accepting pronouncements from central headquarters. This is how we can work together with the largest number of people. If you work among students in this way, we will indeed be able to forge ahead.

On the Youth Movement

Discussion and Question-and-Answer Session†
during an Independent Anthroposophical Higher-Education Course

STUTTGART, MARCH 20, 1921

Question: What was the Youth Movement, what is it, and how can it lead people to Anthroposophy? People who have gone through the Youth Movement see Anthroposophy as an extension of what they were looking for in the Youth Movement. They would like to hear something about the significance of that movement from the perspective of spiritual science.

Rudolf Steiner: The Youth Movement emerged at a time when I myself was no longer young, so the people who participated in it must be at least outwardly better informed than I am. To outer view, the Youth Movement is not an abstract unitary movement but one made up of individuals with a great variety of ideas and worldviews who find their way to each other, perhaps on the basis of feeling. This is one aspect of the Youth Movement, but there are other forces involved. It is not held together by personalities, and its intrinsic cohesive forces are more basic than the forces of any worldview, for example. There are many people in the Youth Movement who cannot formulate what they want clearly or consciously. Another aspect of the Youth Movement is that it emerged simultaneously in different countries. We cannot say, for example, that the Swiss and German youth movements influenced each other. The Youth Movement rose up out of fundamental forces in many places at the same time. It is a universally human phenomenon.

We must consider the Youth Movement's characteristics scrupulously. When we first encounter such a movement, we sense that it can be understood only from very profound perspectives. If we approach the Youth Movement with the historical knowledge of spiritual science, we recognize its connection to the reversal that took place† within individuals and in human history at the end of the nineteenth century. We can come to this conclusion by observing the qualities of statements made by people who were adolescents or children at that time. Having observed such statements closely, I have come to realize that the Youth Movement is indeed related to the great reversal at the end of the nineteenth century. It is one of the symptoms of the dawning of a new era. When we are intimately associated with a movement, we do not recognize all aspects of its being. We learn about some of these aspects only when we distance ourselves from it. Thus, some historical connections can be recognized only from the perspective of a later point in time. Through spiritual-scientific methods, however, we can achieve the necessary distance; we can learn to observe precisely and gain insight into the connections between events. Someday, for example, people will be able to think about the end of the nineteenth century and realize that it signaled the arrival of an important impulse that still remains hidden today.

This universally human impulse appears to be alive in the hearts of those who turned to the Youth Movement. Their hearts are illumined by this tremendously significant turning point at the end of the nineteenth century. It is not always especially important to get into discussion on such matters, but it is important to recognize the vital impulses at work and to acknowledge that those who joined the Youth Movement sensed the presence of these impulses. The purpose of spiritual science is to consciously intercept the impulses at work in humankind's development. Without spiritual science, we believe, we cannot understand major catastrophes in the world. Philistines (materialists) who cannot understand such things take Anthroposophists for eccentric muddled thinkers and fail to realize that they themselves are the muddled thinkers. People who have grown up with old ideas can no longer keep up. Their brains are decadent, full of old stuff they have carried over into the twentieth century.

There is nothing contradictory about Youth Movement members finding their way to spiritual science. In fact, we might say they are predestined to do so. The Youth Movement is characterized by an emotional relationship to what spiritual science accesses on a more or less conscious level. We must not become conceited. Our knowledge must not lead us to say things like "Our era is alive in me." But we have been shaped, at least in part, by the impulse of the end of the nineteenth century. We must take an outer view of such things in place of the patriarchal perspective of our forefathers, which is inadequate for the times we live in.

Question: How can we find a bridge between the Youth Movement, with its resistance to old worldviews, and Anthroposophy? We experience a certain resistance to Anthroposophy. Many people find it somewhat gruff. Anthroposophists lay out the path too specifically and emphasize spirit too much for the liking of young people who are simply trying to find themselves.

Rudolf Steiner: This is related to the impulse I mentioned just now. We can also approach the same question from the opposite perspective. You see, in our era, Anthroposophy offers a means of approaching certain spiritual phenomena. People who find their way to Anthroposophy are no longer rooted in the immediate cultural past. Friedrich Nietzsche[†] is an example of someone who was stuck in the past. He lived during a time of transition, and destiny condemned his sensitive soul to suffer everything possible at the hand of nineteenth-century culture. As a student during the Positivist period, when he became familiar with the works of Wagner and Schopenhauer, he suffered under what his culture found most uplifting. He remained trapped in nineteenth-century culture, and we can see how he first suffered and then collapsed under it.

Some of his contemporaries were able to extricate themselves and eventually found Anthroposophy. In some respects, they were like orphaned children struggling to find their feet on unfamiliar ground. Anthroposophy stood on its own, abandoned by the past. Anthroposophy is not simply a matter of assuming a worldview. Being an Anthroposophist involves participating with your whole being. People who choose not to develop a relationship to Anthroposophy are exposing themselves to risk. If we who do develop this relationship make no attempt to bridge the gap between ourselves and these other "orphans," they may, under certain circumstances, miss out on the connection to humankind's further development.

I can certainly understand objections such as yours. Nonetheless, we must make an effort to find the bridge. If we avoid the bridge out of anxiety, we run the risk I just described, and we will get nowhere at all. Something changed in the Youth Movement not long ago. It had been all about coming together, about people wanting to find each other. In the past few years, however, this has changed for some individuals, who attempted to shut themselves off from others. Within the movement this manifested as subtle but pervasive differences between national groups. Lack of spiritual content is leading to isolation of individuals.

There are many different routes to Anthroposophy. We must move beyond collisions with individual Anthroposophists to attempting to experience Anthroposophy as such. At present Anthroposophy is actually the only nondogmatic worldview, the only one that is not set on very specific ways of doing things and makes an effort to take a variety of perspectives. Anthroposophy's main concern is life, not the forms things assume. But, of course, we are forced to use familiar forms in order to be understood.

An American once asked me whether I thought that what I had written on the body social would still be relevant in future ages. I told this person that my writings are structured in a way that allows for metamorphosis. In the future they may lead to very different conclusions. The important thing is for life to encounter life.

Comment from a participant: An immediate concern of young adults is to bridge the gap between what they have been taught and real life. We can't do anything with what we learned. For example, teachers who were part of the Youth Movement have been fighting for a long time for what is now happening in the Waldorf School. This is one place where bridges could be built. Also, the thought content of various Anthroposophical courses has been experienced in the Youth Movement on an unconscious level for a long time.

Rudolf Steiner: In our times, thoughts are how individuals find access to the general development of humankind. Thoughts are the connection. This is simply a fact that we must take into account. It is completely possible to introduce Anthroposophy to adolescents and even to children, though we cannot do so from an old person's perspective. For example, to introduce children to the idea of the immortal soul, you describe the butterfly in the chrysalis. Children relate to that immediately because it is the truth. When a butterfly emerges from its chrysalis, nature is showing us a parallel, on a lower level, to what happens to the immortal soul. On the other hand, if I approach teaching from the perspective that children are stupid and I am intelligent, the children will never learn anything, especially if I do not believe what I am telling them. This example illustrates one way of introducing Anthroposophy to children. In history lessons living aspects of history must be brought to life in the right way.

Question: By now many former members of the Youth Movement have gone over to the Philistines (the materialist camp). The Youth Movement focuses heavily on life's emotional and psychological aspects. It strives to relate to feelings and to the natural world, and these efforts have caused people to resist much of what comes from the past. People wanted to live according to laws of their own, but they never got beyond the feeling level. They failed to realize that being true to oneself becomes truly fruitful only when it is thought through, and so they did not think things through to the end. If we recognize Anthroposophy's significance for young people, we can then show them, in philosophical terms, that they need Anthroposophy, that Anthroposophy wants what they want, only more consciously. To date, there have been three ways of dealing with the sexuality issue—Kurella's body-soul,[†] asceticism, and young marriages—but these ways have not offered real solutions.

Rudolf Steiner: These three ways all attempt to use old, dogmatic thinking to solve a new problem facing humanity. Thinking alone, however, does not encompass the entire being of a free individual.

I see Anthroposophy as something living, something capable of transforming individuals into beings different from what they were before. Through the substance of Anthroposophy, we become free. After a brief period of development, we become really free human beings. A question that has passed through life cannot be resolved by thinking about it. If tackled from the perspective of freedom, however, it will be solved through real life. We must not be concerned about possible undesirable social consequences. Suppose we want to understand how conception results in the birth of a male or a female being. If this ever became a matter of rational control, there would surely be fewer men than women on the Earth.† But despite the fact that this process manifests as the sum of many individual incidents, the inner laws governing it ensure social balance. [Rudolf Steiner refers to his book, *Intuitive Thinking as a Spiritual Path*, and then continues:] Our life cannot be transformed all at once, and change certainly cannot be programmed. But we can prepare for change by developing an independent attitude as a basis. This problem must be solved on an individual basis. Especially with regard to the sex issue, young people's literature is highly dogmatic.

Question: In the beginning the Youth Movement was very romantic. Based on what they encountered in nature, people realized that the divine cannot be grasped exclusively through reason. Anthroposophy is concerned with efforts to understand; it wants to raise everything to the level of consciousness. Most people cannot bridge the gap between these two approaches.

Rudolf Steiner: This kind of thinking is overly self-centered in that it does not consider how to connect with the development of humanity as a whole. In modern times conceptualization and mental imagery have come to the fore. They are how we experience the world today: We must pull ourselves up out of the dimness of feeling and arrive at light-filled mental images through thinking. Thinking makes us truly human; it transforms our emotional activity. We become more human as a result of what thinking releases in us. We attempt to dwell in feelings when we shy away from clarity. Feeling that passes through thinking can become very intense.

When people say that they are "living in nature," they often imply that they are attempting something out of the ordinary. We need to realize, though, that this longing to connect with nature is nothing new; we are simply regaining what we once lost. This longing must be alive in modern individuals, who inherit too little from the old and thus have to acquire it for themselves. In this context I recommend Schiller's treatise "On Naïve and Sentimental Poetry."† And my *Intuitive Thinking as a Spiritual Path* is based on a natural relationship to nature.

Question: A divide exists between young people who are now in secondary school and older young adults. Young people today are different from the youth of the Youth Movement. The adolescent spirit of the Youth Movement was described as the "romanticism of outrage," whereas the spirit of modern secondary school youth would have to be described as the "resignation of rebuilding." All of the profound experiences of the Youth Movement—outings by night, campfires, aimless wandering—look like Bolshevism to modern adolescents. They reject all of that and long for authority, for limits to abide by. Is this just a transient reaction or should we see it as the dawn of a new era among young people?

Rudolf Steiner: The generation now between the ages of thirty-five and fifty years old grew up in difficult times. The spiritual focus of the late 1800s and early 1900s was on material things, and all the goodness of the spiritual life of the 1850s and 1860s was buried. Most of the people who are actively doing something in the world today are too old—over fifty years old—and young people with good intentions cannot get a foot in the door. Between these groups is an inwardly passive generation, the parents of youngsters now in high school. This generation has a bad influence on adolescents, who look up to them as their leaders. Authority is acceptable in itself, but it depends on the personalities who exercise it. What ideals is the generation between thirty-five and fifty passing on to its children? We can only feel sympathy for these adolescents.

Question: Would you find it desirable to form an organization of Youth Movement members who are also Anthroposophists?

Rudolf Steiner: You know I do not think much of organizing. In my *Toward Social Renewal* (CW 23), I deliberately talked about the body social and not about organizing. We've had more than our fill of organizing in recent years.

Question: What I meant to ask was whether common tasks would emerge for young people in the Anthroposophical Movement or whether each person would have an individual task.

Rudolf Steiner: In the future any task an individual undertakes will be a common task, and everyone will have to make common tasks their own. It will not work any other way. But we can accomplish this only through association, not through organization.

How Can Anthroposophical Work Be Established at Universities?

Concluding Words at a Student Gathering during the Second Anthroposophical Higher-Education Course

DORNACH, APRIL 9, 1921

At the initiative of German students, a meeting to discuss this question took place on the afternoon of April 9, 1921. Rudolf Steiner spoke the concluding words.

Dr. [Walter] Stein has already pointed to the three most important things to consider here, whether or not you choose to organize. But there is one thing I would still like to emphasize: In a movement such as ours, it is essential to learn a bit from the past so as to avoid its mistakes in subsequent stages. To the extent that Anthroposophy meets with understanding among students and present forces and opportunities permit, disseminating the various branches of Anthroposophy among students as positive spiritual content will be of primary importance. In our experience real achievements depend on positive foundations.

Years ago, as I told you yesterday, we attempted to establish a world association of sorts for Anthroposophy.† This association was intended to function entirely according to the rules governing formal organizations, but it never got off the ground. For the sake of the necessary cohesion and cooperation, the proponents of Anthroposophy then joined forces to form the Anthroposophical Society. For the most part these people were already actively involved with Anthroposophy. If an organization is to survive, it needs a preexisting content.

As Dr. Stein suggested, students will need to work on problems of general interest, rather than simply extending our work on current Anthroposophical issues in the narrower sense. Initially, of course, your work will not produce material for dissertations. Recently, students in their first few semesters have been asking me how they can relate Anthroposophy to their specialized fields of study. What can they do to incorporate Anthroposophical work into preparing to write their dissertations and pass the state exams? I have always told them that although I am available to offer advice, I really recommend simply getting through their official studies as quickly as possible. For their dissertation or their state exam paper or the like, I advise them to choose any academic subject that makes sense in the context of their studies. No matter what topic they choose, the Anthroposophical approach to it will undoubtedly be diametrically opposed to any other approaches. I advise them to write their dissertation in a way that the professor will be able to understand and grade but to keep a second notebook for the Anthroposophical aspects they think ought to be included. I tell them to finish the dissertation as expediently as possible, submitting only the first set of papers. Later, the thoughts they compiled in the second notebook will be a real, active contribution to Anthroposophy.

Significant specialized issues often come to light only through rigorous academic work on specific topics, but there is a certain risk involved if there is any lack of clarity in your collaboration with your professors. I do not recommend submitting Anthroposophically oriented dissertations, which most professors will find unsuitable. That would simply slow us down in terms of your availability to work with the Anthroposophical Movement, and we need all the academically trained coworkers we can get. I do not mean this in the outer sense of needing people who have been given an official seal of approval. First, we need people with the inner discipline required for scholarly work, which, of course, is best learned by doing independent research of your own. Second, we need coworkers who are no longer students and will not be held back by concerns about completing their specialized studies, and we need them as soon as possible. (Not surprisingly, this is a difficult situation, especially in Switzerland.) In the first few semesters, of course, it is easy enough to join such a group if you are so inclined, but maintaining the connections you make there becomes more difficult in the final semesters when you are busy with other things.

In any case, what I wanted to say specifically with regard to scholarly contributions to Anthroposophy is this: During this transition phase, you must produce two versions of your work, one your professors will understand and one you save for later. Of course, I do not mean that you must reject any very specific opportunities that present themselves; students certainly can be alert to such opportunities and take advantage of them to serve our movement. I almost do not know whether to hope or to fear that our good friend Professor Römer† of Leipzig will be overwhelmed with huge numbers of Anthroposophical dissertations, though I am sure he would be pleased. It would certainly demonstrate that he is not the kind of professor we were just talking about.

At this point, however, we need to expand on the type of collaboration with students that we in Dornach have already discussed. You can work out the organizational details among yourselves later. It would be good if the Waldorf teachers, along with some of our other members, such as Professor Römer and Dr. Unger,† would share their thoughts with you and give advice on topics for dissertations and other scholarly papers, without compromising your individual initiative in any way. We are seeking an intimate exchange of ideas with you, though it need not take the form of an actual organization.

The economic factor is very, very important. Our university system—actually, our entire system of higher education—will suffer a great deal under current economic problems. We must realize that the only way to improve this situation is by building up institutions such as Der Kommende Tag in Germany and Futurum† here in Switzerland.These organizations will also restructure the economic situation of students. I assure you that these efforts are designed for rapid growth. We do not have the leisure to take our time; economic organizations such as these must make rapid progress. Perhaps the most important thing students can do to help is to promote understanding of these issues. In other situations, we have seen students intervene successfully on our behalf with parents or relatives. It is not true that all students have only poor friends. And once a beginning has been made somewhere, the activity becomes self-perpetuating. Imagine it like an avalanche. If it gets off to a positive start, it becomes self-perpetuating. So please study the prospectuses put out by Der Kommende Tag and Futurum and try to get others to understand what we are attempting to do.

This understanding is extremely difficult for older people to achieve. We have had nibbles from older adults who tried to understand the intentions of Der Kommende Tag or Futurum, but in case after case they could not break free of the old economic biases that led straight to economic depression. Like cats landing on their feet, they always fell back on these old biases. I believe the clarity of your understanding will have some effect on older generations. There is no other way forward. I assure you that as soon as these economic institutions of ours acquire sufficient means to work on a large scale—which is the only way to do any good—and as soon as we can overcome the heated resistance of the proletariat, which opposes any economic improvement in the situation of students, our first concern will be to work on behalf of students.

Then there are our conflicts with outsiders. The Anthroposophical Society has existed in fact if not in name since the beginning of this century, and all of its efforts have been positive, at least inasmuch as I myself was involved. Initially, we let our opponents upbraid us and do whatever they liked. Then, of course, they said that we had failed to disprove their statements against us. It is very difficult to make people understand that the burden of proof rests with the accuser, not with the accused. We have also repeatedly experienced very strange views coming from academics. Seemingly honorable instructors and professors as well as pastors and other university-educated people have uttered accusations against Anthroposophy and Anthroposophists, and their standards of proof reflect very poorly on their training as scholars. This is why I felt obliged to say that Professor Fuchs[†] must be a very poor anatomist. How am I supposed to believe that he examines his specimens carefully if he did not even look at my baptismal certificate? Presumably, the way in which a person acts in one situation can be generalized to his or her other areas of activity. The mental habits revealed in this instance are typical of academic work today. What is now being presented in universities and technical institutes is essentially no better founded than statements like Dr. Fuchs's. In general, academicians have developed extremely sloppy habits. What is now needed is to raise the conflict to a higher level.

One of your fellow students suggested quite understandably that we need to become a fighting organization. I sympathize with his suggestion, but it really is not necessary. We must simply avoid what has already happened so many times in the Anthroposophical Society, namely, the need to use heated words to defend ourselves against vicious attacks, as in the case of a Mr. von Gleich. Having read that I had given winter lectures, Mr. von Gleich† invented a character named Winter and dragged him into the conflict in a very nasty way. I don't think it is overstating the case to call this behavior oafish, even if it is coming from a general. It is pure oafishness. To this day Anthroposophists who defend themselves and the society are still taking the blame instead of those who behave like Mr. von Gleich. In a number of instances we were told that we were being too "aggressive." In many people's eyes, defending yourself in this way is aggressive. Without becoming a fighting organization or anything of the sort, we must nonetheless be alert to such attacks and repel them. You, too, must take a concrete and positive stand, and whenever you are obliged to defend yourselves, you must be backed up by others.

It is important to track the symptoms of philosophical, academic, and religious activity in our time and to take an interest in them. Consider this single instance: I was once obliged to give a similarly unfavorable description of some philosophical scribblings by Count Keyserling.† With incredible superficiality, he had introduced the crazy idea that I had taken Haeckel's views† as my point of departure. This statement is not only objectively untrue but also subjectively untrue—that is, a lie—because we have the right to expect people who make such statements to check out their sources. If Count Keyserling had bothered to look, he could have read the chapter I wrote on my discussions with Haeckel during my earliest years as an author. This chapter appears in my introduction to Goethe's scientific writings. It is all there for you to look up, if you like. And now Count Keyserling has published a booklet entitled *Der Weg zur Vollendung* (The Path to Perfection).† I will not describe this booklet in greater detail, but I would recommend that one or two of you buy it and lend it around. It would be a waste of money if you all bought it, but I do recommend reading it so that you can get an idea of what Keyserling says, which flies in the face of all wisdom. I do not recall the exact wording of the sentence, but it goes something like this: "Well, if I was incorrect in saying that Dr. Steiner took Haeckel as his point of departure, Dr. Steiner could simply have set me straight because [please note this carefully!], I do not have time to research Steiner's specific sources."[†]

So this is the current state of scholarly ethics! Someone who is establishing a "school of wisdom" feels justified in publishing statements that he has not confirmed because (by his own admission) he has no time to research them! An author who considers himself well-bred—judging by his repeated conspicuous references to the Almighty—has been caught in the act. This unjustified lumping together of views is typical of the moral morass of modern writing. Our only recourse is to say to these people, "No one is asking you to research Steiner's sources, but if you have no time to ensure that you know what you are talking about, keep your mouth shut!" We must not succumb to any illusions here. We must abandon any conventional authority principle or the like so that we can independently confront and inspect what is being said and written nowadays. Unfortunately, we will find much of it of similar quality.

You will find it instructive to read a few of the sentences formulated by Roethe,[†] the great expert on German studies from Berlin. (I am referring to the form, not his view, which one can respect.) We need not become a fighting organization, but we must be alert and ready to take a concrete stand against symptoms of decline in our culture. But does this require an organization of Anthroposophical students? In such cases, we can take a stand simply as alert, decent, and academically conscientious individuals. If we are also organized for positive action, others will back us up. We do need backup, but setting ourselves up as a fighting organization would not be a smart move. The point is to work really seriously to improve current conditions; part of this work is to make note of the terrible and very obvious damage we encounter in various fields—there is plenty of it—and to take a stand against it in any way we can.

You can take positive action even in the smallest circles, simply by setting a small number of your peers straight with regard to such issues. In connection with to the World School Association, I told someone here yesterday that simply telling two or three other people about it would be a very valuable beginning. In the absolutely worst case, if you cannot find anyone else, tell yourself! One person's enthusiasm can make an issue accessible to others. We once experienced this very graphically in the case of a physician who was a member. His colleagues proved very receptive. We must avoid making enemies by strutting about like gamecocks and provoking conflict. We must not, however, avoid fights that others initiate. Claiming that we started the conflict is a very common tactic among our opponents, so we must have adequate backup to repudiate their claims. When we are attacked, we must defend ourselves. When we do so, however, we always get to read about attacks *by* Anthroposophists. We must not allow our opponents to turn the tables on us.

With regard to the World School Association, let me just add that I feel it would be best if the association were established independently but allowed to emerge simultaneously in the Entente nations (The Allies in WWI) and neutral countries as well as in German-speaking Central Europe. This would require a certain degree of vigilance, but I believe we are capable of that. It would be especially important for Switzerland to expedite the process, and it would be good if it could happen now. I assure you, in terms of morale and so on, we are standing on the razor's edge. We would already be at war again if the opportunities that existed in 1914 were present again today. If the World School Association were founded in Germany today and somewhere else only a week later, for example, we would not be able to pull it off. It simply would not happen, and it would be impractical to attempt it.

On the other hand, we also must not deny our actual positions in any way. This institute of higher learning is called the Goetheanum.[†] We gave it that name here, during the World War, and the other nations involved in Anthroposophy accepted it. We never denied our reasons for naming the Independent School of Spiritual Science the Goetheanum. On the other hand, it would also not be good if what happens in Germany appears to be an imitation of what is happening on the other side. We in Switzerland must be fully aware that the founding of the World School Association will take a bit of skillful action in the context of international culture. It is imperative that the association emerge from nowhere, so to speak, in Central Europe, in the Entente nations, and in neutral countries simultaneously.

For the moment, I cannot be sure that it will emerge in even one or two places. A committee was formed yesterday, but its enthusiastic members went to bed a few minutes after last night's gathering ended and postponed their meeting to tonight. We must wait and see if it happens. We have had a variety of disconcerting experiences that we will have to take into account. On the other hand, I am convinced that we will succeed if the necessary impetus and enthusiasm for what I and my friends have called "passion for truth" can be found among your fellow students.

I recently read aloud an article from the feature pages.[†] I assure you that what happened recently in Stuttgart is only a beginning, not the end of the matter. I can also assure you that things will get much, much worse. I have been warning my friends here about this for a long time, and now what do I read in the feature pages? "Spiritual sparks are already flying aplenty, like flashes of lightning hissing toward the wooden mousetrap, and some clever reconciliation on Steiner's part is needed to prevent a real spark from putting an inglorious end to Dornach's pride and joy."[†]

I believe we must become better organized and, above all, more vigorous in our responses to such provocation, which will become ever stronger. I believe that you, my dear student friends, need to contribute all your youthful enthusiasm to the "passion for truth" we mentioned so often during this course. Youthful enthusiasm for truth has always been a very positive impulse in the development of humanity. May it be the same in the near future for the issue you acknowledge as good and right.

Anthropoposophy and the Youth Movement

Discussion and Question-and-Answer Session during an Independent Anthroposophical Higher-Education Course

STUTTGART, SEPTEMBER 8, 1921[†]

We see the Catholic youth movement as our most determined opponent, and we would like to ask you, Dr. Steiner, to speak in more detail about that. We imagine our work in the Anthroposophical Movement as follows: While recognizing that we need to increase our knowledge, we see our specific task as fostering community. We want to continue with communal activities such as evening gatherings, hikes, festivals, and so forth, but we will gradually allow them to be pervaded and transformed by the spirit of Anthroposophy. Here, too, we would like to ask you for specific suggestions. We imagine inviting younger members of the Anthroposophical Society, students, and others to our gatherings. In conclusion, I would like to ask a practical question: Is it possible for a young person from the Youth Movement to serve as sponsor for someone seeking to join the Anthroposophical Society?

Greeting: First of all, I would like to thank Dr. Steiner on behalf of all of us for agreeing to meet with us in spite of his very busy schedule. The suggestions he gave us at Easter[†] have continued to work in us. We heard little from each other in the meantime, but when we met here and began to talk together, we noticed that each of us had come a bit further. Some problems that still existed at Easter are no longer problems. Already today, we arrived at some concrete conclusions. We believe that our unique position as mediators between Anthroposophy and the Youth Movement results in specific tasks for us in both movements. We want to bring Anthroposophy to the Youth Movement, which is probably best done on a one-to-one basis. This individual activity, however, will be supported and promoted by more "official" collective activity. Our aim is to establish a network of representatives throughout Germany with its center in Tübingen.

These representatives will meet with young Anthroposophists in their area, attend Youth Movement conferences, and take advantage of their personal connections to distribute written material. In addition, an article on the Youth Movement and Anthroposophy† will appear in an Anthroposophical periodical. The representatives will work closely with the main Association.

Rudolf Steiner: Before I answer your practical question, let me address your last point about bringing Anthroposophy to the Youth Movement. To do this, you will need to have real insight into prevailing inner and outer conditions. For the most part, you are already aware of the history of the Anthroposophical Movement.† From the very beginning, our movement had to take realistic possibilities into account. There was no other way for it to work. In the early stages of the Anthroposophical Movement, humankind was not really ready for it, but we could not wait for universal readiness to get the movement started. Nonetheless, there were some people who had been searching for something out of the indeterminate depths of their souls, and some of these people had not yet found Theosophy and mysticism. Some of them did not know that Anthroposophy existed, yet they longed for something more profound than what their lives offered.

For example, I was once invited to attend a meeting of a club whose members all had this longing, though they differed widely in their abilities and education. So I went, because I had more time then than I do now, and I made a strange discovery. At the club, to my surprise, I recognized a number of people who had attended my lectures at the Berlin Workers' College, where I was then teaching. The longing I mentioned was present everywhere, and we depended on it. Without it, the Anthroposophical Movement would have gone nowhere. At that time, it was impossible to do things the way we do today. It was difficult, however, to make Anthroposophy understandable to the people who had this longing. Many of them were unable to follow, and they wanted something else. Nonetheless, there were always a few who could follow, and they became this movement. As a result, however, our movement still shows traces of its childhood illnesses: unclear mystical striving and the like, which you can also still find here.

Diverse individuals want to hear about subjects of concern to them. Suppose, for example, that someone seeking the answer to a medical question makes the acquaintance of an Anthroposophist who tells him to read this or that verse from Dr. Steiner's Calendar of the Soul.† Furthermore, the Anthroposophist tells him that Steiner habitually shows you something other than what you're looking for, but you will eventually find what you are looking for, because it passes from the verse over to you.

We had to depend on such incidents. And we should not forget that in its early stages, the Anthroposophical Movement had rough edges that did not make a good impression at all. That also had to be taken into account. We would have gotten nowhere by beating our heads against the wall—have no illusions about that. Of course, we had to count on the intrinsic longings of modern youth. But as you become more involved in the Anthroposophical Movement, you must not lose sight of the fact that the Anthroposophical Movement itself is ready to break with old biases. By now we can manage without them, and it is quite possible to break away from everything that is materialistic. This is what I wanted to say initially, in the hope of avoiding having you say that Anthroposophists are awful people, which would be quite possible from your perspective.

As to your question about building community: Of course, we do not prohibit hiking together; in fact, we encourage it. Building community, when carried by the spirit of Anthroposophy, can assume all kinds of different forms. You talk about it as if it were something very new, but you must not forget that we old folks were also young once, and even in our day there were people who wanted to build community. I still remember a circle we formed in Berlin. In doctrinaire terms perhaps it was only a clique, but even cliques can have worthy goals, and every community begins with a clique. The community-building process attracts all sorts of hangers-on, depending on the character of the individuals involved. The very name of our group in Berlin was calculated to raise the hackles of bourgeois materialists. We called ourselves the "Criminal's Table."† Otto Erich Hartleben† was one of our members. I do not mean to say that we went around breaking into houses or anything of the sort. I mention this group only to illustrate that the community-building impulse, as you yourself expressed, did not begin with the modern Youth Movement.

There is no reason why members of the Youth Movement cannot sponsor their fellow members who wish to join the Anthroposophical Society. That is certainly possible, but this leads me to your other question.

You were completely justified in introducing the question of the Catholic youth movement into the discussion. You must be extremely careful with regard to that movement. Never lose sight of the possibility that you could be influenced in one direction or the other. Many of the individuals in the Catholic youth movement are hopeful and capable people. On the other hand, the greatest mistake you could possibly make would be to fall into the Catholic youth movement as such, because it is not based on the needs of young people themselves. Let me describe the difficulty in just a few words. The entire Youth Movement came together on the basis of the needs of individuals. What holds it together is nothing more than what lives in the hearts of individuals. That is not the case with the Catholic youth movement. Unlike any other truly future-oriented movement, the Catholic youth movement has been tremendously consistent in championing an element that has remained static, through tradition and so forth, throughout humankind's development. The Youth Movement must be decentralized. Of necessity, however, the Catholic youth movement is centralized. The greatest danger is that you will succumb to Catholic principles yourselves. Do not underestimate the possibility!

Suppose a movement appears, saying "As good Catholics, we want to do whatever it takes to bring people back to a living Christianity, and we do not want to have anything to do with the Jesuits." This may sound quite tolerable. To gain the right perspective, however, you must know that such a movement can be set up with programs against the Jesuits, but it can all be changed by some Jesuit father. Part of the Jesuits' program is to recruit and enlist its own opponents into its ranks. You would not believe how many people fall for it, but just look at the Young Catholic movement of many years ago. They rallied against Jesuitism, but fifteen years later they were in the Jesuit camp. This is something that may not be evident from looking at the movement's program.

In this situation, you will never be able to see clearly unless you are alert to the fact that the Jesuits are broad-minded in a certain respect because they reckon with the most powerful of their opponents. You cannot be careful enough to avoid falling into the Catholic youth movement as such. When I meet people whom I once knew well and with whom I had a lot in common, I find that many of them have fallen under the spell of the Catholic Church. The Catholic Church has a tremendous power of attraction, and its spell is very strong. Taking all of this into account, you need to be prepared for a trap. That is why I believe you will be able to move forward only if you guard your independence zealously in relationship to the Catholic youth movement. You must realize that your collective strength depends on finding people who have nothing up their sleeve and absolutely cannot be influenced. You will find a brand on the Jesuits; nor can you expect them to show who they really are. I'm telling you this simply to describe the situation and to warn you that you may find yourselves in rough water if you are indulgent toward the Catholic youth movement, even though it is now up in arms against the Jesuits. Check out where these people are in fifteen years, and see where they have landed.

An article on the Anthroposophical Youth Movement would accomplish several different things. As I have often told you, much of what comes from the Youth Movement arises from deep within the human soul. This is very important, and most of it can be understood only by someone who grasps what the Youth Movement is. I can well imagine that such an article would have very positive effects, and it would certainly be good if it were written by young people. But there is a type of opposition that goes hand in hand with individualism, for better or for worse, and you must be prepared for it, though it may not become outwardly evident. And although many people say Anthroposophists do only what they are ordered to do, in reality individualism is nowhere as pronounced as it is in the Anthroposophical Society. Each member of the society does only what he or she really wants to do. This has distinct disadvantages.

When you are dealing with a movement, it is quite true that you need some sort of common ground. And when you choose your representatives, you must make sure they will not quarrel among themselves but are really people who put the greater whole above personal issues. This will always be necessary in the Youth Movement. Evaluate your people carefully, because you need to know and trust your representatives. This is what little I have to say to your questions.

Question: How should we foster community?

Rudolf Steiner: You know, if you grasp the spirit of Anthroposophy, you will come to understand that individual community-building activities are of secondary importance. In the case of already extant individual communities, it is certainly good to cultivate them out of their own essential being. It is also good for them to continue doing what they have always done. Adding this or that to your agenda is not the point. Anthroposophy can work within any existing form. It is best not to attempt any outer changes in what you have been doing so far; just think about how to add Anthroposophy. As an esoteric force, Anthroposophy could gradually find its way into everything.

Comment from a participant: Anthroposophists always object that, through hiking, we fall into rapture.

Rudolf Steiner: Well, really, hiking as such is not an activity that promotes rapture or passion. Hiking is a rapturous activity only if the participants themselves are already rapturous.

Comment from a participant: Anthroposophists in particular always accuse the Youth Movement of being incapable of any activities other than hikes and celebrations.

Rudolf Steiner: You must understand that the Anthroposophical Movement is also made up of individuals, and its founding members are not predisposed to hiking. They have totally different ways of being and working together. You cannot expect them to have much sympathy for the Wandervogel.† It is only natural that they will have all sorts of complaints, but that is nothing to worry about. It certainly does not mean that you need to give up hiking. The Anthroposophical Movement could have developed just as easily among the Wandervogel. We must always keep the whole breadth and scope of Anthroposophy in mind and not get stuck in details. We cannot expect the Anthroposophical Movement to accommodate all sorts of wild fanatics—such as people who say, "We don't need to think at all; all we have to do is go hiking." I do not mean to suggest that all efforts at building community take such extreme forms, but many do. The Anthroposophical Movement was initiated by people whose feelings were very different from those of modern young people. Although it is quite appropriate for young people to maintain this movement, it did not appear first among the young. From its inception, it was somewhat elderly; there was nothing youthful about it. I encountered a characteristic example of this elderly attitude in one of my first lectures. I spoke in my normal tone of voice, and afterward one of these elderly people approached me and said, "You drive away the spirituality when you talk so loudly. You mustn't speak so loudly when you're talking about spiritual science." Incidentally, this person later became one of Anthroposophy's most loyal adherents and remained so until his death. It is best to simply avoid clashing with this elderly attitude. You do not need to confront it; simply go about your business.

Question: Dr. Steiner, could you share your thoughts about solstice celebrations?

Rudolf Steiner: At Easter I advised you to stick to realities that are accepted by Anthroposophists but can be experienced everywhere, and I told you about the effects of a longing that appeared in the late 1880s, emerging from the depths of human souls, and then formed the basis of the modern Youth Movement.

In earlier times people perceived the existence of very real powers that worked in human beings and even right into the seasons and changes of the year. Their effects were set in place at the summer solstice. You will grasp the full scope of what I said if you can imagine these ancient times when people related to natural laws in very different ways. Because they were very closely connected to nature as a whole, the thoughts they grasped at the summer solstice were most fruitful in terms of understanding these laws. We must turn to somewhat radical means of expressing ourselves if we want to formulate our own thoughts about what was then alive in human beings. The people of ancient times thought of how bulls were led out to inseminate the cows at certain times of the year, and they imagined that the human soul also had to be exposed to fructification at certain seasons. Now, in fact, the Earth sleeps in summer; its condition is then like that of a sleeping human being. The Earth sleeps in summer and is awake in winter. During sleep our ether bodies are at their most active, and the same is true of the Earth in this state. That was when people felt most connected to the Earth, and so they held their biggest celebrations around the time of the summer solstice. In the south, however—in Africa and so on—the winter solstice was considered the greatest festival. These celebrations were attempts to come into contact with what emanated from the Earth's waking ether body, in polar contrast to the temporal experience of the human spirit. All of our time-related habits are of similar origin.

In those times, awareness of all such things appeared in people as a feeling for certain natural laws. It is quite true that this awareness is now resurfacing. It was painful for me when some professor came up with the idea of doing away with Easter as an astronomically determined "moveable feast" and fixing its date on April 1. He thought this was a really good idea, but it would have eliminated our emotional connection to events in the entire cosmos. Our human sensibility would perish if cut off from cosmic events, because this connection keeps humans alive and young. If you feel the need to experience the spirit of the solstice and know that this was once done out of the noblest feelings, it is good to encourage celebrating the festival. But it is important to do so concretely, knowing that the summer solstice is different from the winter solstice, and to think about this difference on such occasions.

Question: about the ordering of life (Lebensgestaltung/Lebensreform).[†]

Rudolf Steiner: We will be able to have an impact on life only if the Anthroposophical Movement manages to intervene successfully in society as a whole. Of course, as long as the movement remains at all sectarian, it will also be called a sect.

Now that Anthroposophy has discovered methods of healing, people will come wanting to be healed. Meanwhile, however, people also stand up in the name of some political party and rail against the law that permits anything like the Anthroposophical Movement to exist. This is a real, concrete example. People want to encourage Anthroposophy in private, but they shy away from its public manifestations. But Anthroposophy can and must work on a large scale; only then will it be accepted. Individuals must have the courage to present the Anthroposophical spirit to the public at large. This is why I strove from the very beginning to establish an Anthroposophical therapeutic institute, a research institute, and so forth. Anthroposophy must be the foundation of our work. This will not be possible if current trends persist. The impact also depends on the strength of will of publicly active individuals who base themselves on Anthroposophy. Abstractly speaking, it can always be said that we cannot hope to accomplish our intentions in the next few years.

When I first went public with my thoughts on the threefold character of the body social, people came to me and told me that my timing was bad; it could take a hundred years to implement. All I can say is that if everyone thought like that when contemplating action, nothing would ever happen at all. That is not the right attitude. For me the question is simply, what ought to be done? I must say, the Anthroposophical Movement would never have gotten as far as it has if I had not repeatedly asked myself that question. Acting on the basis of Anthroposophy requires cultivating one's will. We need people who will take Anthroposophy as their foundation without reservation—the more, the better. Our job is not to consider how long it will take for people to become receptive to our ideas. Our job is to work to make them receptive. We must do everything possible, as if that receptivity were already a reality.

People always wonder whether we can actually do that. This is just evidence of a certain amount of fear. People are afraid to act. It is like reflecting on whether one can actually approach the essence of the thing itself through thinking. I imagine it in this way: Here is a bowl of soup, and lying next to it is a spoon. The spoon is your thinking and the bowl of soup the thing itself. What happens if you stop to ponder whether the spoon you have been given has a real relationship to the soup or what will happen if you take the spoon in your hand and eat? This type of questioning will never satisfy your hunger; you must simply pick up the spoon and eat!

Question: about the adult education movement.

Rudolf Steiner: I have become convinced that nothing positive will come of the adult education movement. The instructors simply take the developments of older cultures and graft them onto adult education. Would it be better if we founded institutes of adult education based on modern culture? The instructors should attempt to imbue their courses with life to the greatest extent possible, as I did when I was teaching in Berlin. Basically, though, it is a waste of effort. It would not be right to stop making an effort altogether, but we must realize that our work is contributing to decline, not ascent.

I said this not only because instructors choose contents with no future viability but also to show that we must get beyond our current methods of instruction. The underlying spirit is more important than we think. Attempts at adult education may be based on noble principles, but principles have no effect. Very, very clever people imagine that if they get ten or twelve individuals together and figure out an ideal school program, some good will come of it. They work out the best possible programs for adult education courses, but the program is not the important point. People are coming up with ideal programs all the time. In a school, however, the important thing is to do everything possible with your specific students. You cannot stick to any program. We have to realize that we must extricate ourselves from this way of thinking and base ourselves on real life.

From spiritual science we must acquire a sense for life's realistic possibilities. We must not function in programmatic terms. We have to express ourselves in such terms, but they are not the point. The point is to imbue every subject with life instead of with dead matter, which is what is happening in adult education.

You might say, well, I want to work somewhere. I have a mission I want to bring to people who I believe are capable of achieving a certain level of culture; let us call it level A. Now, everyone knows that A is not the best that can be achieved; we would really need A plus B. But since that is not possible for the people you are working with, you decide it is better to achieve only A. But if you look at it that way, you do not even reach level A, but only A minus B.

Question: about Muck-Lamberty.†

Rudolf Steiner: You will find similar people everywhere. Let me remind you of Häusser,† who is active around here. To the consternation of various people, he showed up at Siegle House and gave a very vehement sermon. But let me warn you about these people—they work almost hypnotically rather than through healthy reason. Their energy is intense, but it is crazy energy, not healthy energy. It is important to realize that any movement seeking a broader audience must be healthy. If the Youth Movement intends to serve humankind, it, too, must be healthy. We are looking at phenomena that develop energy, but in this case it is the energy of madness or of animals. The energy is much less important than what it expresses. In reality, we can penetrate to the core of a subject through the spirit of Anthroposophy only by excluding all traces of hypnotic suggestion. We must not allow ourselves to be overpowered by such energy, though I must admit I have seen it enable people of very limited abilities to do incredible things. Especially in a youth movement, you must be on your guard against mental intoxication. That is how you should relate to such phenomena.

I would like to point out a very simple means of protecting yourselves. In all movements, including the Anthroposophical Movement, there are individuals with a terrible mystical bent. An old friend who lives in Rome once said to me, "Oh, Anthroposophists are all so above it all, and their faces are so long that their jaws are in their laps." People such as these are everywhere; that is the one extreme. The other is the boundless superficiality that allows people to gloss over everything. For you, the important thing is to hold yourself together, not to be overly influenced by other people's energy. There is only one way to do that, and it is something everyone needs—humor! All these long faces and all this superficiality are equally harmful. Humor is what you need to put them in their place. If you can laugh at them, you see them for what they are worth. I do not mean that you should be ironic or sarcastic but simply see them for what they are. For the sake of healthy judgment, humor is needed everywhere. Instead of becoming like the long faces, the Youth Movement should encourage really healthy humor.

I have met surprisingly many pessimists in the Youth Movement, and their pessimism puts them at risk. We are all so clever nowadays that we do not even notice that our whole culture is going mad. Just ask those "mystics"—they will tell you all about how dangerous the outer world is and how we expose ourselves to risks with every draft of air. If people were really so dependent on outer influences, everyone alive today would be hysterical. We would all be powerless to confront every draft of air. Thank God, that is not what people are like. The important thing is to cultivate a higher sensibility, so you can feel every breath of air but not be blown over by it.

Question: about Fidus[†] and Gertrud Prellwitz.[†]

Rudolf Steiner: Some people write books and make public appearances without any real experience. Fidus and Gertrud Prellwitz are classic examples. Such people know absolutely everything, or so they believe. For example, they know what real Anthroposophists are like. They are typical of modern intellectuals. Gertrud Prellwitz is no different from the rest of them, and so humor is the only appropriate response to the situation.

The same is true of the other extreme, the people who come every few minutes saying, "Oh, dear, something terrible has happened! My child is developing a very unnatural sexuality." Well, if you ask the child's age, it turns out that he or she is only five years old. Believe me, sexuality comes out only at puberty, and a child really makes no distinction between scratching his itchy nose and scratching somewhere else. Reading sexuality into everything produces some dreadful theories. It is just nonsense to see erotic activity in a five-year-old. In such cases, healthy thinking is more important than theories because most theories are just nonsense. All people need to do is to consider how terribly shortsighted the conclusions are. In some cultures, eating was accompanied by feelings of shame, so it would be possible to develop similar theories about eating. But you will find that if you are really involved in life's far-reaching issues, you will not have time for this type of theorizing.

Comment from a participant: These issues ought to be taken more seriously.

Rudolf Steiner: I have to say, the way you asked the question was like building a house and not even having the floor in place yet.

Comment from a participant: Muck-Lamberty bases his craft on art and so on. And the "Neue Schar"† wants to reshape life from the ground up.

Rudolf Steiner: But what is the reality of the situation? In the real world, it is only possible to grow forward, not backward. Thinking about sexuality will not move us forward. If the foundations are sound, healthy sexuality will develop all by itself. It simply needs to be incorporated into life as a whole in the right way. It appears in individuals at a certain age, but it also develops in a specific cultural context. All we can do is allow it to emerge naturally. If the other aspects of our life are healthy, a healthy sexuality will result. We do a great deal of damage by attempting to program this aspect of our lives. If healthy prerequisites are in place, it develops appropriately in the context of society as a whole. I cannot count the number of people who have come to me asking about the possibility of prenatal education. The theories about it are simply awful—as if we were breeding children in hothouses. What is important is that the mother is healthy, that she leads a healthy life. If the mother stays healthy, the baby will be fine. It just does not make sense to ask such questions. They get asked only because we are living with a surplus of intellectual productivity—people need subjects to write about and are not willing to wait for actual experience. So they write, and in some cases movements develop based on what they have written, but these movements lead nowhere.

Comment from a participant: This movement developed quite unconsciously, not as the result of thinking. People are living together in small groups and looking for a certain natural lifestyle.

Rudolf Steiner: What do you mean by "a certain natural lifestyle"? Let us assume that there is a little circle of farm boys here, a circle of decadent nobility there, and over here a group of ordinary healthy people. Each group develops differently and leads a life of its own. You cannot say that any one theory applies equally to all of them. The point is that development is always based on a specific foundation. I do not want to be sarcastic about these issues, but it does not make sense to think about how a newborn relates to sexuality. At the right moment we need to have the courage to identify what is right and what is possible. That is why it is so important to develop a sense of humor in this regard. Aristotle pointed out this middle route between the rigid tightness of philistine (materialistic) values and loose dissoluteness.†

Comment from a participant: We need to make very clear distinctions here, because Muck-Lamberty and Gertrud Prellwitz are not the same at all. Humankind learns about these subjects from older people. Stammler† and Fidus have spread false stories about Muck. Muck sought out young people with whom he hoped to demonstrate that something exists that is equal from human being to human being. Folk dancing was one of the outer forms they used to express this. People flocked to him but left equally quickly. The hypnotic effect was short-lived. Those who remained represent a legitimate spiritual force. The artisan's community is one of the healthiest movements. The people in Naumburg are attempting to develop an economy based entirely on brotherliness and to be independent of everything they repudiate. The sexuality they developed was healthy until Gertrud Prellwitz intervened with her theories,† but by now the crisis has been overcome. The people there have moved beyond Gertrud Prellwitz, and their spiritual movement is merging into Anthroposophy.

Rudolf Steiner: It is always possible to see the good side of things, but it is important to maintain the necessary perspective in this case. For example, it is an undisputed fact that some of the people who came to the Anthroposophical Movement from spiritualist circles have become capable supporters, but this is no reason to defend spiritualism. In the Naumburg case, we must take the location into account. Naumburg has a history of such movements, but they come and go. It is easy to take a very one-sided view of such instances. Naumburg proves nothing, just as it proves nothing when such people find their way to a student movement. Although I cannot defend spiritualism, I also cannot deny that some capable people have come from that movement, just as they could have come from anywhere else. We cannot base our opinions on such factors. Muck-Lamberty wanted to make humankind happy; he stood for purity and artisanship, and so forth. He arranged for itinerant teachers to live together with small groups of young people. He stood for purity, and he fathered two children out of wedlock, [by choice]. [The note taker was unable to record the chaotic discussion that ensued.]

Rudolf Steiner: It is certainly necessary for us to engage in Anthroposophy as such, and it seems unlikely that we have to fear any such thing. We must start from the beginnings we have discussed today.

Question: An educational question: How do Anthroposophy and the Waldorf School relate to the existence of independent school communities and rural schools where teachers relate personally to their students as friends? I have heard Anthroposophists say that these schools must be avoided because they attempt to realize an antiquated educational ideal by emulating the ancient Greeks.

Rudolf Steiner: This is the situation: The Waldorf School is based not on a specific program but on a science of education exclusively derived from Anthroposophy's insights into human nature. It places the highest value on treating individuals as they want to be treated in their most profound depths of being. Children are not overtly asked what they want, though they are asked this on a certain level. This is the main point. Related to it is the fact that the Waldorf School is truly a democratic, comprehensive school. It places working class children next to children from the upper classes. To the greatest possible extent, it accomplishes the goals of a so-called democratic comprehensive school. For the rest, we take the position that we live in a world that can be restored to health only by adopting major, all-embracing cultural impulses that are impossible to implement through countermeasures that remain isolated exceptions to the rule. My point is that we must accept what already exists. For example, my educational efforts are adapted to the relevant circumstances of the location. If I have an opportunity to found an Anthroposophical school in a particular city, I do so based on actual conditions there.

Of course, there is nothing to be said against the adoption by a rural boarding school of our educational methods. On the other hand, I cannot believe that such schools have lasting benefits to society as a whole, because they take young people out of their social context and educate them in isolation. This factor is not taken into account, but we must always have an eye for the whole. For example, an excellent physician once said to me, "This man does not have a normal heart. We must do something about it." My response was, "If you fix his heart, he will not survive, because his entire body has adapted to the abnormality." For similar reasons, I have concerns about rural boarding schools. Taking young people out into the country allows them to develop a positive sense of community in isolation, but these schools would prove their worth only if their students can later hold their own within the body social as a whole. The entire body social must become healthy. Anthroposophically based discussions of such issues cannot be the same as discussions in any other context. But I assure you that we are not being one-sided: I recruited an excellent teacher from a rural boarding school to teach in Stuttgart. He likes it better here, so he must find it an improvement over his previous situation. We must be able to recognize the good wherever it exists, and we must not believe that we have a program that can be imposed everywhere.

Comment from a participant: In these schools, where young people live together, it would be crucial to foster a lifestyle that is not estranged from the rest of the world.

Rudolf Steiner: And do not forget the individual! Later, these young people will need to be able to function as individualities again. If you were to study the issue, you would find that rural boarding schools tend to foster self-serving characters who think everywhere else has to be just like school. They become terribly critical social eccentrics, and nothing in the world seems right to them. We must take care not to want the impossible.

What was I supposed to do? If I had started from an abstraction, I would never have founded the Waldorf School. Boarding schools such as those run by Wyneken and Lietz[†] can do anything they want, so they are easy to get started. Essentially, rural boarding schools function only on the basis of isolation from society. Such schools will not have many working class students.

Comment from a participant: I used to teach at an independent school that is now disbanding. But we had more scholarships than other schools. Wealthy parents paid tuition surcharges that allowed us to offer scholarships to poor children.

Rudolf Steiner: The antisocial aspect of private schools, even the Waldorf School, is that even they have to be financed somehow. This situation will improve only when we succeed in implementing the threefold ordering of the social body.

Comment from a participant: Boarding schools emulate family life, but the structure of the modern family is not always the most desirable.

Rudolf Steiner: We must always consider the reality of the situation. For example, boarding schools have always existed in England. People there know the light and dark sides of boarding school life.

[Rudolf Steiner concludes the address.]

ADDRESSES GIVEN IN 1923[†]

"All knowledge,
even purely scholarly knowledge
must merge into pure artistry."
—Stuttgart, February 14, 1923

The Cognitive Task of Academic Youth

Address Given after the Burning of the Goetheanum on New Year's Eve, 1922/23

DORNACH, JANUARY 6, 1923

All the extraordinarily loving words and expressions of intimate connection to what we lost through this terrible catastrophe would fill a book, so let me simply read the names of those who signed these words of concern and devotion to our cause. These words indicate how deeply our communications have affected the hearts of many individuals. They are also tokens of intensely felt wishes and actively willed decisions to work to regain what we have lost. I find it appropriate to convey all this to you because for many of you, the extent to which others share in our work and loss will certainly be a source of strength. Our cause is not intended to be merely theoretical. Our cause is one of work, of human love, and of devoted service to humanity, and thus actions or intentions to act have a place in what we say here. I will read only the names of those friends not present here, since the hearts of all of you who have shared these days of painful togetherness have already expressed themselves, often mutely but nonetheless profoundly and clearly. [Reading of the names.]

We may safely assume that what we are attempting here is deeply rooted in many hearts, and I would like to use the time reserved for tonight's lecture to take a break from reflections on the theme of our gathering and to honor the fact that this course has drawn nonresident friends in great numbers in addition to those customarily working for the Anthroposophical cause here in Dornach. I am thinking especially of the younger friends in attendance. For all those who take Anthroposophy seriously, it has certainly been very gratifying to see these young people find their place within our movement in such beautiful, profound, and heartfelt ways.

We must be absolutely clear about the significance of the fact that young souls involved in mastering scholarly and artistic subjects are finding ways to work together in and with the Anthroposophical Movement. The young friends in attendance at this course may have seen the Goetheanum for only the first or second time and surely did not expect to leave it in its current state when they returned home. My thoughts turn first to these younger friends, because all who take the Anthroposophical Movement to heart must actually share directly in the concerns of any groups or individuals within the movement. For the most part, our younger friends are attempting to find their way to Anthroposophy from intellectual life. In particular, I would like to begin by addressing those who come from academia. It is there that they first felt the urge—though it cannot be said that academia produced that urge—to join forces with others in common striving within the Anthroposophical Movement.

What drove these young people to us was primarily the sacred earnestness of efforts to fill the human soul with intellectual or spiritual life. The spiritual life of Anthroposophy, however, does not come easily, nor does it come through the direct perception favored today. It is no secret—not even in our literature,[†] which grants access to Anthroposophical work to anyone anywhere—that the route to Anthroposophy is difficult, but only because it relates to the most profound and powerful human dignity as well as to the specific needs of our era. Anyone who does not underestimate the signs of decline in our time must acknowledge the need for progress of the sort that is at least attempted in the Anthroposophical Movement.

We must certainly not forget that there are multiple ways for modern human beings to approach Anthroposophy. One way is by attempting, with real inner devotion, to achieve personal perception of spiritual worlds, thus convincing oneself that everything we communicate from spiritual worlds is founded on truth. It is indeed essential for some individuals or perhaps even an unlimited number of people today to follow this serious, difficult path. On the other hand, I must emphasize repeatedly that anyone who applies unbiased, healthy common sense is capable of fully grounded inner insight into the truth of Anthroposophy.

This is a fact that must be emphasized repeatedly to avoid any appearance of validating the completely unfounded objection that only clairvoyants who can see into the spiritual world can relate to the truths proclaimed in the Anthroposophical Movement. Today our intellectual life in particular and our civilization and culture in general impose many biases on us, and these biases make it difficult to convince ourselves of the truth of Anthroposophy without benefit of clairvoyance. The Anthroposophical Society, however, is here to point out the way and to work to eliminate more and more of modern civilization's biases. If the Anthroposophical Society does its job in this respect, we have reason to hope that the necessary inner powers of cognition will indeed become available to those who (for whatever reason) cannot aspire to the exact clairvoyance described here, so that they will nonetheless be able to convince themselves fully of the validity of Anthroposophical knowledge.

But how little inner, personal connection young people in today's civilization have to their fields of study, to the knowledge and insights they are meant to achieve! For the most part, individual areas of expertise are presented to young people superficially and in systematic ways unsuited to expressing the full value of so-called empirical insights, which are often extremely significant. Any academic discipline or specialty cultivated today includes detailed truths that are sometimes quite shattering. If these truths were presented to young people in the right way, they would serve as microscopes or telescopes for the soul and could reveal formidable existential secrets. If they emerged from the human depths of individuals in academic life and were fostered carefully and used properly, they would be tremendously informative and extremely compelling for young hearts and souls. But today these truths are embedded in unresponsive systems and are often presented to young people with total indifference. As a result, students' relationship to the informative possibilities of many different fields of empirical scholarship remains highly superficial. We might even say that many if not most young people in academia pursue their studies without any inner involvement whatsoever. They allow the subject matter to pass in front of them like a panorama that repeats as needed until they pass their exams and find a teaching position.

Yet another unique path to Anthroposophy is accessible to young academics. If our educational system lived up to its possibilities in terms of scholarship, cognition, and inner vitality, academic studies could and should offer the most solid point of departure for achieving independent perception—I say quite deliberately *independent perception*—of Anthroposophy's spiritual treasures.

It sounds almost paradoxical to say that student's hearts should be involved in everything presented to them, but the possibility does exist. For someone with the appropriate subjective disposition and innate energy, even the driest book or lecture can be deeply moving, despite the lack of any compelling energy on the part of the author or lecturer. When we meet the best and brightest of the young friends joining the Anthroposophical Movement, we are sometimes deeply touched to realize how little the "education industry" has given both their hearts and their heads. These harsh words may seem unforgivable to some of you, but I am sure most of the young academics present will understand. This situation is not their fault. It is their destiny in the context of modern civilization.

The developments in the natural sciences that I attempted to describe in this course have brought our civilization to the point where young people ought to be experiencing profound trepidation. Even without Anthroposophy, they should experience some sort of trepidation as a consequence of their fully human involvement in scholarly attempts at understanding. Any serious and conscientious student of the modern natural sciences can experience some aspects of what confronts human souls struggling with the problem of cognition. Anyone who takes the scientific perspective is confronted with great cosmic problems that are often disguised as petty formulations of facts. These formulations compel us to seek solutions to the soul riddles presented by scientific facts. Without tackling these riddles, we cannot go on living; we feel anxious.

If only our scientific studies would fill us with this trepidation! It would produce not only a longing for the spiritual world but also the ability to perceive it. If presented to human souls and hearts in the right way, even inherently unsatisfying insights and perceptions can kindle higher strivings. In the context of our modern pursuit of knowledge, it can be shattering to realize that there is no basis for experiencing its impact on the human being as a whole. Unless endowed with special gifts and longings, young people face insurmountable obstacles to approaching their highest humanity.

If we turn away from the sciences and consider the humanities, we find that they, too, if presented from a fully human perspective, would produce a soul sensation of being unable to breathe. All the abstract ideas and documented research findings and everything else we find in the humanities today, if presented to young people with human involvement, would result in a compelling urge to get out into the fresh air. And that breath of fresh air is what the Anthroposophical worldview is meant to bring to the modern humanities.

Anyone who has followed the gist of my lectures on the development of modern science[†] will certainly not be able to say that I have been excessively critical of it. To the contrary, I have attempted to prove in these lectures that the modern natural sciences—and, ultimately, the modern humanities as well—have served and must continue to serve as foundations of civilization upon which we can continue to build.

But we cannot help being human; we cannot help being creatures of body, spirit, and soul. Of necessity, young people today are confronted with knowledge that does not embrace their full humanity. Nonetheless, the noblest and most forceful human strivings could still be kindled in these young people if they were introduced to this inherently unsatisfying but necessary knowledge through the full humanity of others, in the highest sense of the word. If that were the case, our young people would need to hear nothing more than the achievements of the modern physical sciences and humanities to develop both the innate urge and the ability to receive spiritual science in full humanity. The seed thus planted in them would then grow into the Anthroposophical science we need to ensure the survival and progress of human civilization.

I believe that if our young friends reflect on these seemingly paradoxical words, they will find a characterization of the most significant anguish imposed on them during their academic studies. I assume that this anguish is why most of them have come to us. But for many, this anguish already belongs to the past, and it is too late to catch up. Anything missed at the appropriate point in a young life is no longer available later in the same form. The substitute for it is to recognize the unique task of young people in cultivating modern Anthroposophical activity.

Your task, should you choose to accept it, is to do whatever your own individual convictions tell you to do on behalf of the Anthroposophical Movement. Do what you recognize as necessary for the survival of human civilization. If you do this, the consciousness of having done your duty toward humankind and the cosmos in an age of extreme human difficulties will persist in your hearts for the duration of this lifetime and beyond. This consciousness will more than make up for what you have lost. If we have a right sense of the young people's situation today, we will also look in the right way at the fact that students have found their way into our circles. And as a result, we in the Anthroposophical Society will gradually develop a talent for establishing connections to young people who for one reason or the other are not members.

From our current sorrowful situation, I hear words resounding that I can also impart to the oldest members of the Anthroposophical Society, namely, that in the Anthroposophical Society today, human beings who truly understand themselves as such can experience something that must be considered seriously if human civilization is to survive, if forces of decline are not to gain the upper hand over forces of ascent. In the context of modern culture and civilization in general, it sounds almost comical to say that we need to ensure that human souls and spirits can act appropriately in the time between falling asleep and reawakening. In the Anthroposophical Movement, however, you have learned that the human spirit and soul are seeds we contribute to the future and to eternity. The aspect of the human being that stays behind in bed when we sleep and is visible as we carry out our daily work from morning to evening is not carried through the portal of death into the spiritual, supersensible world. Through the portal of death, we take only our subtle spiritual aspect, which also exists outside the physical and etheric bodies when we sleep. For the moment, let us disregard the significance of sleep for human beings here on the Earth. Through Anthroposophical spiritual science we realize that this subtle substance, which is imperceptible to ordinary consciousness but alive and active in the time between falling asleep and reawakening, is the aspect we take with us through the portal of death. It is the guise in which we perform our tasks in worlds different from this earthly world, and our ability to perform these tasks depends on the extent to which we have cultivated this soul-spiritual aspect.

In the spiritual world, which is all around us just as the physical world is, live human soul beings not currently incarnated in physical bodies. They may have decades or even centuries to wait before they incarnate on the Earth again. These souls exist in spirit as we physical human beings exist on the Earth. Historical events among physical human beings are shaped not only by earthly individuals but also by forces streaming in from human beings in the period between death and rebirth. These forces are quite real. Just as we stretch out our hands, these beings stretch out their spirit hands into our immediate present. Historical writing based entirely on earthly documentation is dead and dry. In truth, the history that takes place on the Earth is codetermined by spiritual forces belonging to those between death and rebirth. Our history is the result of collaboration between us and human beings currently not incarnated on the Earth.

We sin against humanity by failing to educate our young people in the right way. But what if we fail to educate our own spiritual aspect so that it can develop ever more consciously after passing through the portal of death? If we fail to do this, we sin against humankind's evolution, against the noble work that should be done by unembodied human beings working out of invisible worlds. Between death and rebirth individuals who neglected to cultivate their soul-spiritual aspect while on the Earth experience clouding of their consciousness instead of increasing illumination. If we are to become fully conscious of our humanity, we must include our spiritual aspect.

Modern human beings with an appropriate understanding of the Anthroposophical Movement's impulses need to take Anthroposophical knowledge seriously. Knowledge acquired through Anthroposophy is a life-giving treasure, a cosmic life force. We sin against humanity in a higher sense when we neglect to cultivate what earthly humanity needs for its continued development. The absence of this aspect of our humanity necessarily leads to the decline of earthly life. In addition to what we gladly gain from spiritual science on a more or less theoretical level, it is essential that we also sense the profound seriousness of joining forces with others on behalf of an all-encompassing human concern that we grasp only in the spirit. This concern belongs to young and old alike. It is not limited to any specific group of people. To me, it seems to be a unifying concern that can bring young and old together so that a single spirit prevails within the Anthroposophical Society.

My hope is that young people will contribute the best they have to offer, that older people will learn to understand this contribution, and that understanding on one side will meet with understanding on the other. Only then will we move forward. May the sad days we have just been through and the pain and sorrow that have overcome us now fill our hearts with resolve—not with mere wishes or promises but with resolves so deeply rooted in our souls that they become actions. Even in small circles, we will need actions to compensate for our great loss.

Youthful deeds, if they take the right paths, are deeds the cosmos can use. And as older people, the most beautiful thing we can wish for is to work together with individuals still capable of youthful deeds. If we truly know this, dear friends, young people will also approach us with understanding. We will be able to do what is needed to compensate for our great loss only if the young people who can bring us what the future needs can also see—to their great satisfaction, no doubt—good examples of what older people can do to compensate for this loss. Let us make every effort to see what is good and powerful in one another's contributions, so that our strengths enhance each other. Only then will we move forward.

Restructuring the Anthroposophical Society

Address and Discussion in Preparation for the Delegates' Assembly

STUTTGART, FEBRUARY 8, 1923[†]

Rudolf Steiner: By now at least a draft of a circular[†] to the Anthroposophical Society is available as a basis for further discussion. It might be good if you would discuss your own wishes with the advisory committee that will be in place until the delegates meet. Unlike the former Committee of Thirty, this committee consists of representatives of existing establishments, not their entire membership. It includes two members of the old executive board: Mr. Leinhas of Der Kommende Tag and Dr. Unger representing the remainder of the old board. The other members are Dr. Rittelmeyer, representing the movement for religious renewal, Wolfgang Wachsmuth, Mr. von Grone, Dr. Palmer, Dr. Kolisko, Miss Mücke of the Philosophisch-Anthroposophischer Verlag, and Mr. Werbeck of Hamburg, who represents all other out-of-town interests. I have asked the seven Stuttgart members to work with you to take whatever steps you find necessary. I must leave for Dornach early tomorrow morning and will be back only on Monday. I regret not being able to take part in the next round of discussions, but I believe this is for the best. My absence should not make any difference; you can conduct discussions with these individuals on your own. They represent a full spectrum [of the Society's membership]. Young people are represented by Mr. von Grone and Wolfgang Wachsmuth, whom I expect you will find sympathetic. They are complete newcomers to board membership. In addition, Dr. Palmer has stated his readiness do everything possible to build bridges to young people.

The appeal to the members of the Anthroposophical Society was drafted by those who have led the society up to now, and it contains the essence of what the society must say at this point. From February 25 to 28 delegates of the branches and groups will gather for a general assembly, which will be an opportunity to hear the full spectrum of views on restructuring the society. Our options are either to restructure the Anthroposophical Society or to dissolve it and found something completely new. Founding something new would have been easy in 1918, but now we are publicly involved in concrete developments we cannot pull out of, so the society will have to change from within. The society itself must become more open; we must make it impossible for individuals to feel constrained within it. I think we will be able to do this, but I would like to hear your thoughts on the subject. That it has taken us so long to get this far must be attributed to the deliberateness that comes with age. We would be happy to hear what you have to say right now.

Comment from a participant: A young representative talks about the situation of younger people in the society, referring to what Dr. Steiner said about phases in the society's development in his last lecture to the Stuttgart Branch.†

Rudolf Steiner: What you have said about partitions separating the first, second, and third phases of the movement, which are very different, is quite accurate. We must also consider the fact that each phase lasted approximately seven years and that the society itself is now in its twenty-first year. Clearly, the impulses that led earlier members to join and participate are not the same as the impulses at work in primarily academic youth circles. The people who joined during the first phase were motivated by completely unconscious longings and came with general human interests. They were unaware of their connection to contemporary circumstances and were at an age when people tend not to be able to verbalize that connection with any degree of clarity. This was almost equally true of the second phase. Anthroposophy moved on, but Anthroposophists—with some exceptions—were not especially interested in contemporary issues. For the early joiners, the third phase felt strange and uncomfortable. They were thrown in with newcomers who were dissatisfied not with contemporary circumstances in general but with their very specific experiences in modern educational institutions. These newcomers came to Anthroposophy because they felt out of place in the modern educational system, and their impulses were different from those of the early joiners, who saw Anthroposophy in the contemporary context only to a very limited extent. I have often talked about Anthroposophy in the context of our time, but very little of what I said sank in. You, however, arrived with longings that actually speak to the core of Anthroposophy.

And then there was a strange misunderstanding about our higher-education courses. I do not mean to suggest that they are not valuable, but they were a misunderstanding. You were not looking at all for the content of these courses; you were looking for Anthroposophy as such. Your wishes were misunderstood by the academics who joined the Anthroposophical Society in its earlier phases. They had wanted to merge their academic work with Anthroposophy, but you did not accept that. As time passes, you will discover that you are not in conflict with the bulk of the Anthroposophical Society. Your conflict is really only with our academic members, who wanted to present Anthroposophy through biology, chemistry, physics, or history. That is not what you want. You want pure Anthroposophy. The academic element that infiltrated the society is like a mountain standing in your way. Getting to the other side of the mountain is both difficult and necessary for you. This situation is not unique to you; it is common to the society as a whole. I am sure this challenge can be overcome if there is goodwill on both sides. On the other hand, if we want to move ahead with our work, a bit of specialization will also be necessary.

Comment from a participant: A participant talks about some wishes young people have with regard to restructuring work in the branches, especially lectures and reports.

Rudolf Steiner interrupts: This little book by Albert Steffen about the Educational Course at the Goetheanum† is very valid, because it reproduces the contents of my lectures in a truly artistic way. This is no mere journalistic report; it stands on its own. This is the first time such a thing has been done. We will see if it becomes common practice. It would be good if it did.

The appeal to members will essentially make two points. It will emphasize first the need for internal work in the Anthroposophical Movement and, second, the need for the Anthroposophical Society to present a strong, united front to fend off opponents as they appear—not with polemics, but with really relevant work in full view of the world. We cannot work effectively if one of us says one thing and someone else refutes it. If we do nothing about our opponents, Anthroposophy will fail. Addressing our most important opponents does not give us access to the public. When the Pan-German nationalist groups† spread slanderous statements about Anthroposophy among their membership, they are preaching to the choir. We have no way of reaching their audience. You have to know your audience. There are certain things you cannot say to a Catholic audience. If our rebuttals are wrong, they are wrong. But if they are right, they do not do us any good, either—in fact, they harm us, at least among Catholics.

As our work in higher education develops, people like Leisegang† will start coming out of the woodwork. I am really concerned that the old reactionary forces are getting ever stronger. When we first established the Hochschulbund [Federation for Higher Education], the chances of holding back these old forces were much greater than they are now. I am afraid that you are going to endure a great deal of hardship. But even if Anthroposophy is killed, it will rise again, because it is a necessity. Either the Earth has a future or it does not, and the Earth's future is inseparable from Anthroposophy. If Anthroposophy has no future, humanity as a whole will not have a future either. The intention alone is enough. Disseminating Anthroposophy can take place in different stages. I believe that it is imperative for you to get over the mountain I described earlier and to do so in a peaceful manner and to the benefit of the society.

If we successfully refute their antagonistic statements, it simply makes them angry. Being in the right harms our cause, perhaps more so than being in the wrong. Antagonism of this sort can be defused only through positive work, by making ourselves as strong as others are. Dr. Rittelmeyer recently said, as I myself have often pointed out, "We have no idea how potentially inflammatory the situation is out there." In the near future, this antagonism toward us will be expressed in terrible ways. We must present a united front. All of our movement's positive manifestations, such as the Movement for Religious Renewal,[†] actually put the society at risk. No one had expected us to enter this field.

Comment from a participant: A participant talks about changing young people's relationship to the society.

Rudolf Steiner: Keep in mind that old, historically mature cultural streams require very different soul attitudes than do young movements. We simply cannot imagine anymore how difficult it was to be a Christian in the early centuries of Christianity. Nowadays being a Christian is easy. When I say it was difficult, I am not referring to the possibility of martyrdom but simply to the inner, personal difficulties. It was difficult to see oneself as a Christian. Today, in a certain sense, it is equally difficult to be a good Anthroposophist. Our long-time members have carried the burden of being associated with an emerging spiritual movement, and this difficulty is reflected in their entire soul attitude. As a result, they are less understanding of certain phenomena. Those who have been Anthroposophists for longer than you young people sometimes talk at cross-purposes when they speak to you.

I recently encountered a very blatant example of this. These friends had had discussions with you, and after the meeting they all felt that the gap had been bridged and that everyone understood each other down to the last detail. They were quite sincere in feeling this way. The mood among you was quite different—you felt that no meeting of the minds had occurred and were ready to go out and organize the opposition. This situation reflects how easily one can succumb to illusion concerning the circumstances of life, when one is in a certain way of life that I have characterized. Being an Anthroposophist is hard, and it is also hard to overcome a certain rigidity. These people are sincere in taking illusion for reality. You, on the other hand, approach the situation with a certain freshness of soul, so you are less likely to have these illusions than someone who is already tired. Many of us are tired, worn down by the difficulties we have faced. That is why there has been so much talking at cross-purposes.

Comment from a participant: A participant talks about his original plan to redirect forces that are being used, especially by young people, to oppose Anthroposophy and to organize them for productive purposes.

Rudolf Steiner: We need to take a realistic look at some of these things. Somewhere in the future the educational facilities you imagine must exist. Meanwhile, however, even if all of our hopes for the future are still nothing more than seeds, it is not right for higher education to be a mockery of what it should be. I am really concerned about how far we have to go. The whole system of higher education is in bad shape. A century ago, at least it presented a unitary worldview, but that is long gone and with it any sense of human dignity. Mr. Leisegang, who aspires to become a full professor and probably soon will, has just published the first volume of a work on Plato. Never mind how he treated me—he treats Plato much worse. He makes a caricature of Plato, but people do not notice. You know, what really concerns me is how far we are from being able to create a college.

Comment from a participant: A participant tells of a prison camp where the prisoners created a college, as an example of how to create a college for spiritual science.

Rudolf Steiner: We cannot establish a college today because the first prerequisite is to have scholars available to serve as instructors. We have the ideas. We have thought about how to get started, but it will be difficult to establish a completely new and different way of educating people as long as the people who work in our movement have to starve, to put it bluntly. It is getting more difficult by the day because inflation is making it almost impossible to pay salaries. For purely spiritual reasons, I must take every opportunity to emphasize two things: First, we must work with great intensity to become as strong as possible. Second, we must spend all our energy on increasing the size of our circle of friends. Current circumstances make the numbers important. On the spiritual level, the opposite must be true, of course, but in view of current circumstances, this is how it is. Expanding our circle need not happen at the expense of superficiality, but we must make every effort to have a sufficient number of friends. If we do not, individuals and our movement as such may not survive. That is simply how it is. As young people, you must not be afraid of being as strong as you can in order to achieve the expansion we need.

Comment from a participant: A participant talks about how difficult it is to communicate with older people.

Rudolf Steiner: All judgments aside, the lack of understanding is mutual! That older people are the way they are is not their fault; it is their destiny. But the resistance of young people to their elders is simultaneously a means of protection and a weakness!

Become geniuses at being interested![†]

Three Main Questions for the Anthropsophical Youth Movement

Address and Question-and-Answer Session

STUTTGART, FEBRUARY 14, 1923

I believe I can safely assume that you are all familiar with the appeal that has been issued to the members of the Anthroposophical Society in Germany.† In Anthroposophical circles we have realized that it is time to set a new course, and we are aware that this shift also requires a change in the society's leadership as it has been exercised in Stuttgart up to the present. The details of the change will be discussed at the upcoming delegates' assembly.† I believe that you will be especially interested in everything that happens there. When the outer circumstances of your life led you to seek Anthroposophy, you found the society in a certain condition. You imagined that there must be someplace where young people could find what they seek from the depths of their souls but cannot discover in modern worldly institutions. You were embedded in these institutions and discovered that their recent historical development did not correspond to the demands of the human soul.

Perhaps you looked for a place where this demand for true humanity could be met, and eventually you believed you had found it in the Anthroposophical Society, but the reality did not live up to your expectations. Not all of you felt conflicted as the result of this situation. You were dissatisfied with some things but let it go at acknowledging your dissatisfaction. Both old and fresh realities within the Anthroposophical Society are forcing us to face the fact that the society simply has not kept pace with the development of Anthroposophy. We must seriously consider whether to create something completely new or to allow the old Anthroposophical Society to continue, but with a new impulse. These questions are being considered by individuals who were involved more or less closely in leading the society. They are looking at many old sins—mainly sins of omission—and debating whether to abandon some bureaucratic structures. With the understanding of the representatives of the Anthroposophical Society in Germany, they are attempting to create a basis for the society's continuance.

Developments in recent years have brought together a large number of very good workers in Stuttgart. As individuals, they are all excellent people, and collectively they are a truly great movement in their own way. But they also get in each other's way, as one of the leading individuals put it. This has proved unproductive in many respects. Individuals have done their jobs very well. We have good reason to be satisfied with the performance of the Waldorf School. But despite the presence and activity of Anthroposophists, the Anthroposophical Society has been gradually disappearing and falling out of favor. We must put an end to this process, or the society will fall apart completely.

Clearly, you were very aware that this was going on and formed your own opinions about it. The society needed a new form, and it had to come from the old backers. After all, the bulk of the Anthroposophical Society's membership has contributed twenty-three years of work. Many of them are in a very different situation but still find something that persists: if the branch falls apart, the individual Anthroposophists remain, and Anthroposophy continues to spread. An example of this is Mrs. Wolfram, who led the Leipzig branch for years before stepping down. Recently, she founded a local group of the Bund für Freies Gesitesleben [Federation for Independent Spiritual Life] in deliberate contrast to the local Anthroposophical circle. As the example of Leipzig illustrates (the current branch leader is a former student), replacing old forces with young ones is not enough. We must create a balance between the results of two decades of work and the fresh forces of new arrivals.

Our appeal to members is intended to represent this balance in the right way. Many members joined the Anthroposophical Society seeking a calming element, so it was always very unpleasant for them when the need arose to use pointed language against outside opponents. We will not be able to avoid this in the future, either, because the opposition is assuming ever stranger forms that require an atypically defensive position from us. We must not lose sight of this fact. For older people who became accustomed to the calming element, being good Anthroposophists today is difficult.

It is very bad when our experiences of Anthroposophy become habitual. Anthroposophy actually needs to be acquired anew every day. It is not enough to simply remember what we have already covered. The difficulties of the old Anthroposophical Society are due to the unfortunate fact that human beings are creatures of habit. Anthroposophy, however, must not become a habit. Difficulties also arise because Anthroposophy challenges us to rise above all egotism, even with regard to our knowledge. Like other living things, human beings can be self-centered, of course, but Anthroposophy and egotism are a bad match. It is possible to be egotistical and still be a tolerably good materialist or even a tolerably good person in general, but you get into constantly recurring contradictions if you are egotistical and an Anthroposophist.

This dilemma is due to the fact that human beings actually do not live entirely on the Earth. When we descend to the Earth from our pre-birth existence, a bit of each of us remains behind in the astral realm. Similarly, when we wake up in the morning, not all of our supersensible being enters the body. We leave part of our existence behind in the supersensible world. But since social structures are based entirely on earthly circumstances, it is impossible to establish a totally satisfactory social order in which human beings can be completely happy. I have said repeatedly that organizing social life in a threefold way is not heaven on the Earth; it simply demonstrates the possibilities of the body social. To claim more would be deceiving, because human beings are not exclusively earthly beings. We must be aware of this fact if we are to sense our full humanity, but if we do, we can never be satisfied with a merely materialistic worldview. We are ready for Anthroposophy only when we truly sense our full humanity—that is, when we realize that we cannot descend to Earth completely, when we acknowledge the needs of our supersensible aspect.

Obviously, you yourselves felt something of this sort quite instinctively and found your way to the Anthroposophical Society as a result, but now this situation has led to certain difficulties. On the one hand, Anthroposophy must never become a habit. On the other, Anthroposophy cannot be taken up by beings who are exclusively Earth-oriented. Anything that merges into egotism becomes Earth-related. Consequently, people become worse human beings when they are both supersensibly oriented and egotistical: the supersensible being assumes the character of a material being. Spiritual feeling and sensing are incompatible with egotism. At this point, obstacles begin to appear.

But this is also the point where the Anthroposophical Movement coincides with your search, which is based on the circumstance that all connection to the spiritual world has been lost. In your search for your humanity, you are attempting to escape from our superficial institutions. You must attempt to come to grips with what already exists while being aware of your inner being. If you can relate the difficulties you encounter to the difficulties of others, together we will find our way to a strong Anthroposophical Society—including those circles seeking inner experience—and a strong Anthroposophical Movement in the near future.

If you choose this path, you will experience privation and difficulties, because humankind does not want such a movement to exist. More experiences are in store for you before you will be truly ready to join our cause with your whole being. Then Anthroposophy will assert itself under all circumstances. The breakdown of the civilized world is so pronounced that Europe cannot survive for long if it does not turn to the spirit. Only spirit will allow our civilization to rise again. Hence it is absolutely necessary for human beings to seek the spirit, and you have made the right choice. The next step is to decide on our work for the near future. We are meeting today to hear about how you imagine this work and what your intentions are.

Question: A participant asks what form scholarly work should take today.

Rudolf Steiner: With regard to scholarly work, none of what will need to be present in the future exists yet, which is not to say that there is absolutely nothing now. Already present in all branches of academic knowledge are the outer facts that we must move forward into areas that will be needed in the future if human souls are not to become corrupted. A number of fields of scholarly research have already produced significant results, from the smallest collections to the London Museum. With regard to the academic knowledge of the future, however, current researchers are inwardly dead and therefore cannot do anything with these resources. Because they arrived at this body of material through an automatic, unconscious development of sorts, they do not know what to do with the information they have.

The dilemma for Anthroposophists is not that it is impossible to approach these fields from the Anthroposophical perspective—the comprehensive ideas and spiritual perceptions are already available—but that the body of facts needed for academic research is monopolized by people who do not know what to do with it. The people who ought to be describing the contents of our culture stand there empty-handed. Meanwhile, the body of facts is not being presented to university students in ways that encourage seeing these facts in the right light. For example, when you are shown a skeleton in zoology class or a plant in botany, you do not get anything out of it. You simply learn that the skull goes here, the shoulder blade there, the tibia down here, and so on. A table or a machine could be described in the same way. When your instructors show you a skeleton, you cannot develop any feeling for the process of its growth and development. It is shown to you as if it were nothing more than a machine that can be broken down into its component parts.

But what do you see if you first learn to imbue your perceptions with soul? For example, if you look along the spine of a dog skeleton[†] from back to front, you can see that moon forces are at work in the tail end and sun forces in the skull, while Earth forces work along the legs. This becomes a matter of direct perception if we do not prevent people from seeing it by failing to teach them how to perceive in this way. As I just said, we would have to be able to see it in the same way that we see (and remember) a sculpture of a human figure—the fact that it represents a human being is a matter of direct perception. In the same way, we ought to be able to see that sun and moon forces are active in the skeleton of a dog. We simply need an adequate basis for such perceptions.

At the moment, however, those who have access to the facts do not know what to do with them, and those who actually need these scholarly resources do not have access to them. This is why we say there is nothing there, but we might equally well say that everything is already there. The great difficulty is in finding one's way. If students today have not been gifted with exceptionally favorable karma or if their souls have not been guided in ways that allow them to acknowledge the existence of a spiritual world, they are led away from that world, and the fact that a spiritual world exists seems simply ludicrous to them. Students today realize, for example, that an embryo develops within the mother's body, but it does not occur to them that a human or animal embryo would have to be seen as the product of elements of reality—specifically, that embryonic development depends on protein breakdown in a certain part of the maternal body. This breakdown, however, is interrupted by the intervention of cosmic forces, and the entire macrocosm is then reflected in miniature in proteins that are reconstituted as soon as they are broken down. As a result, the form of the cosmos asserts itself in the development of the embryo. The maternal organism simply supplies matter, which must first be broken down so the cosmos can build it up again. Considering embryonic development from the perspective of modern science is like taking a paper rose and claiming that it is freshly picked from the bush. Such examples make it obvious that a complete reversal is needed not only in all areas of academic knowledge but also in art and religion. Even in religion, the worst sort of materialism prevails.

In Germany the situation is especially difficult right now. People are gradually losing the courage to go on living. This courage, however, can come only from the supersensible world. Of course, doubt is possible, but doubt comes from the sense-perceptible world, whereas the courage to overcome doubt and to perceive in the right way comes from the supersensible world. During the course of scientific lectures that I gave in Dornach at Christmas, I pointed out that wherever atoms appear, death is present. Atomism is the science of dead matter. Many of the facts confirmed by modern science are pulling it closer to Anthroposophical scientific view. Facts pointing to spiritual science can be found everywhere. Radium, for example, is the most striking example of decaying matter spitting out atoms. Facts pointing to the spirit are everywhere, but superficial science lacks the courage to follow these pointers.

Also, a much faster-moving global economy† replaced our many different national economies in the nineteenth century. The slower tempo of national economies is evident even in the smallest areas. The trains that the old national economy used to run were much slower than those arriving in Stuttgart today, which are run by the global economy. Attempting to revert from a global economy to national economies will simply destroy what has already been accomplished.

Question: A participant asks how to develop a relationship to architecture and sculpture.

Rudolf Steiner: One's worldview is very important in this regard. The modern worldview that takes mere logic and sensory observation as its starting points is forced to imagine that the world ceases to be accessible at a certain point. We have set outer, natural limits that we can no longer get past. Our logic consists of inner laws that we impose on ourselves; it does not include nature at all. All knowledge, even purely scholarly knowledge, must merge into pure artistry. We must teach ourselves to be artists so that we can shape forms as nature shapes them. We can learn this as soon as we discover where nature becomes an artist. We must deepen our knowledge of nature to such an extent that we see plants, animals, and humans as artists. Only then will we recognize the infinitely interesting static and dynamic proportions encompassed by the human body, for example. We will see how each bone represents a system of beams or girders. We will understand the difference between standing with legs apart in the frontal plane and stepping forward. Each human body is a very subtle architectural structure.

Older religious creeds taught their candidates for initiation about the miraculous ways in which human bodies are embedded in the cosmos through their dynamic and static proportions. When we look at a statue of the Buddha, we see the dynamics and stasis of the human body. The broad base of the legs, crossed below the torso, emphasizes the structure and static character of the torso. Architectural forms are derived from how human beings move and stand. A perfectly proportioned building is nothing other than a perfect, idealized human being standing and walking. Each culture's architecture understands and represents the dynamics and stasis of human bodies in its own particular way. Assyrian and Babylonian culture represents the proclamation of the Logos through the human body bending forward, Greek culture through the standing body at rest. To achieve a living knowledge of all architectural forms, we must simply know how the human body takes its place within the cosmos. Today architectural imagination is severely limited. Nonetheless, modern architecture must be born out of our own experience as human beings, out of the "know thyself."† This is what we attempted in the Goetheanum.

When we move from the proportions of human movement to proportions of human form, we shift from architecture to sculpture. Sculpture is the experience of the proportions of human form. The transition from architecture to sculpture means that movement shifts from balance to form. The more our knowledge of the human being advances, the more possible it will be to develop art and differentiated architecture and sculpture that will reflect the nature of the human being. To make this transition to the human form, however, we now need an independent social realm based on selflessness and love. The Greeks were still able to experience their own individual forms through individual embedding in the cosmos. In contrast, modern human beings must discover sculpture by synthesizing their perceptions of other people. The Greeks did not need to observe other people; they discovered sculpture by experiencing their own bodies.

Art is based on revealing hidden forces of nature. We need art in order to understand the human being and to understand nature. Modern sculpture needs to incorporate a living, artistic view of the human. In the human being, we must learn to see Luciferic activity in the form of the head, as I attempted to show it in the group sculpture in the Goetheanum,† and the counter pole of hardening, the activity of Ahriman, in the bony skeleton. Their interaction then shapes the ideal human body. We must again achieve the human form.

Hebrew culture followed through with the moral impulses inherent in its religion in a profound way, but it did not dare to make an image of its god. As human cultural development continued, we gradually achieved a logically empirical conception of human nature and lost the artistic aspect of our understanding. The result was the separation of worldview and art. On the one hand, we have our logically empirical worldview and, on the other, artistic imagination. As yet, no connection has been established between consideration of laws uncoupled from the human being and artistic arbitrariness. The architecture and sculpture of the future will need to be created out of an understanding of the entirety of the human form.

Comment from a participant: What can you say about the difficulties students have in getting Anthroposophically oriented papers accepted?

Rudolf Steiner: The Anthroposophical Society must realize how important it is not to allow Anthroposophical accomplishments to go unrecognized. It must learn to appreciate works such as Dr. von Baravalle's, or Caroline von Heydebrand's pamphlet on the negative aspects of experimental psychology and educational experiments.† Assuming that our research institutes succeed in answering the questions I have posed in my lecture cycles on natural history, we must gradually reach a point where even our opponents develop respect for the work done under the auspices of the Anthroposophical Society. We must train ourselves and others to acknowledge individual accomplishments in Anthroposophical settings. When this becomes a matter of conscience in the society, professors will no longer be able to reject Anthroposophically oriented papers without cause. People with practical experience in our research institutes must support the efforts of students working on dissertations or papers for seminars. The Anthroposophical Society must develop enough clout so that professors will refrain from rejecting Anthroposophically oriented papers of adequate substance for fear of having the society breathing down their necks.

[Rudolf Steiner asks whether student representatives will attend the delegates' assembly.]

Comment from a participant: A student representative talks about the delegates' assembly.

Rudolf Steiner: It would be good if you could be as thorough and serious as possible answering the three primary questions involved here:

First: How are things going with the student and youth movements in general?

Second: What are those who sense their full humanity on the basis of Anthroposophy experiencing in universities?

Third: What do students and other young people expect of the Anthroposophical Society?

We need a vivid understanding of these issues in order to act on them effectively. In the early 1870s Nietzsche gave a vivid and brilliant account† of the state of our educational institutions. He described what schools ought to be like and what he expected of them. Unfortunately, Nietzsche's contribution to this subject has been almost forgotten. Today we would have to ask for even more than Nietzsche did. The three questions I just listed are the most important. All will go well if we have people at the core of the Anthroposophical Society who are not only highly interested in their areas of specialization but also attentive to everything going on in the society and in the world at large. Such interest and attentiveness have been lacking, as evidenced by the fact that the development of the Movement for Religious Renewal went almost unnoticed until its first public appearance. Universal attentiveness and interest must enter the Anthroposophical Society. Thoughts do not grow; they remain unchanged. Attentiveness and interest, however, can grow and bear fruit.

Above all, we must clearly and decisively seek out and follow the path to supersensible worlds. If we do so, we will also find the right relationship to our fellow human beings. And the opposite is also true: Having found the right way to relate to human beings, we will be on the verge of entering supersensible worlds.

Essays on the Youth Section of the Independent School of Spiritual Science†

Announcing a Section for Youth

NEWSLETTER, FEBRUARY 24, 1924†

It has become evident that a Section should be added to those the Executive Council of the Anthroposophical Society is already endeavoring to establish at the Goetheanum. If the Executive Council's intentions are met halfway by the people in question, forming this Section is indeed feasible. Throughout the years, a certain contrast has always been recognized between youth and old age. This platitude offers consolation to many concerned about phenomena in the life of young people today. This facile consolation, however, is potentially harmful. The "spirit of the present" should guide our understanding of both the questionable aberrations of today's young people and their all-too-justified striving for something other than what older people have to offer.

Of immediate concern to us are the young people whose circumstances lead them to pursue academic careers. They are presented with academic knowledge—secure, solid knowledge that is supposed to fructify daily life. It would make no sense for us to complain about this knowledge after the manner of many laypeople, yet we cannot deny that it petrifies young souls before they have a chance to recognize its solidity and fruitfulness.

The greatness of science today is due to its vigorous opposition to a worldview that includes the spiritual since the middle of the nineteenth century. At that time it was recognized that human knowledge stands on shaky ground when the valleys of objective research are abandoned for the heights of an all-embracing conception of the world (weltanschauung). Frightened by experiences of these heights, people then attempted to divorce science from the comprehensive worldview [which includes the spiritual]. They clung to the "facts" in the valleys of nature and avoided the high paths of the spirit.

For those who actively combated the mingling of science and spirit, opposition to the comprehensive worldview provided a certain inner satisfaction. Young adults today, however, are no longer happy with this antagonistic stance. The struggle against the "uncertain" and "visionary" character of the worldview no longer engenders satisfaction in their souls because it has died out, and so, there is nothing left to fight against. Espousing the separation of science and the comprehensive worldview has become meaningless because the worldview [that includes spirituality] is dead.

Out of the depths of undivided human nature, young people today have made an important discovery that is based on feeling rather than intellect. They have discovered that life without the all-encompassing conception of the world is unworthy of human beings. Many older people succumbed to the power of the "proof" against the comprehensive worldview. Young adults are no longer impressed with the power of rational, intellectual proof. They instinctively sense that such proof is impotent wherever the human heart speaks out of invincible impulses.

Young people are presented with scientific knowledge that owes its certainty to a total absence of the worldview that includes spirituality. The youth want this comprehensive worldview. Science, however, needs the perspective of youth.

Here at the Goetheanum, we hope to understand young people and accompany them on their search for ways to achieve a worldview that includes spirituality. We hope that, in the light of this all-encompassing worldview, true love for science will be engendered. Rather than losing science to dreamy spirituality, we want to really find science through conscious spiritual experience. The Executive Council of the Anthroposophical Society seeks the understanding of young people. If this understanding is forthcoming, the "Section for the Spiritual Striving of Youth" will become a productive force in our life.

On the Youth Section of the Independent School of Spiritual Science

NEWSLETTER, MARCH 9, 1924

I. What I have to say on this subject to our older members

The announcement of the "Section for the Spiritual Striving of Youth" at the Goetheanum has met with a resounding response from young adults. Representatives of the Independent Anthroposophical Society and younger members living at the Goetheanum have informed the *Executive Council* of the Anthroposophical Society that they are ready to support the *Executive Council's* intentions with all their hearts. I see these two statements of intent as valuable starting points for a wonderful part of our Society's work. If we succeed in bridging the gap between old and young in today's culture, the Society will have accomplished something important.

If we read between the lines of these letters, we can hear our young people speaking in a tone of voice that is new in humanity's development. We sense that their inner vision is not focused on preserving and supplementing our inheritance from the past. They are turning toward the dawn of a new life that originates in realms that reveal the eternal, free of temporal constraints.

If we older people hope to be understood by today's youth, we must allow the eternal to become the driving force in our approach to temporal concerns, and we must do so in ways that young people understand. It has been said that young people are unresponsive to their elders and reject their hard-won insights and mature experiences. Such statements originate in older people's displeasure with the behavior of youth.

It is true that young people have isolated themselves from older adults, preferring the company of their peers, and that they do not want to listen to what their elders have to say to them. This state of affairs is cause for concern, for these young people will also eventually grow old and abandon their current behavior. They want to be young in the right way and wonder what that entails. They will no longer be able to ask this question when they themselves grow old.

In the opinion of older people, the young should lay aside their arrogance and look up to their elders to find the goal on which their youthful spiritual vision is focused. Such statements suggest that young people are at fault for not being drawn to older people. But if older people were truly "old," young people would indeed look to them as examples. The human soul—especially when young—is naturally drawn to and attempts to unite with that which is foreign to it. But in older people today, young adults fail to see any human element that is both foreign and desirable, because these older people are not really "old." They have absorbed a great deal of information and can talk about many topics, but this knowledge has not matured in them. They have grown older in years but their souls have not kept up. What they say using their old brains is no different from what they once said using young brains. Young people sense this lack of maturity in older people. Instead, they sense young soul-constitutions like their own, but in aging bodies, and they turn away because this discrepancy feels untruthful to them.

For decades, older people have cultivated the notion that we "cannot know anything" about the indwelling spirit in the world's objects and processes. Young people who hear such statements naturally feel that older people have nothing to tell them. Young people are quite capable of "not knowing" without any help; they will listen only to old people who have actual knowledge. Talking about the impossibility of knowing is somehow tolerable if it is done with the freshness of youth, but hearing such talk coming from old brains is a desolating experience for human souls, especially young souls.[†]

Young people today turn away from older people not because the latter have grown old but because they have remained young—that is, because they don't understand how to grow old in the right way. Older people today lack this self-knowledge. Growing old in the right way means allowing the spirit to unfold in our souls as befits an aging body. When we do this, we show young people not only *what time has done to the body* but also *what eternity reveals through the spirit.* Young people will find their way to older people who seriously attempt to experience spirit. To say that we must act young when we are with young people is just an empty phrase. As older people, we must understand—and demonstrate to young people—how to be old in the right way.

The young are fond of criticizing what comes toward them from older people, and they have every right to do so, because the burden of what older people have failed to accomplish on behalf of humankind's progress rests on the shoulders of the young. It is not appropriate, however, for older people to simply join in the criticism. To avoid confrontation, young adults may tolerate such behavior for a while, but ultimately they get tired of the overly strident tones of these "old young folks." There is more vitality in the criticism of young voices.

In the context of its search for spirit, Anthroposophy is attempting to find a setting in which younger people enjoy associating with older people. The *Executive Council* of the Anthroposophical Society has every reason to be pleased at how its announcement has been received by young people. The Society's active members, however, must not leave the *Executive Council* in the lurch. In addition to positive responses, I have also received letters whose contents *must* be heard by all whose hearts belong to the Anthroposophical Society. "There could come a day when we 'young people' will feel obliged to break away from the Anthroposophical Society, just as inner reasons once compelled you to leave the Theosophical Society."

This day could indeed come if we in the Society fail to make the "Youth Section" a reality in the near future. It is to be hoped, however, that the active members of the Society will follow the lead of the *Executive Council* at the Goetheanum so that young people will increasingly feel the need to join forces with Anthroposophy.

Today I have been talking to older members about young people. In the next issue, I will speak to young people about what is on my heart.

* * *

Newsletter, March 16, 1924

II. What I have to say on this subject to our younger members

In the words of the letter sent to members by the committee of the Independent Anthroposophical Society on the occasion of my announcement of a Section for Youth, I consider "the youth issue" so important that "it can become the subject of a spiritual-scientific discipline of its own." This is indeed how I feel about this issue. Anyone who has read the account of my life in our weekly publication "The Goetheanum" will understand why. When I was as young as those who speak through this letter, I felt quite isolated by a soul-constitution that has now become evident among young adults in general. At that time, my age peers felt differently than I did. According to this letter, our culture no longer "allows young people to acquire a comprehensive worldview in the course of preparing for a profession," and "aspiring to such a worldview" is incompatible with "professional involvement." In my youth, this culture was still in its ascendancy, and young people experienced it as the flower or culmination of the latest stage in humankind's development. They felt liberated from the vagaries of ideological aspirations and secure in the prospect of professions resting on the "secure" foundations of "scientific knowledge."

I, too, observed the "flowering" of this civilization, but I sensed that it would bear no real fruit for humanity. My young peers, swept along by the experience of flowering, felt otherwise. In their enthusiasm for the sterile flower, they failed to notice the absence of fruit.

Today everything is different. The flower has faded, and instead of fruit we confront an entity that is remote from life and petrifies our humanity. Young people today feel the chill of a civilization devoid of spirituality. In contrast, my age peers still took pleasure in the sterile flower—at least in the superficial levels of their consciousness—because its sterility had not yet become evident. And as a flower, the bloom was indeed glorious. Enjoying its splendor, however, hid the deeper layers of our consciousness, the layers where our longing for true humanity is alive and invincible. Young people today can no longer take pleasure in the wilted flower. The uppermost layer of their consciousness has grown barren and the deeper layers are exposed. The longing for an all-encompassing conception of the world is revealed in their hearts and threatens to wound their soul life.

For young people today, being young exposes the longing for spirit and has therefore become a riddle to be solved. Although the Age of Light has dawned, it remains unrecognized because most human souls are still filled with the aftereffects of past darkness. But anyone who senses the presence of spiritual beings knows that "light" has dawned.

I would like to ask the young people of today not to be too harsh on the "old folks" like me who were young forty years ago. Of course some of us remain superficial and flaunt an emptiness that we mistake for superiority. Others, however, are simply resigned to a fate that has deprived us of the living, vital experience of our true humanity. Fate set us down in the last phase of the Dark Age, when experiencing matter dug the grave of spirituality. Today's young people, however, are standing at the grave and finding it empty. Spirit cannot die and cannot be buried.

This light will become perceptible only when the riddles of existence are reborn and formulated anew. Being young is one of the first of these riddles. How do we experience being young in a world of age and rigidity? On the feeling level, this question is alive in young people today. Because being young has become one of life's riddles, any active and vital attempt to solve it can happen only in the context of an independent spiritual-scientific discipline. In the context of this discipline, we do not talk about being young in empty phrases. Rather, we seek the light that must shine on youth so that it can perceive its own humanity.

Today's young people aspire to a comprehensive worldview that will imbue their life's work with warmth. They are afraid of professions created by a civilization devoid of such a worldview. They seek professions that derive from our humanity instead of killing it. Finding one's place in the world without losing one's humanity in the process requires a living, vital relationship to the world on the soul level. Such a relationship, however, can develop only through the experience of a comprehensive worldview. This attitude frames the Executive Council's announcement of its efforts to bring young

Anthroposophists together in a Youth Section to engage in activity that acknowledges our true humanity.

But there is one more thing I would like to say to our younger members. If we succeed in supplying the Youth Section with the right content, active Anthroposophists who have understood how to grow old in the right way will want to make common cause with you. If this happens, I hope you will not say that you don't want to sit at the same table with old folks. Anthroposophy is supposed to be ageless; it dwells in eternity, where all human beings come together. You young people are seeking a field of activity within the Anthroposophical Society where you can be young together. But "old" Anthroposophists totally imbued with the life of Anthroposophy will be drawn to youth. They will discover that what they have acquired with age can be communicated best to young people. And young people will struggle in vain to achieve true humanity, if they avoid contact with the maturity that will also come to them one day. In the cosmic cycle, what has grown old must always be rejuvenated, or it will lose its very essence and succumb to insubstantiality. And from Anthroposophists who have grown old in the right way, young people will learn what they need to know to avoid experiencing their own aging as undesirable, yet inescapable.

* * *

NEWSLETTER, MARCH 23, 1924

III. More of what I have to say to our younger members

Wherever the Youth Movement appears today, it arises out of a sense of something lacking. But what is missing? Our modern culture is full to overflowing with things worth knowing, so why does young people's conscious experience focus on a lack?

The obvious conclusion is that this excess confuses young people so they cannot understand its contents. But experience shows that this conclusion is false. In fact, young people understand perfectly well what our civilization offers them. Anything that can be grasped through thinking can be understood, and in spite of its excesses, modern culture can be grasped almost entirely through thinking alone.

When young people begin to relate to our culture, they realize that they understand it. Their healthy instincts tell them that understanding through thinking will be their destiny in the longer term. "Understanding," however, is not satisfying for young people. They need to experience with full hearts, with their entire souls, things that they are waiting to *understand* with maturity. Young people sense that growing old means gradually transforming experience into understanding.

What today's young people receive from our culture allows people to grow old but not to be young. Our civilization has almost nothing to offer the first phase of life. To absorb the contents of our culture on its own terms, we could not set foot on Earth before age twenty.

Our civilization has lost the spirit; its thinking encompasses only material things. Such thoughts can only be understood, not experienced. Once understood, they are incapable of transformation and lie heavy in our souls like stones. They are complete as soon as they arise; they are not capable of growth. But young people must grow, and they want the contents of their souls to grow with them.

Real spiritual science also manifests only in thoughts, but its thoughts can be perceived and experienced. No one can receive them with a greater degree of maturity than he or she already possesses. These thoughts, like their human recipients, grow and mature. If I'm eighteen years old and you present me with thoughts derived from the material world, I receive them in the same way that I would at age forty or fifty. But if people who are seventy make it possible for me to experience thoughts of spiritual origin as they relate to those individuals' unfolding humanity, these thoughts unite harmoniously with the makeup of my eighteen-year-old soul and continue to grow and mature along with me.

Materialistic ways of thinking and perceiving insist that young people fill themselves with "old" contents. But young people want to experience their youthfulness. Experiencing the old means missing their youth. The Youth Section at the Goetheanum wants to provide young people with living insight that allows them to experience their own youthfulness in a living and vital way. Today's civilization provides no thoughts that allow people to experience being young. Real spiritual science will provide such thoughts.

When we older people hear young people talking today, we are often surprised at how old they sound. They are simply echoing what they hear from their elders. They take in "old" contents but do not unite with them; they feel untrue to themselves when they attempt to experience them. They make statements they do not experience as true. Meanwhile, their own truth remains hidden within, unrevealed even to themselves. It suffocates them like a nightmare developing from within.

Young people want to be *free to breathe* so they can make the nightmare disappear. They want to *wake up* into healthy perception of spirit and to be fully conscious of being young. The thoughts available in our materialistic culture, however, reduce awareness of youthfulness to the level of a dream—that is, a state of suppressed consciousness. As a result, youthful consciousness navigates the realities of the mechanical world in a suppressed state. The hammer strokes and electrical impulses of this world beat on young people's dreams but cannot induce wakefulness because they are not human; they exist outside of human beings.

Spiritual science exists for souls who want to wake up. It attempts not only to convey knowledge but also to make life accessible, to free people to transform life into knowledge.

Philistine, materialistic would-be poets will object that taking away young people's dreams and waking them up would deprive them of the best of their youthfulness. Anyone who talks likes this does not realize that dreams are most valuable when illumined by the light of wakefulness. Our mechanistic civilization does not shed joyful light on the dreams of youth. Instead, it crushes them as they arise and makes them burdensome and oppressive.

What the Youth Section hopes to accomplish can be expressed here only in images such as this. The Youth Section will not publish "programs," nor will it provide explanations of the "essence of youth." It will attempt to allow life to arise from its young founding members' sense that something is missing. The result will be a "wisdom of youth" that can continue to unfold anew each day.

Beginning immediately after the announcement of the Youth Section, young people living at the Goetheanum have enthusiastically expressed their intention to work in this Section. In my first appeal, I said that the Youth Section will be effective if its intentions are understood. I sincerely believe that enthusiasm will produce the right kind of understanding. I do not mean the rational understanding I mentioned earlier. Young people can do without that. I am using the same word to mean something quite different, namely, the understanding that arises out of the whole human being instead of out of intellect alone.

The Executive Council can only hope that its efforts will continue to meet with enthusiasm and that the life-force of spiritual science will prove adequate to supply worthy efforts to support. The Executive Council aspires to live together with young people in such a way that they are able to bring their youthfulness to older people in true humanity. We believe that is what young people are lacking and what their hearts desire.

On the Youth Section of the Independent School of Spiritual Science

NEWSLETTER, MARCH 30, 1924

Once again, I would like to address our younger friends in the Anthroposophical Society on the subject of the founding of the Youth Section. Within the circle of our young people, two contrasting opinions have become apparent. One group experiences a searching that feels inherent in being young. This group is drawn to Anthroposophy in the hope of finding what they are looking for. They realize that this search leads into the depths of the human soul and that contemporary culture cannot lead us there. These young people seek esoteric knowledge because they sense intuitively that it is the only way to experience the true inner content of being human.

These young people will find it easy to accept what the Executive Council of the Anthroposophical Society hopes to accomplish by establishing a Section for Youth. Although the primary concern and explicit task of the Executive Council is to cultivate esoteric activity, its members respect the independence of individuals and will not stand in the way of their personal efforts. In guiding the Youth Section, the Executive Council will ensure that esotericism is given its due, in the belief that a true "youth wisdom" can also be found in true esotericism.

There is another group of young people, however, who have a different opinion. They will easily be tempted to interpret "being young" in such absolute terms that even striving for esoteric knowledge seems foreign to them. Their primary aim is to immerse themselves in their own youthfulness and to understand it, oblivious to anything that comes toward them from outside. Presumably, these young people also hope to find what they are looking for within the Anthroposophical Society. If that were not the case, they would not have joined. But they believe they need to bring the right spirit to Anthroposophy through their own youthful activity. It would not occur to the Executive Council to react to this group with superficial criticism. Nonetheless, some of these young people will easily see the Executive Council's intentions in the wrong light. The Executive Council has come to the insight that the stream of eternity that young people are seeking flows in the esoteric knowledge to which the Anthroposophical Society aspires. This insight cannot be abandoned. In esotericism, young people will discover how to be "young" in the best and truest sense of the word. Knowing this, the Executive Council cannot make the mistake of believing that youthfulness itself is a prerequisite to the emergence of esotericism in its true form.

My intention in making this statement is not to suggest a difference of opinion between some of our young members and the Executive Council, because I do not see any such difference, and in fact no difference is possible in the context of a practical view of the world. The Executive Council, aware that its tasks derive from the spiritual world, will always follow the paths laid out in that world. In our particular field of activity, there can be no "differences of opinion."

It remains possible, however, for young people to take an opposing position by one-sidedly emphasizing a certain aspect of their own striving over another. This would cause immeasurable damage to the Anthroposophical Youth Movement. It will not happen, however, if young people pay closer than usual attention to a behavior they have learned from our culture, which has grown all too old. This is the tendency to speak in abstractions. I commented earlier on how poorly such abstraction is suited to youth, and in reality, no one in the Youth Movement wants it. Nonetheless, it is present when young people talk about youthfulness and about their ideals. It is an alarming bit of "oldness" in today's youth. Closer consideration, however, reveals the legitimate experiences of young adults as questions that the esotericism of the Anthroposophical Society at least attempts to answer.

On the basis of this practical insight, it will certainly be possible to reconcile differences in individual opinions within our Youth Movement.

Involvement with esotericism offers a way for young people to transform their vague ideals into reality. For some of our young members, direct experience of esotericism could easily remain concealed behind a curtain of theoretical "old talk." This way of talking, however, is an acquired behavior not intrinsic to youth.

If young adults understand *themselves*, they will also understand the Executive Council of the Anthroposophical Society.

The Independent School of Spiritual Science

In the school of spiritual science,
the immediate human element must come into its own

NEWSLETTER, APRIL 6, 1924

This institution cannot develop from the top down on the basis of abstract speculation. It must develop from the bottom up, out of the needs of our membership. The Executive Council's plan to establish a Youth Section is based on the deepest aspirations of young adults in the Anthroposophical Society, and this Section will take shape in a way that addresses their needs as they emerge.

The same must also become true of the other Sections. For this to happen, however, all needs that emerge among our membership really must flow through the Society as a whole and ultimately come together in our expectations vis-à-vis what we expect at the Goetheanum. We must become increasingly aware that the purpose of the Christmas Conference was not simply to form an administrative board. We must not forget that administration is necessary and must be implemented with care and precision. The main issue is, however, for our membership to truly see the Executive Council as the focus of the Society's spiritual interests. All of these spiritual interests should flow together in the Executive Council.

It should never occur to this Executive Council to attempt to limit the initiatives of individual parts of the Society in any way. Rather, we should all feel the need to bring everything that appears in the context of the Society to the knowledge of the Executive Council so it can then harmonize the intentions of one group of individuals with the aims of another. This Executive Council will not attempt to work one-sidedly "from the top down" as public authorities do. Its job will be to present an open, understanding heart and mind to whatever the membership attempts to bring to fruition. In turn, it hopes that its own initiatives on behalf of the Anthroposophical Movement's goals will be actively accommodated by the members. This is what I meant when I said at the Christmas Conference that this Executive Council will be one that takes initiative.

The more we see the Executive Council in this light, the more it will be able to offer appropriate advice in all matters of concern to the Society. The Executive Council's intention is to "advise" rather than to "decree," which would be completely at odds with the spirit of the Anthroposophical Society, as the Executive Council well knows. In offering advice, it will appeal exclusively to our members' independent insight. But the Executive Council's advice will be appropriate only if all members feel the need to keep it informed of their intentions and efforts.

To the extent possible, the Executive Council at the Goetheanum wants all of its resolutions and programs to relate directly to activity within the Society. It is the hope of the Executive Council that the immediate human element, which also works in all details in highly individual ways, will come into its own in our Society, especially with regard to what must be done on behalf of the Independent School of Spiritual Science.

Addresses Given in 1924

"I have never seen anything inscribed
in the subconscious of young people but this:
The world must be constructed anew from the ground up."
—Arnheim, July 20, 1924

The Nature and Aims of the Youth Movement

From Rudolf Steiner's Report in the Weekly Newsletter
What Is Happening in the Anthroposophical Society:
News for Members, Vol. 1, No. 24

JUNE 22, 1924

"I was able to meet twice with the Breslau youth group of the Anthroposophical Society—a fact that is deeply satisfying to me. Individual members of this circle spoke with open hearts and earnest souls, and I saw receptive hearts and souls before me as I spoke. We spoke of the character of the Youth Movement and the goals our times demand. The participants displayed a great deal of idealism, concern, and goodwill. It is to be hoped that young adults will make a concerted effort to make a reality of what impels their hearts toward the spiritual world and that they will not be weakened by lack of unity."

* * *

Address and Question-and-Answer Session
at the Breslau-Koberwitz Conference

BRESLAU, JUNE 9, 1924

From the conference organizer's welcoming address: We would like to thank Dr. Steiner, Mrs. Steiner, and the other members of the Executive Council for being with us today. Let us be aware of the tremendous significance of Dr. Steiner's presence among us, in light of the cosmic scope of the tasks he faces, so that we may receive what he has to say to us with the respect it deserves. Let us greet him as someone who knows how to be young, younger that we ourselves can be. Our seeking is all we have to offer him; more cannot be expected of us. Our numbers include not only graduate students but also business people and civil servants. Most of us are not members of the Anthroposophical Society.

Comment from a female participant: When we look at flowers, stones, or stars or whenever we look out into the world, we become prematurely old. We cannot find a way of looking at these things that allows us to be youthful, so we give up looking outward and attempt only to experience the youthfulness within ourselves. But to find our place in the world, we are looking for a worldview that allows us to be youthful. We have approached Dr. Steiner with this in mind.

Rudolf Steiner: Many thanks for your warm words of welcome. I would like to return them in kind, because I have believed for many years that what is going on in your hearts, souls, and minds is of tremendous importance for the future. Let me assure you that anyone involved in the world in an unbiased way takes today's Youth Movement very seriously indeed. It may seem that this is not the case if you survey older people rather than your own age peers, but I assure you that the members of the older generation who are pursuing spiritual endeavors certainly do take the Youth Movement seriously.

Several years have passed since a small group of young people joined the Anthroposophical Society, wanting to do more than participate as listeners. They appeared with all of the thoughts, sensations, and feelings shared by young people today. This small circle of young people in Stuttgart posed a question to the Anthroposophical Movement: What kind of space can you make for us within your movement? I believe I really understood that question. It is not always easy to understand the questions truly seeking individuals ask of our times, and young people are quite rightly asking a number of questions that cannot be formulated completely clearly. Perhaps we will have time to talk about this phenomenon at some point today or in the next few days.

Although all times have had their youth movements of sorts, there has never been one quite like what is emerging now. When I talk to older people about the burning issues of the modern Youth Movement, they often comment that young people have always wanted something different, always felt differently from older people, but in the end everything stays more or less the same. These older people say that today's Youth Movement is no different from what younger generations have always wanted compared with older generations. Such comments are totally inaccurate, and this gives rise to a huge problem. In all earlier times, at least to a certain extent, even the radical young people involved in youth movements aspired to follow in the footsteps of their elders and were able to acknowledge and respect the institutions older people had established. Today this is no longer the case. Within and outside academia, young people must find their way into old institutions where they feel totally out of place. Within these institutions, young adults experience the behavior of their elders as mask-like and dead. In contrast to the vitality of their own inner humanity, they experience nothing but masked faces all around them and are driven to despair. The older people they encounter bear the stamp of their specific classes, occupations, or ideals but do not appear as complete, inwardly alive individuals.

You see, that first contact between the Youth Movement and the Anthroposophical Movement seemed like predestined connection, and to this day I believe that their inner destiny brought these two movements together. When I call on my own decades of experience in striving for a community of spiritually seeking individuals and compare it to the Youth Movement that has appeared since the beginning of the twentieth century, I must say that an ever broader cross-section of the Youth Movement is now feeling something that went almost unnoticed forty years ago because it was sensed by only a very few individuals. Your words of welcome beautifully express how difficult life has actually become for young people today.

What I am going to say next may sound somewhat abstract, but on the feeling level it is quite concrete. Today we are standing at a turning point in time unlike any other in human history (or even in pre-historical times, to a great extent). I am not fond of talking about times of transition, since every moment is a transition from past to future. But in our time we really are facing an unprecedented turning point. Significant events are taking place less on the conscious level than in the subconscious depths of human souls, and these events are actually spiritual processes. They are not limited to the physical world. It has been said that the so-called Dark Age† came to an end at the turning of the nineteenth to the twentieth century and that a new Age of Light is beginning. Anyone who can see into the spiritual world knows that this is true. Admittedly, not much light is present yet, but that in no way changes the reality. People are accustomed to the old darkness, which will persist for a while just as a rolling ball keeps on rolling out of inertia. The inertia-driven aspects of our civilization have one thing in common, namely, the need to have everything confirmed or proved. It is difficult to find living words to describe these things, because the things themselves are dead. Our culture accepts only what has been confirmed. Every scientific truth and every scholarly statement must be confirmed and every individual officially validated. Anyone entering a profession requires outside confirmation or certification. In academia we say: Prove it. If it cannot be proved, it does not count; we cannot understand it.

I could say much more about this need for confirmation or proof, which sometimes appears in strange guises. In this connection, let me tell you a little story about when I was young, though not quite as young as you are now. As the editor of a periodical, I became involved in a trivial lawsuit. When I went to court, I represented myself and won the case. The plaintiff, not satisfied with the outcome, decided to appeal. When I appeared in court again, the lawyer for the other side said to me, "We don't need you; we need only your lawyer. Where is he?" Now you see, I had not brought a lawyer with me, because I was the person involved, and I thought I could handle it myself. Not good enough. It took all the ingenuity I could muster to get the case postponed. It was made quite clear to me that I must not show up myself next time. I would have to send a lawyer, because it was not customary for defendants to represent themselves on appeal. I went away much relieved and forgot about the whole thing until the day before the case was to be heard again. Unwilling to be told again that I was superfluous, I walked around downtown until I found a lawyer's office and went in. I did not know the man or anything about him. He asked me who had recommended him, and I said "Nobody." I thought any lawyer would be able to handle the case as well as any other and simply chose the first one I found. He handed me a piece of paper and told me to write down what he should say the following day. I did, and I stayed away from court, as was expected of me. After a few days I received a letter from him saying that we had won the case.

I could tell you hundreds of similar examples from my one life. Your presence as an individual does not matter. What counts is that everything runs according to plan and design. Young people sense this. They do not want everything confirmed and proved; they want something different. They want to replace confirmation and proof with real experience. Older people do not understand what "experience" means; the word is not in their conversational vocabulary. The very idea of "experience" horrifies many people, especially when you talk about spiritual experience. This is what we are encountering during the radical transition from the Dark Age to the Age of Light.

It is quite natural for this transition to manifest in two different movements. That is why the Anthroposophical Movement and Youth Movement are linked by destiny. Regardless of their class, occupation, or age, the Anthroposophical Movement unites people who have sensed that now, at the beginning of the twentieth century, individuals must find their place in the cosmos in a very different way. We need not just confirmation and proof; we need actual experience. That is why the meeting of our two movements seems karmic to me, and their meeting led to the development of an Anthroposophical Youth Movement of sorts within the larger Anthroposophical Movement. Soon after the refounding of the Anthroposophical Movement at our Christmas Conference at the Goetheanum, the decision was made to add a Youth Section to cultivate the sincere and heartfelt interests of today's young adults.

This highly gratifying step in the development of our Anthroposophical Youth Movement took place in the first few months of this year.† Since then, efforts have stagnated somewhat, owing to difficulties in the Youth Movement. In the chaos that prevails at present—most notably, the spiritual chaos—it is inherently difficult to get anything started; in fact, it is much more difficult than it has ever been before. I am actually not at all inclined to boast, as those of you who know me can attest, but I must say that I have had some very peculiar experiences indeed. In his very kind words of welcome yesterday, Headmaster Bartsch† said that the Anthroposophical Society here experiences me like a father, and I must admit there is some truth to that statement. But fathers are old, or at least no longer very young. In contrast, when we started the Youth Section in Dornach, I encouraged the young people to speak clearly and concisely, and a number of them stood up and spoke very sincerely. Then it was my turn to speak, and at the end of the meeting, someone who knows me well told me that I sounded like the youngest of the young. That is what can happen today: First you are addressed as the old father and then as the youngest of the young. The concepts have become somewhat fluid. But climbing up and down the ladder of age like this offers opportunities to see what moves the hearts and minds of people of different ages.

As I said, the Youth Section has entered a period of stagnation, but it will come out of it. The reason for this stagnation is that it is truly very difficult for young people to think and formulate what they so clearly feel. Along with spirit, our culture has also lost the individual! From the perspective of the underpinnings of our existence, I can see that young people who have only recently descended from the spiritual world into physical existence are asking something very different of life than those who preceded them did. Why is this so? You do not have to believe me, but for me this is not a matter of mere belief but of direct perception and insight.

You see, before we descend into physical, earthly existence, our experiences in the spiritual world are much richer in content and much more powerful than anything we experience on the Earth. I do not mean to undervalue earthly life—without it, freedom could never develop. Nonetheless, life between death and birth is much grander. Souls descending to the Earth—the souls living in you, my friends—perceived a tremendously important spiritual movement that runs its course behind physical existence. In Anthroposophical contexts I have called this the Michael Movement.† The power guiding our time could be given other names, but I call it the power of Michael. In the spiritual guidance of the Earth and humankind, this power strives to restructure the soul element on the Earth. The people who became so intellectually clever in the nineteenth century did not suspect that the spiritual world had already abandoned their "enlightened" soul makeup. Its time was over. A Michaelic community of beings that guide humankind but never descend to the Earth is striving to introduce a new soul makeup for humankind. The death of our old civilization has come.

The Movement for the Threefold Social Order failed due to the death of this old civilization. While that movement was active, I often said that our public life now has a threefold structure consisting of empty phrases, conventions, and routines instead of spirit, law, and economics.† Empty phrases substitute for spirit and culture, and routines—rather than human goodwill or human love—dominate our economic activity.

Human beings are stuck in an old soul makeup that is now meant to be superseded by a different one that once again arises out of and is experienced within the individual. Bringing about this change is the goal of the spiritual beings that have assumed leadership of our time and can be recognized in the signs of the times. Souls now descending into earthly bodies have seen the Michael Movement; they descend to the Earth under its influence. Here, however, they are forced to find their place within a human race that actually excludes the individual or transforms individuals into masks. Thus the Youth Movement is a marvelous reminder of the most important impressions of pre-earthly life. Although nothing of these indistinct, subconscious recollections, nothing of this striving for the renewal of the constitution of the human soul, can be found on the Earth as yet, this is what is really going on in young hearts and minds today.

The Anthroposophical Movement is an earthly manifestation of the Michael Movement and is charged with bringing its intentions to human beings. The Anthroposophical Movement attempts to look up to the Michael Movement in the context of earthly life, whereas today's young people bring recollections of the Michael Movement with them from their pre-earthly existence. Karma brings these two groups together. To me, everything that has happened in the Anthroposophical Movement in connection with the Youth Movement seems innately determined not by earthly circumstances alone but also by spiritual circumstances inasmuch as they involve human beings.

These underlying circumstances explain why your Youth Movement arouses such great hopes in me for the future of real Anthroposophy.

Of course, we are forced to realize repeatedly that both the Anthroposophical Movement and the Youth Movement are mere beginnings. We recently looked on as the Independent Anthroposophical Society was founded alongside the Anthroposophical Society in Germany. The Independent Anthroposophical Society chose or elected its own board of directors, which I believe had seven members—no, someone just said there were nine. In any case, one after the other, individual members were eased out, and understandably so. In essence, the Independent Anthroposophical Society wanted to encompass the youth experience, and the board members questioned one another's ability to have that experience until only three remained; those three continued to question each others' qualifications. This strange process may sound comical, but it is really very serious. It is also indicative of the joint destiny of the Youth Movement and the Anthroposophical Movement.

When we explore great questions of destiny, we often make very significant discoveries that are symptomatic of the scope of the destiny in question. When we founded the Anthroposophical Society, our Executive Council members also quarreled terribly, and I realized that a few of them would soon stand alone, if they ushered the others out. That would not have been the end of the matter, however. The disagreements would have continued until the left half of the one remaining member was arguing with the right half—in the case of the Independent Anthroposophical Society, about which side had the real "youth experience." This sounds ironic, but it is not. It simply points out that the so-called youth experience lies deep within human souls and cannot necessarily be clearly formulated in words. Clear words have already been spoken to excess in the age of intellectualism. Now, however, we must have *experiences*. You have claimed the right to persist in a state of unclarity, but your differences must not tempt you to go your separate ways. Even if you do not agree, you must come together and speak your minds.

Regardless of what you may feel, think, and perceive as individuals, I would like to ask all of you sitting here to stick together with an iron will. Sticking together is what is most necessary if we hope to accomplish anything today with regard to life's great issues. We cannot be constantly checking to see whether someone else's opinion differs slightly from our own. In spite of the greatest possible differences in feelings and perceptions, we must come together and stay together. Eventually, you may realize that the greatest achievement of your youth was knowing how to stay together despite your different perceptions. What young people today yearn for above all else is to find other people. You do not find other human beings, other individuals, because they are all dead behind their masks. Wherever you look, you see only masks. So, of course, you go looking for real human individuals, and your search is tremendously poignant. You look for ways to come together; you seek yourselves in others. This is totally understandable. Human individuals have become spiritually absent, but you look for them because you feel they have to be there somewhere. You look for them primarily in togetherness, in associating with others.

But we must not lose sight of the fact that many young people experience a very tragic aspect of this search. They hope to find real human individuals by coming together with others, but togetherness does not fill them with what they are looking for, and they become even lonelier. Two distinct phases of the Youth Movement emerge—a phase of togetherness and a phase of great loneliness. How many young people today continue to make their way through the world alone, aware that they are not met with understanding anywhere?

Now the fact is that we cannot find the real individual in another person if we do not know how to seek spiritually. The simple truth is that human beings are spiritual beings, and if we approach others superficially, we cannot find them even if they are there. It is truly sad to watch people pass each other by in life as they do today. We are right to be horrified by the many barbaric aspects of earlier times, but at least back then human beings were able to meet as real individuals. Today this is no longer possible. No one knows the other person. People cannot get along because they do not listen to each other. They just keep yelling in each other's ears, shouting out their own opinions and their own perspectives. All we have today are points of view with no further content, because what is validated by these points of view is unimportant.

The longing to perceive with the heart rather than the intellect resonates in young people. So you can trust my sense that a connection of destiny exists between the Youth Movement and the Anthroposophical Movement. You young people are coming to Anthroposophy not simply to try one more thing after having tried many others. You come out of destiny. That is why I am sure we will be able to work together. We will be able to come together, and no matter what else ensues, the human element (in the broadest sense of the word) that is alive in young people will have to come to expression. Something completely different would happen if spirit did not well up out of your youthful life. Unless you are filled with spirit, being young is no longer an option after your early twenties. Physiologically, we cannot preserve youth. We must grow old, but we can and must carry something of our youth with us as we age. Our understanding of being young must allow us to take something with us as we grow older. Unless the depths of our souls are touched by spirit, we cannot survive the years between twenty and thirty without falling into gray and abject misery. My greatest concern is whether our work together can help you survive this transition. I have seen any number of people succumb to depression and indifference in their mid-twenties. In essence, now that the Dark Age has ended, the subconscious depths of young souls are crying out for spirit. It is quite all right that many of you are not members of the Anthroposophical Society. I myself was not a member until Christmas, and even then I joined simply because membership is required of those on the Executive Council. But your membership or nonmembership is not important. The important point is that you are seeking truly concrete spiritual experiences.

So much for my words of introduction. I hope that you will have much more to say. Just as I asked the young people in Dornach to speak out openly so that we could work together, I also ask you to speak frankly. Choose a moderator or proceed however you like. I am sure the Dornach Executive Council will listen attentively to what you have to say. We have much to learn from you as we develop the

Youth Section, and so we will attempt to relate to you as sons, not fathers.

Question: Our young friends talked about wanting to do something together but finding it difficult because they were always so worn out from their professional commitments. Performing the Christmas plays seemed to work best. Then there was some conversation about the Michael idea.

Rudolf Steiner: Yes, the question is this: How can we survive in professions as real individuals and with some kind of inner enjoyment, without allowing our souls to be deadened? This question is not so easy to answer, but perhaps my own experience can help clarify it. When I was your age, a number of my friends asked the same question. After a period of wandering about on their own, these hotheads—that is what such people who wanted to develop themselves independently were called back then—forced themselves to take professional jobs, but their souls withered terribly. As a rule, I do not enjoy talking about myself, but in this instance it is unavoidable. In the context of my life as a whole, I could not have organized Goethe's literary legacy, nor would the Anthroposophical Movement have happened, if I had gone into a profession. These experiences make me feel qualified to begin to answer this question. The problem of how to engage in professional activity and simultaneously preserve your inner joy in life is basically unsolvable. You must either enter a modern profession[†] or resign yourself to not having a career. You must also realize that until professional activity is transformed to accommodate real individuals, our professions cannot be expected to provide inner satisfaction or happiness. Give up on the idea of finding satisfaction in a modern profession. This problem must be solved outside work, which means that you must make all the more effort in the little time your job leaves you. You are right, performing the Christmas plays is very heartening, but being young is not a prerequisite. Some of the people who have taken part in those plays have souls as gray as their hair.

Celebrating inspiring Michaelic festivals would help a lot in summoning this energy. This is something we really must manage to do. We can already sense the life of the future in embryonic form, and we need to foster it through festivals of hope and expectation. Hope and expectation (not sharply defined ideals) must bind us together in these festivals. The image of Michael with his guiding eyes and hands and his spiritual armor must stand before us. We *must* develop such festivals. So why have they not happened? As insistent as I have been about the need for the Anthroposophical Movement to give birth to these festivals, I will prevent them from happening until we are strong enough to bring them about with the necessary dignity. The times are too serious for playing around. That is why we must wait until we are strong enough. What we need is not vague, foggy attempts to develop the Michael idea. We need to be conscious that the world of the human soul is being reestablished on a different foundation and that the Michaelic principle is guiding this process. To foster this consciousness in ourselves, we can work together toward a Michaelic festival that creates a home for our hopes for the future and the spirit of expectation. The satisfaction we get from these efforts, which can take place after work, will help us resign ourselves to the unsatisfying aspects of our jobs. I hope what I have said will encourage you, not depress you.

Let me describe a unique feature of Anthroposophy. If you are ambitious about self-education, you read books, ordinary scholarly writing. What kinds of claims does this writing make? For one thing, it claims to be clear-cut, to be interpretable in only one way regardless of whether the reader is eighteen, twenty-five, thirty-seven, or eighty years old. Its truth is supposed to be absolute, that is, to have the same effect on you regardless of your age. That is not the case with Anthroposophy. If you are eighteen, you will absorb Anthroposophy differently than you would at twenty-six, because it grows with you. It adapts to the age or youthfulness of the individual. When you become involved in this new worldview or soul makeup—or whatever you want to call Anthroposophy—and let it come to life in groups you form for that purpose, you will realize that it allows you to be young and act young. Our older members complain that young people do not understand Anthroposophy, but that is a good sign. Anthroposophy is meant to be experienced, not understood. But you are clinging to one last bit of conservatism that you must relinquish, namely, the belief that you can find your place in a modern profession and enjoy it. You will need to find another way, outside your work. When you finally meet enough like-minded people, their energy will eventually transform the professions into jobs people can enjoy.

Question from a participant: On the job, we are forced to be different people. At night we do our exercises and take a few steps up the ladder, and during the day we are dragged down again.

Rudolf Steiner: You cannot take your search for satisfaction to work with you. There are simply too few like-minded people to engender the energy it would take to transform our professional working lives. It could happen if everyone who feels, however dimly, that something else is possible would come together, but no matter what profession you are involved in, I am sure you have found that a number of your associates do not feel as you do. They feel no need to spend their evenings in youth gatherings. They are content with their jobs because they have no capacity for dissatisfaction. It does not occur to them that they ought to enjoy their work.

During the second half of the nineteenth century, when I was attending academic conferences, I repeatedly encountered a characteristic phenomenon that drove me to despair: Scholarly discussion was restricted to the few hours of official proceedings. When we socialized, anyone who said a word about work was ostracized. "No talking shop" was the rule—ample evidence that people really were not at all interested in what they did for a living. This is true regardless of your line of work. For the most part, people are victims of their times, and they could still be won over to something better. Modern spiritual movements must become stronger so that people who feel oppressed by their professions are not simply squelched by those with no such needs. So the more we relinquish instant gratification and put our efforts into developing a spiritual community with a common goal, the better it will be. That is what we need to keep in mind.

Question: A participant asked about the difference between young and old. Old Anthroposophists want to consume spirit, while the young want to create out of it. The others want to put on the brakes; they are sarcastic about what young people are creating.

Rudolf Steiner: This contrast between young and old need not be so pronounced. Tolerance of others seems the best approach to me, as I said before, since we cannot possibly fit everyone into the same mold. It is inevitable that those temperamentally suited to it will attempt to reach out into the world on the basis of what is available to us. It would be sad if that were not the case. On the other hand, we must acknowledge significant differences in strength. There will always be stronger elements, individuals who are capable of taking action long before others trust themselves to act. Comprehensive action, however, will be possible only if these different shades of temperament come together, which is possible in our context. If it happens, the Anthroposophical Movement will be able to accomplish a great deal. Unfortunately, it is not happening yet.

I think that if the Youth Movement finds its way to Anthroposophy, these different shades of temperament will come into their own. I personally have no objections to any youth movement based on the temperament you represent. I have absolutely nothing to say against it. In my own youth, however, I saw young people beating their heads against the wall. Subjecting yourself to an unknown destiny is all right for those who want to do it, but it is not for everyone. Constructive action, however, will be based less on criticizing those who act differently than on pointing out positive accomplishments. It is truly important to acknowledge positive steps. Even among the young, people do too little of this. Your positive accomplishments remain unknown in wider circles. This is a danger, even though it is not as crass among young people as it is in sects. We must avoid sectarianism. The universally human element must always prevail.

Question: A participant asked about the differences in age (eighteen to twenty-five) and educational level of the participants.

Rudolf Steiner: Basically, the fault lies in the fact that egotism plays such a tremendously great role in our culture. As a result, people cannot feel their way into other people and their situations. Each person talks and acts only out of himself or herself. Just think about how different everything suddenly becomes if you manage to feel your way into the other person. Let us assume a sixty-year-old is talking with a five-year-old boy. I really think the five-year-old is much more able to feel his way into the sixty-year-old than the other way around. We need to learn to creep under another person's skin. Anthroposophy allows us to do this because it is flexible. When you have spiritual interests in common, the age difference between fifteen and twenty-five easily disappears, especially after you have been together for a while. But when you have only egotistical interests to keep you together, fifteen-year-olds and twenty-five-year-olds cannot understand each other. The point is to overcome egotism and discover a certain degree of objectivity. Egotism is the signature of our time, but it cannot persist when we begin to be truly interested in other individuals. We can overcome egotism completely if we first manage to overcome it in the context of something difficult to internalize, such as Anthroposophy. In this process we strip off egotism, and we can then find our way into the other person. This is one of the fruits of Anthroposophical efforts.

You find yourselves unable to understand each other because you are not meeting as real human individuals. If you are not an individual but simply a template, which is more or less the case today if you are twenty-five, how are you supposed to understand others? If you are twenty-five and a graduate student, you are not an individual; you are a clothes rack decked out with your college entrance exams and your fear of defending your dissertation. At fifteen, you are a clothes rack laden with report cards your parents still have to sign. These objects do not understand each other, but we do understand other people as soon as we meet as individuals. The same is true of different professions. We are not true individuals; we are simply impressions of different circumstances. The significance of the Youth Movement lies in the fact that it does away with all this. It wants individuals. When you are not at work, you want to be individuals, and you will be when you clearly grasp these ideas.

Hermann Barr† once described what it is like to be a newcomer in a big city. He was invited here, there, and everywhere—someplace different each day of the week—until he could not tell the lady on his right from the lady on his left or the Sunday ladies from the Monday ladies. They all became confused in his mind. In those social circles people all look very much alike because they all reflect the same circumstances.

Question: Should we simply give up on having a career and devote ourselves to Anthroposophy, or is there some way to imbue our professions with warmth?

Rudolf Steiner: That is a very individual issue.† You must never hesitate to do what you recognize as right. Sometimes it is possible and sometimes not. If you can do it, you should already have a sense of the possibility, and then you can go ahead. Of course, you can also become a martyr, though I would not recommend that as a general rule. It would be different if everyone did it, but if only one person out of a hundred is prepared for martyrdom, nothing comes of it because the other ninety-nine shoot that person down. Your question can be answered only on an individual basis. For me, the answer was to avoid entering a profession. Of course, you can say that means I am not qualified to give advice on the subject, but I have been in the position of making that choice. The fact is, however, that professional activity has become so deadened and life so complex that it is difficult to accomplish much from within a profession. But if you have a good nose for the possibilities, you can do it.

Comment from the questioner: I am not attacking Anthroposophy. We must simply understand the positive aspects of the Youth Movement.

Rudolf Steiner: The point here is simply that Anthroposophy can help the Youth Movement experience how to act positively, in harmony with the entire cosmos, by excluding negativity. By its very nature, Anthroposophy cannot be adopted by anyone who does not experience it, so it excludes activity that is not free. I have never made a point of proselytizing on behalf of Anthroposophy. I simply stated what I knew. I know that if I talk to a thousand people, what I say will really take root in only five. This has never worried me. Something similar happens with the fish in the sea. Of a thousand eggs, only two or three survive to become adult herrings. If success is your goal, you will not achieve it. Your cause itself must motivate you. The attitude I hope to see prevail among us is tolerance—allowing each individual to do what he or she can, without saying "Young people should not do this" or "The Youth Movement shouldn't be like that." We need to bring together as many people as possible, and people should act out of their own individualities to do whatever they can.

The difference between fifteen and twenty-five can be overcome if you are all young, as in fact you are. What makes you different from each other is not very great; you have a basic structure in common. After all, the others who have not joined your movement are going to the movies instead of youth group meetings!

Another important point is that too much thought may have gone into providing a form for your activity. Sincere individual relationships are much more important than any form. If you like each other, you spend time together without looking for forms. It may even be a mistake to look for a form. It is important to be able to come together and enjoy each others' company even when you disagree significantly. Human feelings provide the healthiest form for interaction. In fact, any attempt at formal programming will disrupt the Youth Movement. We have considered many possible activities for the Youth Section at the Goetheanum, and many of them will become realities once a certain stagnation has been overcome.

A striving for light—and not necessarily an abstract spiritual light—became apparent when Kali Yuga came to an end. If this striving is so strong in us that we cannot help but pursue it, we need no further forms. Having specific forms is only disruptive. The life within individuals must emerge and merge. Even if only two or three people out of a large gathering are truly enthusiastic about their cause, others will gather around them. The individual, human element must emerge. We will surely find it if we come together with enthusiasm and earnest intentions instead of with floppy arms, legs, and brains. If instead of expecting others to entertain us, we arrive expecting to accomplish something, that is already enough of a form.

It is so difficult to speak in general, programmatic terms. In real life, everything depends on the vitality we bring to what we do. If you are active in a profession and you have to make an extra effort to bring life and vitality into it, your profession will wear you out. We need enthusiasm and especially the enthusiasm of young people, since it is so sorely lacking in older people. Nothing moves; old bodies are full of lead. But I am sure you young people can generate enthusiasm simply by resolving to talk about your individual ideas in the near future with the others present here. That is enough of a form, and we will be sending all kinds of messages and questions from the Goetheanum, which will give you something to do again, so look for opportunities to meet and skip as few meetings as possible. For you, perhaps the first principle of organization is this: We have "x" number of friends who resolve not to skip our gatherings. That is a form in itself.

Question: A participant asked about the young people of the Wandervogel movement.

Rudolf Steiner: In reality, there is no need to make a distinction. The Wandervogel go out into nature seeking impressions of nature, seeking to experience the human element in the natural world, and so on. If, after having these experiences for a while, they go to the other extreme—not wanting to have anything to do with nature and simply reading books—it means that they also did not engage properly in the first phase. Today people can travel all over the world and see nothing. I could show you striking examples of English Wandervogel trips to Italy where the participants saw nothing. They visited galleries but saw nothing. I have met a number of Wandervogel like that.

To see anything, you have to have a heart. But if you are prevented from being a whole human being as early as elementary school, you do not see what is there in the natural world. When you become responsive again to everything in nature, you will also find things in *How to Know Higher Worlds* that other people do not find. This book was written to include nature, not to exclude it. People have told me they could tell from the style that I used a typewriter because I did not have enough time in the day for writing. This is certainly not justified criticism. I do most of my writing in bed, and I have never taken a typewriter to bed with me. That would look rather strange, wouldn't it? But what is important is how things are conceived, and nature was certainly included when this book was conceived.

How to Know Higher Worlds is definitely a Wandervogel book. I do not see any conflict here based on whether one is a Wandervogel or not. By experiencing nature as the Wandervogel do, you will also experience the book. It was not meant to be a book; it simply looks like one. The only way to disseminate some things is in black and white. If the Youth Movement is a success, we will also be able to get away from using printer's ink. We must break through to the human element, but the Anthroposophical Society cannot do everything at once, can it? Unfortunately, its efforts in this direction have been unsuccessful. It was never my intention to permit printing of contents that are best communicated from person to person. I am so glad no one is taking notes today. There have always been people who were willing to take notes, and in some cases bad transcriptions were circulated, so in the end I did have to find a way to get the material printed.

How to Rediscover the Forces Active in Nature

From Rudolf Steiner's Report in the Weekly Newsletter
What Is Happening in the Anthroposophical Society: News for Members, Vol. 1, No. 25

JUNE 20, 1924

"A number of younger members of our society who participated in the Agricultural Course felt the need to meet together at the end of the conference, which they then did early in the morning of June 17. Speaking from the depths of their hearts, these young friends told how they longed to use their own creativity and work to approach spiritual insights that connect human beings to the forces active in nature. These statements came from the innermost souls of young people who hope to transcend sterile materialism, which separates us from the natural world instead of connecting us to it, thus condemning our work to barrenness. At this youth gathering I was given opportunities to suggest paths to follow for this longing to achieve its goal."

* * *

Address during the Breslau-Koberwitz Conference

KOBERWITZ, JUNE 17, 1924†

I

The Youth Movement of today is again turning to the natural world. Young people in the Anthroposophical Movement are also seeking nature but in the sense that they seek the spirit in nature. In the hearts of young Anthroposophists, this seeking manifests as an appeal of sorts to the spirit. Our culture, with its roots in earlier centuries, has not been very receptive to this appeal to the spirit in nature. Of necessity, the spirit has gradually been disappearing from the unique cosmic karma of humankind since the fifteenth century. We are already losing the spirit, and it is easiest to lose with regard to the natural world. Death is inherent in the natural world as a fundamental condition of its becoming. You must not forget that for life to come about, death must always be involved. From the cosmos every living thing receives and incorporates a dead, bony skeleton or other support structure. We carry death with us throughout our lifetime in the form of this nonliving structure, which we cannot do without. In primeval times people knew that this dead element allows life to receive revelations of spirit, and even Roman times produced sayings such as *In sale sit sapientia*—"Sapientia" (wisdom or spiritual light) is inherent in salt. When the traditions of ancient, instinctive clairvoyant wisdom were still alive, people sensed that the dead salts of bones and similar structures were what distinguish us from the beings around us whose lifeless underpinnings do not allow them to absorb as much spiritual light or "sapientia." But now we are living in a time of transition. Young people who approach nature in the style of the last century, through the traditions of the nineteenth century, are discovering the death of spirit in the natural world around us.

Nature constructs a wisdom-filled crystal for itself. We can be charmed by this crystal when we go out into nature, but we must also realize that gods must die—not earthly death but the death of transformation, the transition to unconsciousness—in order to come to life again in that light-filled crystal. When we look at this dead crystal today, we must begin to sense that it shines with the light of divine lives that have been resting there, unconscious, for thousands of years. In our own souls we must find the possibility to discover heart-quickening light, which shines on us from the sun everywhere in the natural world. We must sense it as the light of the gods.

Although it is difficult to express in words, what young people today are seeking is a simple, fundamental fact. Wherever an appeal to nature resounds, it comes from these youthful souls. They want to remember and reconnect with the divine source of everything on Earth and in the starry heavens. In their renewed search for nature and spirit, young people today sense a profoundly serious cosmic karma. Only serious souls can truly grasp this karma in the right way.

Today let us attempt to sense the world of the divine soul that has rested for thousands of years in the heavenly glories of the natural world around us. Seeking souls can find a great deal in that world. The young people of today are seeking very ancient human knowledge, knowledge that was associated with humankind as early as the ancient Saturn epoch. With the coming of the Sun and Moon epochs,† this knowledge lapsed into cosmic sleep, a resting consciousness of sorts, so that its own spirit substance could form the foundations of earthly nature. For today's young, feeling souls who sense this fact but cannot see through nature to the spirit, the earthly natural world is as if covered with snow, even in summer. Death—that is, unconsciousness—is inherent in this "snow" of bright spirit crystals. It challenges the human soul to sense the fiery activity of the living Word, which dates back to even more ancient times, radiating from the Earth's center deep beneath its soul-covering of ice.

Rousseau's time smoldered with desire for nature. In German literature that was the Sturm und Drang period, dominated by the precursors of Goethe and Schiller, though its influence was felt in much wider circles. Let us recall the abstract, literary appeal to nature that resounded through broad swaths of the civilized world at that time. Let us also recall the warm, intense appeals to nature that came from Rousseau's soul. Even today these appeals move many people. "Nature, we want nature again," young people were calling. But what came of these calls?

With almost elderly and uncanny deliberateness, Goethe himself cried out, "Nature! We are surrounded and embraced by it.... Unasked and without warning, it pulls us into the circle of its dance."† Goethe did not want to become conscious of the appeal to nature that was so evident in Rousseau and his followers. When we feel our way into how Goethe then felt about nature and how he approached others' appeal to the natural world, we can feel our skin prickling slightly. We feel the slight shiver Goethe felt in response to this appeal, which seemed unnatural to him. He wanted to be taken into the circle of nature's dance without asking, and he sensed that nature neither asked nor gave warning. The nineteenth century saw a rigid, materialistic response to Rousseau's appeal in the form of so-called scientific knowledge of nature. This response appeared like a realm of demons who first snickered as Rousseau and those around him cried out for nature and then laughed derisively as nature appeared to humankind in its extreme Ahrimanic form.

This is the background of our present situation. When we seek a middle way, we are overcome by a sense of tragic destiny. Since the end of Kali Yuga, young souls have been filled with a subconscious yearning that is extremely difficult to bring to full consciousness. This appeal to nature must resound. The working of ancient gods must be found in the earth, water, air, and fire of the natural world and in all its shining beings. We must rediscover the ancient spirit in nature. But how can we avoid the circle dance of wild demons that answered this call in the nineteenth century? We must not be overwhelmed by them. The twentieth century must not become materialistic. And so today the voice of karma in the souls of young people calls out, "If you allow the twentieth century to become as materialistic as the nineteenth, you will lose not only much of your own culture but much of human civilization in general."

If we can hear such voices at all, this is what we hear, repeatedly and in a great variety of guises, wherever young people gather. It makes many members of today's Youth Movement feel uncertain, pulled first in one direction and then in the other. Simultaneously present in their souls, however, is a certainty that possesses some intrinsic strength, though it is not yet completely clear. We must not allow this strength to be broken. Anthroposophy can help because it believes spirit can be perceived concretely in all the details of the natural world—in plant roots, in the activity of light above the plants, in the warmth that streams its blessings through them. Anthroposophy also believes that the animal kingdom, which is in need of healing in many respects, exists as a warning call to humankind. Animals are present on the Earth for the sake of human beings. Acting appropriately toward animals and the rest of the natural world requires the ability to sense—and, ultimately, to acknowledge—all of the natural world's individual spiritual beings. We sense this requirement whenever the need arises to speak about spirit not in generalities but in connection with the details of agriculture or any other human activity in the natural world. That is why I was so sympathetic to your request to share a few thoughts today.

[Discussion ensues.]

II

Even today those who have found their way into the Anthroposophical spiritual movement experience uncertainty and feel a need for strong support to find what they are seeking. Why is this so? What happens to young people who feel passionate about meeting other individuals in new ways that contrast with the transmitted wisdom of centuries past? Outer circumstances, at least, almost always force these seekers back into old channels. Since the end of Kali Yuga it could not become clear—and apparently must be unclear—what has approached us as the modern, hidden seeking of humanity: proceeding from "nature" to look into and search in nature; and to seek and search into the spiritual with the "spirit."

As you may know, our good friend Mr. Ritter† has told us about growing up as a farmer's son and then outgrowing his peasant roots. Outgrowing one's peasant roots was something of an archetypal phenomenon at a time when some of you were not yet conceived and others were infants in the cradle. That was the beginning of the age of uncertainty. By now agrarian life as it existed for centuries is nothing but a myth. On the psychological level this life was totally different from our abstract science or our modern culture as a whole. The peasants of old were really much more spiritual than modern scholars. But in the 1860s and 1870s this peasant spirituality died off, and one of the manifestations of its dying was a sudden urge on the part of farmers to send their sons to college. This abstract notion, which appeared in the last third of the nineteenth century, points to something very different from the old peasantry that knew how to live in and with nature. Of course, some sons of farmers had gone to college before, but they did so in order to join the clergy, not to become farmers. Becoming a clergyman was compatible with the consciousness and spiritual seeking of the old peasantry. When farmers sent their sons to institutions of higher learning, they were seeking spirit. In the last third of the nineteenth century, however, these students gradually became poor in spirit, spiritually empty. The farmers who had insisted that their sons go to college began to realize that they were losing their offspring to a very different way of life.

The most I can do is to hint at these things, because they can actually be grasped only in real life. In the spiritual deterioration of the late nineteenth century, the agrarian class developed an active antipathy bordering on hatred of all things spiritual and intellectual. I am thinking of an amusing cartoon from a farmers' almanac. Although it was probably conceived by some journalist, it is nonetheless characteristic of the attitude among farmers in the 1870s and 1880s, when farmers' associations were being founded in Central Europe. This cartoon shows a representative of one such association pulling a pointed cap down over his ears and saying, "We don't want no lawyers or teachers in the farmers' association." Farmers were no longer comfortable with academia in any form, including theology, and they thought the smart thing to do was to exclude the most common forms of scholarship from their associations.

In the late 1800s this view produced individuals who were actually mere "images" of human beings. With a few exceptions the civilized world at the turn of the nineteenth to the twentieth century was populated by images, not real humans. A time had come when what should have been the truth was perverted into its opposite in a very strange way. It was enough to make your heart ache to see these so-called truths. A good example is the theory that actively encouraged overpopulation in certain areas. The fact that many people were being born was taken as a sign of real progress, and this interpretation in turn encouraged increases in population. From the spiritual perspective, however, increasing numbers of souls were coming down to the Earth prematurely, and these "spiritual preemies" never really found their way to the Earth. They came to the Earth without discovering the content of their essential being. Once here, they walked around like mere appendages to their own rationality, like mere shadows or images of themselves, estranged from the natural world. They were a terrible sight to see.

Then, in the early twentieth century, many of the souls being born experienced what was lacking in their immediate predecessors, and they felt the need to go looking for the truly human element. But all kinds of old social establishments remained in place to quash the souls of these young people. If our ability to reshape outer life were as strong as our ability to awaken souls through Anthroposophy, things would be very different, and we would not have to talk about the need for Anthroposophy to become "concrete." In the absence of outer deterrent forces, we would sense how Anthroposophy could reshape the world. Just think about how young people are growing up today. Dr. Ritter had the opportunity to spend his formative years on a large estate that remained spiritually intact, so to speak, while the materialistic world around it went crazy. This is a phenomenon in itself. But such a phenomenon is present today wherever an outer refuge is found for what young people are seeking. In every such instance, Anthroposophy must stand behind it in some way, because when we want to learn, we Anthroposophists do not "study" in the sense of striving for rational understanding, but rather we become "priests" in the best sense of the word. And when the transition from the old priesthood, which has become a falsehood, to the new priesthood happens remarkably fast, then it becomes quite noticeable. For instance, what happened in Köfering is quite remarkable: Anthroposophy shaped first the landowner and then the estate.

In our hearts we must learn to transform artificially thought-out spirit, which remains estranged from nature, into developed spirit, which again finds its way out into the world of natural objects. That is why I have attempted to draw on actual experience during this course. Today the only way to find spirit is to clothe it in words provided by nature, so that our perceptions also grow strong again. Now, in the Age of Michael, you are on the right path if you manage to develop real reverence out of what is already knowable but appears to dwell exclusively in ideas. Transforming such knowledge into reverence is the best path of all. Meditation means transforming what we know—

specifically, what we know about individual concrete things—into reverence, and the results are sometimes surprising.

In making such statements, I expose myself to allegations of impertinence from those who grew old conventionally rather than spiritually in the course of the twentieth century. Unlike you, they have no access to the profound feelings that arise when we realize that the human brain develops similarly to manure, but in a different direction. You also sense that this manure substance is given back to the forces that shape the cosmos. It is received by spirit as the human spirit receives matter from within, but on a much higher level.

When we take in matter from outside, we have no inkling of what we take in along with the cultivated plants we consume. It begins to work in us with divine energy as soon as it touches our tongues and is transformed into taste. We are briefly aware of this sensual experience, but then it disappears from consciousness and reemerges full of profound wisdom. Within the human body, matter that is subconsciously transformed in this way ends up in the "dung heap" that fills the brain, where it allows us to grasp spirit. We must learn that our task as human beings is to transfer this "manure" to the cosmos in the right way. This does not mean making mechanical toys for children out of compressed dung, which is how modern individuals use their brains. Instead of manuring spiritual fields so that spirit can work there, we use our brains to make machines. We must acknowledge that the purpose of the human brain is to manure spiritual fields for the gods who descend to humankind. Considering the brain in this inner light leads to awe and wonder as we learn to divine what is happening in our unconscious and subconscious. We become aware that nature is created in the image of the human being. If we see nature in association with manure, we slowly and gradually become aware of the unconscious workings of the human body.

From within ourselves, we learn to renew the faith that has long since become mere tradition. In our Roman-influenced age, faith, like so much of what comes down to us from ancient, nature-imbued, clairvoyant times, is not understood. For example, consider the saying *Naturalia non sunt turpia*—"Natural things are not shameful." All things in nature are beautiful. If they do not seem so to us, it is simply because we cannot see—or smell—their beauty. Let us compare ancient and modern attitudes in this regard, looking at Western culture as a whole. Washing is a large part of how we in the West imitate nature. Of course, washing is a good thing, but in Europe and America we do enough of it to wash nature away altogether! We dull our senses with washing. You may recall that the ancient Egyptians also did a great deal of washing. Their purification was somewhat forgotten in Greece, though it was reflected to some extent in the concept of catharsis.

What does all this mean? It means that when we are surrounded by the natural world of the Earth's surface, we are in the belly of the cosmic being. Knowing this, we regain a sensation that I myself experienced only as a very small child among metal miners in the mountains. Some of them knew that they encountered spirits underground that could not be found on the surface. They encountered the living thinking of the Earth's interior, the organs with which the Earth dreams and thinks about the universe. When miners looked heavenward, they saw abstract stars, but when they became somewhat familiar with what lay beneath the Earth's surface, they saw truly living images. When we succeed in restoring this element of feeling to our cognition, which had become dead and desolate by the end of Kali Yuga, we gradually free ourselves from the shackles of time that constrain abstract thinkers.

This is why I repeatedly point to Anthroposophy as something that will allow you young people to connect with each other with special intensity. Anthroposophy first appeared to people who grew up surrounded by godless thinking, and these people also approached Anthroposophy abstractly. Consequently, Anthroposophy was well understood in the early twentieth century but in a rather abstract way. By destiny, not coincidence, the first Anthroposophists were retirees. Those of us responsible for Anthroposophy experienced repeatedly that people still active in ordinary careers in our culture might be attracted to Anthroposophy but did not become Anthroposophists, somehow imagining that they might be of more use to Anthroposophy if they did not become members. Typically, they joined only after they retired. We experienced a certain tragedy in the influx of members of this age group.

Then came a very difficult time, the second decade of the twentieth century, when middle-aged people should have become active but failed to do so. These middle-aged people were left dangling between getting their doctorates and retirement, so to speak, though we saw this phenomenon among proletarians and farmers as well as academics. They never really found their direction. To be sure, they were members of the Anthroposophical Society; they saw the need for activity based on Anthroposophy. Then they faced the need to develop a threefold order in the body social as a dwelling place for spirit nature. If threefold social order had captured their hearts, this would have happened, but it failed. We were dealing with adults, people who had finished school but were not yet retired. This is the unique tragedy of that generation.

In any case, it proved impossible to move forward, and the more so because that generation stands there like an abyss between retirees and young people, who no longer have much respect for diplomas. Nowadays, people get diplomas as a matter of habit, but in the 1860s and 1870s, diplomas hanging on the wall counted for much more than actual spirit-pervaded, flesh-and-blood human beings. This attitude has vanished. When I meet young people today, I often have to think of a friend I met when he was in his late fifties. At the age of forty-six, having become something of a success in a small city, he wanted to marry the woman he had fallen in love with at age eighteen. But the church containing his birth registry had burned down, and he was unable to marry because he could not obtain a birth certificate. At that time, you had to be entered in a registry somewhere and get certificates to prove that you existed. No one paid any attention to your actual presence; all that counted was the official documents saying you exist.

Young people today are no longer so impressed with certificates, diplomas, and other forms of documentation because they have no faith in the competence of those issuing them. More typical today is the enthusiastic striving of more spiritually inclined young people, including proletarians. But these young people feel separated from old people as if by an abyss, and that abyss is made up of middle-aged adults who were between the ages of twenty-five and forty-eight during the first decade of the twentieth century. Individuals in that generation had an excellent chance of not remaining human, of being reduced to the trappings of their class or profession. But for young people with their yearning for real life experience, the point is not to continue to transform Anthroposophy into abstractions—ideas, concepts, or even fields of study—but to actually act out of an Anthroposophically based understanding of the natural world. This is what I want to emphasize especially strongly today.

We say we are forging the sword of Michael, but there is more to it than that. In the esoteric world, the Michaelic sword we are forging must be placed on an invisible underground altar, where it can be found by receptive souls. This is what we learn as we become familiar with subterranean natural powers. You can help make it possible for increasing numbers of souls to find the sword of Michael. Forging this sword is not enough. We accomplish something worthwhile only by making it possible for people to find it. As young people, you must be strong yet modest in the conviction that you are karmically called upon to seek and find Michael's sword. That will give you what you are looking for in gatherings like today's, and it will also help you understand what I said today about Anthroposophy and the difficulties of those left hanging between getting their doctorates and retirement. If you think of it in great images (that is, in an appropriately instinctive and pictorial way so that the terrible Ahrimanic spirit of abstraction cannot touch you), you will then understand, as people in the nineteenth century did not, why two words ("wander" and "vogel") were combined to describe the striving of young people.

When we hear these words today, we wonder whether any modern traveler understands what "wandering" meant in ancient times. We must harken back to a pictorial form of soul experience. Does anyone thinking about birds today know that we must do as Siegfried did in order to understand the language of birds? To understand the Wandervogel, we must first understand Wotan and Siegfried. We must move away from an abstract conception of the Wandervogel to Wotan, who lives in the surging wind and clouds and waves of the Earth's body, and to the hidden language of birds. We learn this language by activating Siegfried's power of recollection within ourselves, along with his sword, which is simply a prophetic precursor of the sword of Michael. We must find the way from wandering to Wotan to Siegfried, the way that once again makes us receptive to believing in the secret language of birds. This is a path that you all have sensed. If you sense it deep within your souls, you will also find it possible to sense the natural world and to know these things. And if you then also dream a bit, you will learn to live in nature with your heavenly dreams.

Initially, we can dream our way into nature through sensing and feeling, without thinking about it. Your efforts in this regard will allow you to form a community after your own hearts, and after taking a number of steps together, you will find what you are looking for. May we keep this possibility alive in our consciousness and allow it to fill our souls!

The Life of the World Must Be Constructed Anew from the Ground Up

Address during the Anthroposophical Teachers' Conference

ARNHEIM, JULY 20, 1924†

Dear friends, the questions and longings that bring you together as young people are essentially the same as those that have occupied the hearts of modern youth for two decades. Insight into humankind's evolution allows us to recognize that point in time as the end of Kali Yuga and the dawning of the Age of Light. Equating our own time with the dawning of the Age of Light easily gives rise to misunderstanding, since the increase in light is still barely noticeable. In fact, we might say that circumstances have become even darker and more confused since the turn of the century. As with the inertia of external physical objects, human beings also exhibit inertia, tending to remain in a state they have once assumed. Most people today are visibly out of place in the twentieth century. One has the impression that they were alive at least a hundred years ago. It is not that they have simply remained the same age; they seem to have become stuck in a time long before their own births.

Nonetheless, when we consider the beings involved in the Earth's destiny, we find that humankind has outgrown the age when our souls were more or less unconsciously guided by creative divine powers. In our time, some spiritual beings have retired from involvement in human life, while others whose impulses have more to do with human freedom have begun to intervene in our evolution. As a general rule, people today remain relatively unaware that entirely new spiritual powers have become involved in humankind's evolution. Since the turn of the century, however, young people have sensed (at least in subconscious depths) the shakeup that is taking place in humankind's evolution. Of course, people say it has always been like this; in any age, young people have always resisted the contributions of their elders or of traditions. Very brainy people say crown princes are always the emperor's opponents; youth always resists age.

Indeed, this has always been the case to a certain extent, but what is happening among today's young people, in part totally unconsciously, has never existed before. We might say that the discrepancy and contrast between young people's inner experience and its outer expression have never been so great. We have seen all kinds of youth movements, including the Wandervogel and various independent youth groups with different names. We have seen many examples of young people attempting to extract themselves from what old people call culture, to flee to the safe haven of powers they cannot clearly define. But from the very beginning it was quite clear to me that the majority of modern youth have a strangely comprehensive understanding that a great, earthquake-like transformation must now occur in the evolution of humankind as a whole.

Sometimes we perceive such things in very shattering and haunting ways. As an example, I have often recounted an incident that happened to me in Norway. A very young man, a high school student, came to see me, and they wanted to turn him away, thinking that such a very young person would only pester me. In such cases, people's good intentions are not always the right ones. As karma would have it, I met him on my way out the door and asked him to come in. For some reason, despite his age, I felt the need to start a conversation with him. He explained that the students in his high school were longing for something the school did not provide. They wanted to start a newspaper just for themselves, just for high school students. Could I help? I promised to help in any way I could if the project got off the ground. Then I went on talking with this very young person, who was not even close to graduating from high school. It became quite evident that he shared subconsciously in the so-called youth experience, which is something very few old people understand.

I have often asked old people what they mean by "youth experience," and they say only that young people have always resisted the status quo. I have also asked young people who claim to have had this "youth experience," and their answers were equally uninformative. Nonetheless, I knew that many of these young people had a subconscious experience of youthfulness that they could not describe. Very little comes out when you ask them about it, but it is obviously present in their subconscious. It comes out, for example, when they marvel at a natural view. People have always marveled at such things, but not in the way modern young people do. Perhaps modern young people do it much less perfectly, but they do it with a clear feeling of their own helplessness, knowing that the most basic elemental forces are involved in even the simplest act of marveling at nature.

When one encounters such examples, one gains a very deep sense of the inner significance of this entire youth movement. Recall, for example, the monumental appeal to the natural world that came about through Rousseau and his followers. That, too, was a youth movement, explosive in its manifestation, even stormier than today's. And what came of it?—the great intellectual materialism of the nineteenth century, the very thing that makes today's young people feel so out of place in modern culture. The intellectual activity that people enjoy or become annoyed about in conventional ways has grown old. Young people feel much more than that, but I must place great value on the more insightful aspect.

There is so much talk today of revolution and reform, but the desire to revolt has become so deathly old. It is no longer anything that someone born around the turn of the century might want to grow into, if that person is honest with himself or herself. Young people sense this. They feel that they have not had a chance to grow up alongside older people who modeled joy and enthusiasm for the natural world. They feel that their souls were left to their own devices as they grew up, and the result was a cry to "Let me out of here! Get me away from here; it doesn't matter where! Get me away from centuries of tradition!" You can tell that I am not being very specific when I talk about this issue, but a heartfelt lack of precision is exactly what we need now. Our accustomed materialistic, intellectual clarity would only falsify the issue.

When I observed the dawning of this youth experience, I could tell that it was different from the experience of the young people of the 1870s, who also behaved with youthful enthusiasm and saw their elders in shades of gray. But I also saw one of those young people express his enthusiasm by giving a great speech about someone who died in the uprisings of 1848. As I listened to this speech, I thought that he sounded just like a privy councilor, and, in fact, that is what he became. I met others who never grew into any of the traditional professions, and I saw them sink into an early grave because it was simply impossible for them to participate in humankind's current evolution. At that time a youth movement existed subconsciously, almost as if people were ashamed of it. They did not admit what they were feeling and chose to let it waste away rather than allowing it to rise to the surface of their existence. What they felt did not allow them to participate in the normal human developments of their time. Years passed and then decades. Now the vessel is full to overflowing, and the old shame can no longer endure. Young people have been forced to ask themselves why they are suffering and what they long for. This is what we saw flow into various youth associations in the modern Youth Movement.

A relatively short time ago, a number of these young people entered the Anthroposophical Movement. Remarkably, what lived in their hearts met there with some understanding. In the relatively short time that has elapsed since then, young people have grown into a great variety of activities within our movement, but what is most needed in the Youth Movement is the will to meet other people on the human level. Without this, we will not get beyond fruitless discussion. To understand other people on a human level! The contents of our conversations are really terribly unimportant. It is crucial, however, that we feel in our hearts what the other person is feeling. If we can do this, we will always be able to reach agreement. This is something we must understand with our hearts. In this connection it is essential for individual leaders in the Youth Movement to develop more confidence in the Anthroposophical Movement's sincerity and reliability. Without this confidence, the Youth Section will go nowhere.

Initially, I felt compelled to inaugurate the Youth Section because of young friends who clearly and sincerely feel in themselves the longing of young people in the context of our modern lifestyle. If these people really come together in the Youth Section of the Anthroposophical Society, we will make a reality of the "youth wisdom" I mentioned in the *Mitteilungen [News]*. This youth wisdom will not be pedantic at all; it will be worked out among individuals through cordial mutual understanding. Of course, we are feeling our way forward, attempting to understand out of love, as young people do today. We began by attempting to poll young people about how they imagined the Youth Movement. We solicited thoughts of any kind on this subject—or perhaps not thoughts, but more concrete feelings and intentions. We were ready for anything we might hear, but nothing came of this effort. I then decided to take a more pointed approach and sent out a survey to young people[†]—I am sure you have seen it—asking how they imagined the human world would look in 1935 if it incorporated their youthful desires. If you take this question seriously, it can serve as a starting point for a great deal of in-depth thinking and feeling.

Where is our old world headed? We know that we are not living in the three elements of the body social proposed by the Movement for the Threefold Social Order. Today we live in the trinity of fixed phrases, conventions, and routines[†] that have taken hold of all aspects of our life. Since childhood, today's young adults have learned how to behave toward other people, but these conventions no longer apply. Since the turn of the century your souls have received an entirely new impulse.

Decades before the end of Kali Yuga, I felt something emerging that could not be encompassed by any of our traditional vocations. I myself never entered a profession. If I had done so, there would be no Anthroposophical Movement today. The Anthroposophical Movement was created independent of all traditions. The slightest traditional bias would have made it impossible.

Anyone who cannot understand the fundamental need for such a movement is an opponent of the Anthroposophical Movement. In this sense, the Anthroposophical Movement is pure youth, so why shouldn't young people find their way to it? If the Anthroposophical Movement is honest and young people need honesty, what else do we need? Only courage, real courage! We need the courage to say that the life of the world must be reestablished on totally new foundations. This courage is something we either learn very quickly or not at all.

In fact, I have never seen anything but this inscribed in the subconscious of young adults: The world must be constructed anew from the ground up. What they really want is to reestablish the world on new foundations. There are all kinds of reasons to refute this statement, endless discussions, all sorts of cover-ups. They simply falsify this very sincere subconscious statement and the courage it requires. The Anthroposophical Movement can become an institute of higher learning where we study courage. Admittedly, it is difficult for the Anthroposophical Movement to serve as the school of courage today, because for many people, our movement is a sideline, not the first priority in their lives. This is evident in the form of our public conferences. Increasingly, we are invited to give courses at places in the countryside where people spend their summer vacations. Why not offer Anthroposophy instead of the usual concerts? As such, there is nothing wrong with this arrangement, but it is a symptom of the absence of the pervasive courage required to come to grips with concrete issues, to really unite with the spirit of Anthroposophy rather than its shadow. It is a matter of feeling; my intent is not to criticize but simply to point out symptoms.

The Youth Movement must be able to find a connection to the impulses of the Age of Michael, which I described yesterday as the great goal of our century.† To do so, however, young people must learn to descend deeper into themselves and to avoid dreamy abstractions of all sorts. At that point, great problems appear. Materialistic intellectuals do not understand when we say that Michael has lost cosmic intelligence and remains above. Now that Michael appears without the cosmic intelligence he formerly held in trust, it is up to human beings on the Earth to win it back for him and with him. Today such statements are frequently taken as abstractions in poetic disguise, which they are not. Young people who understand themselves will also understand these statements. It is essential to realize that spirit is real and that we must learn to communicate with it. It is also important to understand that spirit behaves differently now than it did not long ago. A century ago sunrise was a misty semblance of the spiritual world, and people understood that spirit was alive behind it. Formerly a faint shimmer, the semblance became flaming as the nineteenth century progressed. Flames emerged from the semblance, and it is simply not accurate today if we follow Herder's or Goethe's example in describing a sunrise. Sunrise has changed from glimmering to flaming, and from the flames emerges spirit that challenges us to act. The spiritual world's gesture toward the physical world has changed.

If people understand these laws of the spiritual world, we can prevent the Youth Movement of the twentieth-century movement from becoming as materialistic and intellectual as the post-Rousseau period became. If young people, with their youthful enthusiasm, can understand the reality of the spiritual world, the Age of Michael will indeed dawn. If they cannot, the twentieth century's materialism will be infinitely greater than what transpired after Rousseau. The nineteenth century—far exceeding earlier centuries that had not experienced Rousseauism—developed an exceptionally upstanding bourgeoisie. We talk a lot here about the principles of Waldorf education and a new science of education, but the most important point is to continue growing. Each day we face the danger that things will go sour on us. When we want to do something, to prepare for something new, it is important not to fall asleep by clinging to old habits. We must make a habit of creating a clear divide between sleeping and waking; we must be able to both sleep properly and wake up properly. At present, we are constantly sleeping when we should be awake. Our constitution does not allow us to realize that unless we repeatedly wake up anew, all of our reform movements and revolutions will do us no good at all. It is much worse when material intellectualism takes hold of our best efforts. Wherever the light is strong, shadows are dark. What is needed is not thinking about what should happen. People need to feel that the spirit outside of us speaks to us from the flames of nature. The sunrise has changed.

But also our heart has changed; we no longer bear the same heart in our chest. Our physical heart has grown harder, and our etheric heart, more mobile. We must find access to our supersensible hearts. This is the way we must understand spiritual science. Spiritual science, as dry as it may sound, has become something everyone is talking about. Science is really suspect. We have to realize that spiritual science must live in our hearts. In this respect, young people have hearts ideally suited to feeling when something is right. It simply requires courage to really think it. In his enthusiasm, Schiller had a lot to say to the world.

He died under strange circumstances. His autopsy showed that his heart looked like an empty sack, totally desiccated and burned out.

All hearts that grasp their own renewal will burn like Schiller's. If we take spirituality seriously, we must have the courage to admit that if we cannot participate in the world as it is, it must be because we have new hearts. This is not just an empty phrase. We must become conscious of having new hearts that feel and experience the world very differently from old hearts. If we take this fact seriously, the Youth Movement will become a flame rising up in response to the flaming sunrise.

This will happen, but not because of any discussions about being young or talk about experiences. Believe me, I have had strange experiences in this regard. In Breslau I was welcomed into the ranks of the old when they called me the father, but in the youth gatherings I was called the youngest of the young even though I was three times the age of most of those present. The point is to be able to admit this [age] to oneself. Flames arising from within must join forces with flames coming from outside. It is not a question of learning or defining anything. The point is to develop a new type of enthusiasm. Nietzsche once said of Michelet†—whom many people thought capable of enthusiasm—that his was the sort of enthusiasm that waited until he took off his coat. Michelet always had time to take off his coat before waxing warmly enthusiastic. It is as if he always had to take off his coat and put on his silk vest to be properly enthusiastic. Real enthusiasm, however, has no time to take off its coat. It does not notice that it is sweating in a hot coat.

That is the enthusiasm we need, my friends—enthusiasm that overwhelms us so that we forget we have our coats on, enthusiasm that develops out of our direct experience of life. We really need to overcome everything that is old and tired. We are not at leisure to wait for clarity. We do not have time to gain clarity in the old way. We must really become enthusiastic, inspired, enspirited. Enthusiasm will accomplish everything. Then the old saying that, "enthusiasm [Be*geist*erung] bears spirit [*Geist*] within it," will become really meaningful. This is only natural. We need enthusiasm. Enthusiasm supports the god within. God is inherent in the word itself.

So that the Michael impulses can become reality, let us become one with the flame that is enkindled today. These impulses cannot become reality without flames. But to live and work out of the flames of enthusiasm, we ourselves must become the flame. Flame is the only thing that is not consumed by flame. When we feel ourselves becoming flames that cannot be burned by flames, we can afford to leave our physical hearts behind like empty sacks because we will possess etheric hearts, hearts that understand that humankind is entering a new age and a life of spirituality. The complete youth experience means becoming one with spirituality.

APPENDIX

The appendix also includes reports on addresses for which no transcripts are available. We would like to take this opportunity to thank Mr. Kurt von Wistinghausen, who reviewed and corrected his account of the missing gathering in Breslau especially for this edition. The letter about choosing a profession was made available years ago by a member from Stuttgart, now deceased. In addition to his account on page 161, Fred Poeppig also touches on the problem of choosing a profession and conveys what Steiner said on this subject in Dornach: "In a different group, which was struggling with the problem of choosing an occupation, Rudolf Steiner advised the participants to meet weekly to talk about related problems. No one was allowed to miss a meeting. He said that by meeting repeatedly to clarify their goals, they would ultimately discover the right way to proceed."

These collected addresses to young people were given during an important period in the history of the Anthroposophical Movement. Because this volume addresses a specific circle of readers (primarily young adults), including a certain amount of documentation in the form of an appendix seems justified. First and foremost among these documents is Rudolf Steiner's "Appeal to the German People and Culture," which he himself mentions, and the "Appeal to Academic Youth," which led to the first higher-education course at the Goetheanum. No less important is the appeal of February 13, 1923, to the members of the Anthroposophical Society after the catastrophic fire, which was followed by the assembly of delegates in Stuttgart in late February, as reported in *Awakening to Community* (CW 257). During this assembly, Steiner suggested establishing an "Independent Anthroposophical Society" alongside the Anthroposophical Society in Germany. This unexpected bit of advice posed new problems for both societies. In a memorandum, Steiner formulated the principles meant to provide the basis for "unification," as surprising as it may sound. As he explained in an address to the delegates on February 28, "As we know, it is impossible for these two groups to reach agreement. Therefore, what I am suggesting is not a split in the society but a means of uniting it. When we stand on spiritual-scientific ground, we unite by differentiating and individualizing, not by centralizing." This memorandum, therefore, is a very valuable document that has lost none of its formative power as the circumstances surrounding its writing recede into the past.

In conclusion, we print two sets of notes by Maria Strakosch-Giesler, a painter who attended the two lectures during the Stuttgart Youth Course in October 1922 and recorded her recollected images. She emphasizes: "In this Youth Course, Rudolf Steiner was attempting to awaken artistic sensibilities in his audience, so these lectures dealt with painting and the world of color." In addition, Steiner offered explanations and addenda on the speech formation classes led by Marie Steiner, which took place almost daily. Marie Steiner's account of this 1922 course on artistic speech formation was published in the afterword to *Creative Speech* (CW 280).

Appeal to the German People and Culture

RUDOLF STEINER, 1919

The German people used to believe that their Federal Building, constructed half a century ago, would stand indefinitely. In August of 1914 they still believed the building would prove invulnerable to the catastrophic war that was then just beginning. Today there is only rubble to look at. Surely, self-reflection is called for after this experience, which demonstrates that the beliefs which prevailed for half a century—and especially the dominant thinking of the war years—were an error with tragic consequences. Where can we find the reasons for this fateful error? This question forces self-reflection on the German people, whose survival depends on having the necessary strength for such self-reflection. The nation's future depends on seriously pondering the question of how it fell into this error. If Germans ask themselves this question today, the answer will be illuminating.

Half a century ago the German people founded an empire but neglected to endow it with a mission born out of the essential content of German ethnicity. In the empire's early years attempts were made to align its inherent possibilities with demands that arose from year to year on the basis of old traditions and new needs. Later, the empire's outer position of power, based on material strengths, was consolidated and expanded. Alongside these efforts, measures related to the societal demands of the new age accommodated some momentary needs but lacked any greater purpose derived from insight into the evolutionary forces that humankind must take into account in modern times.

The German empire emerged in a global context, but no essential goals were formulated that would have justified its continued existence, as the course of the ensuing catastrophic war so tragically revealed. Before the war broke out, the empire's behavior showed non-Germans nothing to suggest that its stewards were fulfilling a unique mission in world history that ought not to be simply swept away. The absence of any such obvious mission shaped the views of the non-German world.

For anyone capable of real insight, these views constitute the deeper reason for the collapse of Germany.

For the German people immeasurably much depends on a bias-free assessment of this situation. Misfortune is encouraging the emergence of insight that has been lacking for the past fifty years. Petty thinking about immediate, momentary demands needs to be replaced by a broad view of life that makes every effort to recognize the evolutionary forces affecting humankind at present. The trivial urge to dismiss anyone who focuses on these forces as an impractical idealist must be abandoned, as must the pride and pretensions of those who think themselves practical but are the very people whose narrow vision, masquerading as practicality, brought about our misfortune in the first place. We must consider what truly practical people, currently condemned as idealists, have to say about what is required in modern times if humankind is to continue to evolve.

"Practical" people of all schools of thought have long been aware of the emergence of new demands on humanity but have attempted to meet these demands within the context of traditional institutions and habitual thinking. Modern economic activity has given rise to these demands. Meeting them through private initiatives seemed impossible, and to individuals of a certain class the shift from private to public activity seemed indispensable *in certain areas* and was implemented wherever this class deemed it beneficial. Radical conversion of *all* individual work to public work was the goal of a different class with no vested interest in preserving private goals as modern economic activity developed.

To date, all efforts with regard to these new demands on humanity have had a common foundation. There has been a general push for the socialization of private activity, which is to be taken over either by communities (such as state or local authorities) that are based on old premises having nothing to do with the new demands or by new communities (such as cooperatives) that are also based on old forms and traditional thinking and are not fully aligned with these demands.

The truth is that no community based on old, habitual thinking can assume these responsibilities. The forces of our times are pushing for understanding of a social structure for humankind that looks very different from anything we see today. To a great extent, our social structures have been shaped by our social instincts. It is the task of our time to become fully conscious of the forces involved. Like the natural body, the body social is made up of different systems. In the natural body, thinking is a function of the head, not the lungs. Similarly, the body social must also be divided into different systems that cannot assume each others' functions. They must work together while preserving their independence.

Economic activity can thrive only if it develops as an independent part of the body social, according to its own forces and laws, and only if its structure is not confused by the effects of another part, such as the political system. The political system must coexist with but be totally independent of the economic system, just as the natural body's respiratory system coexists with the head. These social systems cannot interact healthily if the same legislative and administrative body governs them both. Each must have its own legislative and administrative organ, though these organs must interact. Of necessity, the political system destroys economy activity by attempting to control it, and the economic system loses vitality when it attempts to become political.

In addition to these two systems within the body social, a third must also develop, completely independently and on its own terms. This is the system of cultural productivity, which also includes the cultural portions of the two other areas. This third system must have its own lawful governance and administration. It cannot be controlled by the other two systems and is influenced by them only to the extent that a natural body's organs also influence each other. Already all of the details of what has been said here about the necessities of the body social can be scientifically substantiated and worked out. These brief remarks merely offer guidelines for all those who wish to pursue these needs.

The founding of the German empire occurred at a time when these new needs were beginning to appear to humankind. The empire's administration did not understand how to endow it with a mission based on these needs. Such a mission not only would have provided the appropriate internal structure but also would have justified external policies allowing the German people to live in harmony with other nations.

Now, however, misfortune must lead to mature insight. We must develop the will to establish a body social based on current possibilities. Germany must not present itself to the outer world as it did in the past. Independent representatives of its cultural, political, and economic systems must meet with those who vanquished the old Germany, which was an impractical hodgepodge of these three social systems.

In spirit we hear so-called practical people brooding over the complexity of what has been said here. Merely thinking about the interaction of three corporate bodies is uncomfortable for them, because they choose to remain ignorant of life's real demands and attempt to shape everything according to the comfortable requirements of their own thinking. They must realize that if their thinking does not adapt to the challenges of reality, they will have learned nothing from our recent misfortune and will perpetuate it indefinitely.

Dr. Rudolf Steiner

Appeal to the Academic Youth Association for Anthroposophical Higher Education

AUTUMN, 1920

Your fellow students address these serious words to you in serious times: As we find our way into academic knowledge and the academic system, we experience them differently than do those who had a hand in creating the status quo. With each day spent in academia, we experience a life-threatening power never encountered by those who have spent their entire lives there. The weight of this onerous burden derives from all aspects of academic knowledge and the academic system that prevent them from contributing positive energy to the collapsing cultural, political, and economic affairs of the West.

As we see it, the academic system is facing the test of life itself. Will it pass? We cannot answer this question in the affirmative. Consider the individual disciplines: Theology is paralyzed by moribund dogmatism and a philological spirit that clings to externalities. Spiritual Christianity, wherever it has not been destroyed by a naturalistic view of Jesus, has become orthodox, literal belief. Both facets are equally foreign to the people; both no longer have access to the hearts of broad classes of humanity.

Like the natural sciences, law, political science, national economy, and all of the other sociological sub-disciplines keep their gaze firmly fixed on end results and are incapable of finding the living springs of society's life and development. These springs were broken open by the ground motion of recent upheavals, only to have their waters held back by all the obstacles of outer life—institutions, programs, and attitudes—that originated in the dead thinking of those who took the refuse of academic workplaces and developed it into abstract worldviews and moribund philosophies of life (such as Marxism, formal democracy, abstract liberalism, political phraseology, reactionary historicism, and conservative political fat-cat-ism).

Medicine and the natural sciences are degenerating as the result of spirit-free observation and the accumulation of facts out of context. Born out of the absence of spirit, they find no access to the problems of organic life or to the human heart's longing for liberating world-views. In sickness and in health the human being as such remains inaccessible to us because no bridge has been created between human beings and the natural world. A stillborn, mechanistic science kills philosophical inquiry as it germinates.

The natural sciences do not engender any spirit-releasing philosophical energy, and our philosophy departments are devoid of real philosophy. Specialization has destroyed the university's universality. The study of words is undermining the wisdom of language, history has become a reference list, and cultural history distorts human life into an abstract fabric of causality woven with no understanding of human will. This departmental spirit never became the sun that could illuminate the age of materialism. Not surprisingly, the technical, commercial, and agricultural colleges that are products of this age lead to mere routines rather than authentic practices.

We students are on the lookout for individuals with leadership potential. They have failed us. Left to our own devices, we stand here leaderless. Political activity and the body social have become mechanized and call on us to become cogs in their machinery. We are horrified by the disappearance of moral foundations and ethical momentum from public and private life. Leaders we might freely choose to follow would have the will and strength to carry the full burden of our academic past and present and to wrest from it the fullness of life that is attempting to emerge in us on the basis of true religious sensibility.

We have found the combination of youthful energy and the maturity of serious and thorough science only in Rudolf Steiner. Through his philosophy of freedom, he released a fountain of youth that cannot grow old. On the strength of this freedom, his Anthroposophically oriented spiritual science has for decades united our expert disciplines into a unified, articulated structure in which they no longer mutely confront our individual and societal activity as a sum of specializations. As this new universitas, the product of free human will, they have begun to speak a truly spiritual and social language.

To become organs of this living language of spiritual reality, to become "servants of the Word": that is what spiritual science calls upon us to do! The cultural and social impoverishment of the present day challenges us students to free our life from the restrictive burdens of the corpses of what were once life forces. In his instructions on active self-education and in the philosophical, spiritual-scientific, artistic, educational, social, and economic accomplishments culminating in the Independent School of Spiritual Science at the Goetheanum in Dornach, Rudolf Steiner lays out a path that can lead to increasing independence for the core of our being and to collaboration on the spiritual-social development of community based on a unified core of comprehensive human/moral and nonhuman/natural reality.

We hope to bring these thoughts and insights, in all their binding weight, to the consciousness of every individual student. We are addressing the healthy heads and hearts of our academic fellow-citizens as well as anyone opposed to any sort of petty intellectual materialism and overblown phraseology. We speak as representatives of a matter that is greater than we are, knowing that it will make us greater than we are now.

Everyone who understands these words as an appeal to their active sense of responsibility is asked to sign the accompanying card as a token of support for the impulse this appeal represents, with the understanding that the loosely knit community of signers is intended to serve as fertile ground for furthering spiritual-scientific work and its fruitful social applications. This work has been actively begun at the Goetheanum in Dornach and at Stuttgart's Independent Waldorf School. The forms it may assume elsewhere will not be pinned down in advance through abstract formulations but will develop on the basis of free mutual understanding wherever the will to work is kindled.

Hans Altemüller (medical student, Munich)
Otto Altem¸ller (philosophy student, Münster)
H.v. Baravalle (philosophy student,Vienna)
V.C. Benny (mathematics, London)
Gertrud Bernhardi (Academy of Art, Leipzig)
Franklin Bircher (medical student, Zurich)

Walter Birkigt (business student, Leipzig)
Karl Gustav Bittner (law student, Prague)
Martin Borchart (theology student, Marburg)
Anton Burg (philosophy student, Freiburg)
Dr. H. Büchenbacher (philosophy, Munich)
Wilhelm Chlormann (graduate student in theology, Mannheim)
Kurt Dannenberg (philosophy student, Berlin)
Marie Detusch (medical student, Vienna)
J. K. van Deventer (licensed engineer, Utrecht)
H. J. V. van Deventer (medical student, Utrecht)
H. J. Dibbern (graduate student in mechanical engineering, Stuttgart)
Friedrich Doldinger (philosophy student, Freiburg)
Walter Dollfus (student of law and political science, Bern)
Felix Durach (architecture student, Stuttgart)
Hedwig Engelhorn (graduate student in political science, Freiburg)
Dr. Richard Eriksen (Kristiania)
Friedrich Franke (philosophy student, Giessen)
Verena Gildemeister (medical student, Tübingen)
Norbert Glas (medical student, Vienna)
Emil Gmelin (electronics student, Stuttgart)
Meta Gorgus (political science student, Mannheim)
Walter Gradenwitz (theology student, Tübingen)
Andreas Grunelius (political science student, Tübingen)
Helene Grunelius (medical student, Frankfurt)
Gerhard Günther (School of Applied Arts, Munich)
Alfred Haag (philosophy student, Würzburg)
Gerhard Häcker (chemistry student, Stuttgart)
Heinr. Hänselmann (graduate student in philosophy, Stuttgart)
Carl Hammann (medical student, Tübingen)
Erika Hammann (pharmacy student, Darmstadt)
Maximilian Hans (chemistry student, Stuttgart)
Jakob Hauser (political science student, Zurich)
Otto Hoerler (graduate student in law and political science, Zurich)
Karl Hoffman (graduate student in engineering, Darmstadt)
Johannes Hohlenberg (graduate student in philosophy, Copenhagen)
Rudolf Honegger (philosophy student, Basel)

Paul Hottinger (medical student, Zurich)
Gottfried Husemann (theology student, Tübingen)
Hans Jacobi (philosophy student, Jena)
Erwin Jeangros (graduate student in philosophy, Bern)
R. Jehmlich (Academy of Art, Leipzig)
A. P. Imrie (engineer, Glasgow)
Hans Itel (philosophy student, Basel)
Willi Kirsch (philosophy student, Munich)
Ludwig Köhler (theology student, Tübingen)
Otto Kratz (graduate student in forestry, Giessen)
Eugen Kraus (chemistry student, Prague)
Manfred von Kries (medical student, Freiburg)
Olga Krietsch (mathematics student, Hamburg)
Hans Krüger (theology student, Tübingen)
Ernst Kunert (music and philosophy student, Leipzig)
Hans Erhard Lauer (philosophy student, Heidelberg)
Helmut Lauer (architecture student, Stuttgart)
Kurt Laute (mathematics student, Stuttgart)
Hermann Liebert (medical student, Freiburg)
Bernt Ljungquist (theology student, Upsala)
Erwin Maier (natural science student, Stuttgart)
Rudolf Meyer (graduate student in theology, Hamburg)
Julie Charlotte Mellinger (graduate student in political science, Frankfurt)
Elisabeth Mittag (philosophy student, Stuttgart)
Wolfgang Moldenhauer (philosophy student, Berlin)
Otto Palmer (mathematics student, Stuttgart)
Ehrenfried Pfeiffer (philosophy student, Basel)
Otfried Plass (mechanical engineering student, Darmstadt)
Hermann Poppelbaum (natural science student, Frankfurt/Main)
Josef Prinke (Academy of Art, Prague)
Liselotte Prinz (chemistry student, Leipzig)
Wilhelm Rath (philosophy student, Berlin)
Dr. Franz Reichel (philosophy, Prague)
Hans Reipert (mechanical engineering student, Stuttgart)
Albert Röth (chemistry student, Heidelberg)
Georges de Rubis (engineering student, Berlin)

Wolfgang Rudolph (chemistry student, Stuttgart)
C. Smid-Curtius (medical student, Stuttgart)
Gertrud Schoop (School of Applied Arts, Zurich)
Hedwig Schramm (medical student, Marburg)
Eugen Schwab (natural science student, Stuttgart)
Hans Schwedes (philosophy student, Heidelberg)
Otto Senn (philosophy student, Tübingen)
Henri Smits (graduate student in engineering, Charlottenburg)
Adolf Steinemann (graduate student in architecture, Darmstadt)
Franz Tabuschat (medical student, Tübingen)
Johannes Thielemann (engineering student, Dresden)
Ernst Umlauff (philosophy student, Breslau)
Dr. Hans Hasso von Veltheim (philosophy student, Munich)
Hans Vetter (philosophy student, Tübingen)
Ludwig Waslè (graduate student in agriculture, Giessen)
Ernst Wich (engineering student, Munich)
Germnot Weisshart (chemistry student, Stuttgart)
Marcel Wrzesniewski (graduate student in electrical engineering, Stuttgart)
Paul Zahner (political science student, Zurich)

Association for Anthroposophical Higher Education
Business address of the working committee:
Champignystrasse 17, Stuttgart

Circular from the Anthroposophical Society's Representative Body to the Members of the Anthroposophical Society

FEBRUARY 13, 1923

Dear friends,

The Anthroposophical Society has entered a new phase of its development. It is up to us to grasp this new phase with full consciousness and to shape our Anthroposophical work accordingly. In earlier years it was enough to absorb the findings of spiritual research with open minds and receptive hearts and to prepare a place for them in small circles. In recent years the Anthroposophical Movement has increasingly become a world movement. For those who choose to represent Anthroposophy in public, this state of affairs presents new challenges, owing in part to changing times and in part to Anthroposophy's own inner progress.

Since 1919 a number of individuals, emboldened by the insight that Anthroposophy can enrich all aspects of practical life, have founded a series of enterprises based on the Anthroposophical worldview and its implications for practical affairs. Dr. Steiner accommodated these initiatives in full confidence that those undertaking these ventures were committed to implementing them. The belief has become prevalent in the Anthroposophical Society that Dr. Steiner himself founded these enterprises. In view of this belief, it is our duty to emphasize that this is not the case. The full responsibility lies with the actual founders.†

Wherever Anthroposophy is able to work out of its own inherent impulses, its fruitful consequences are evident, as with creations such as the recently destroyed Goetheanum and the art of eurythmy, which has undergone unprecedented development in recent years under the guidance of Mrs. Marie Steiner. These manifestations of Anthroposophy have found recognition in the world as creations of universal human importance. Similarly, the Independent Waldorf

School and the educational approach based on Anthroposophical spiritual knowledge have attracted great interest in Germany and beyond. In the field of economic activity, it proved possible—despite opposition from outdated views, which is especially vehement in this field—for the company Der Kommende Tag to develop in a way that allows it to accomplish its important task within the limits imposed on it by general economic circumstances.

Dr. Steiner has indicated how scholarly work can be fructified by supersensible insights. As a result, however, our Anthroposophical work has been charged with monumental tasks. Scientists can do justice to these tasks only by incorporating Anthroposophical methods into their research, as Mrs. L. Kolisko† of the Scientific Research Institute did in her work on spleen function. Anyone aware of the inherent difficulties of research in this area to date will welcome her discovery as the epoch-making beginning of a new understanding of the nature of the human organism. Dr. Hermann von Baravalle's† paper "Zur Pädagogik der Mathematik und Physik" [About teaching mathematics and physics] is an accomplishment of similar importance in its own field, and Dr. C. von Heydebrand's† scathing critique of experimental teaching methods is also a real contribution to the field of education. Dr. Heydebrand's writings expose the grotesque aberrations of experimental psychology as applied to education and contrasts them for the first time with the positive results of the spiritual-scientific art of education. But how can we expect non-Anthroposophical scholars to value these accomplishments if they are not fully appreciated in our own ranks?

Above and beyond such positive results, Dr. Steiner has often pointed out how researchers can discover the route to supersensible perception as an extension of legitimate scientific research. If the Anthroposophical Society intends to be the true vehicle of Anthroposophical activity, it must take an active interest in these important tasks. The society's primary task is to foster the process of achieving spiritual scientific knowledge. In many individuals, modern consciousness is now undergoing a transformation that threatens to drive them into psychological chaos that can be counteracted only by the formative power of Anthroposophical work.

Young people have an inherent potential for new developments. Their striving leads them out of the dull atmosphere of lecture halls, which has sometimes been evident even in our own higher-education courses, in search of Anthroposophy as such. Anthroposophy must accommodate their desire for healthy inwardness by grappling with insight, feeling, and moral and religious strivings. The older generation already on the Anthroposophical path of soul development cannot experience opposition to younger adults, because such development awakens youthful forces in all souls. In our attempts at Anthroposophical soul development, there is no distinction between young and old.

Our opponents' campaign of slander demands a clear, factual, and energetically implemented counter-campaign. The opposition that first developed when Dr. Steiner founded Anthroposophical spiritual science would have remained relatively unimportant. Dangerous opposition has emerged only since 1919 and the founding of various Anthroposophical ventures. The latter type of opposition uses the misguided assertions of former members in its efforts to get rid of Anthroposophy once and for all. In this way our unscrupulous opponents have dumped a flood of personal slander on Dr. Steiner.

It is the job of the Anthroposophical Society (and especially of those who intend to represent any aspect of Anthroposophy to the outside world) to energetically counteract these slanderous statements so Dr. Steiner can finally be effectively protected from such attacks. In particular, attacks such as those contained in the "Psychischen Studien" [Psychological studies], which have been accepted without question by almost all of our opponents, must be combated by exposing the true character of their perpetrators and holding them publicly accountable.

For example, there was an individual in Munich who expressed a fanatical devotion to Dr. Steiner in a very annoying way: by attempting to kiss his hands at every opportunity. Out of injured vanity, this person later became an equally fanatical opponent, and all of our other enemies drew from this source. A recent example also reveals the character of our opponents. Under the cover of scholarly interest, a lecturer at an old and famous university attempted to obtain unpublished material from us. Around the same time he also proved his manly courage by asking a few of our members not to ruin his career by treating him like Professor Drews† in the ensuing "polemical discussion" (his words). It is essential to note and publicize the methods of many of these new opponents. In many cases they have abused their official positions or scholarly authority in their attempts to impose a distorted image of Anthroposophy on their contemporaries, often by maliciously taking passages from Dr. Steiner's books and lectures out of context and lumping them together. It is up to us to counteract this distorted image by factually representing Anthroposophy's spiritual assets.

We owe it to Anthroposophy to represent it in its full dignity and in a way that is accessible to all human souls. We can do this only on the basis of independent spiritual experience. Assertions by our opponents—for example, that supersensible perceptions of previous stages of humanity's development have no significance in real life—can and must be counteracted simply by the practical actions of Anthroposophists themselves. If such perceptions are cultivated by individuals and in our branch work, it will become evident what they have to offer in terms of strengthening the personality and illuminating our existence. Instead of being presented in abstract or dogmatic terms, knowledge of life before birth and after death will then be experienced directly, as an ethical force. The reenlivening of Christianity through the findings of Anthroposophical research will no longer be experienced as debatable claims or uncertain promises when it is encountered in the very actions and attitudes of Anthroposophists.

Considering the strength of the opposition, it is equally urgent not to allow any vital spiritual forces available in the Anthroposophical Society to grow weak through isolation or worn out with conflict. These forces must be allowed to unfold fully in voluntary collaboration, and the society's leadership must encourage and help anyone acting out of the spirit of Anthroposophy to become as effective as possible in the service of our common cause. Human relationships among individual Anthroposophists are essential. We must look for new, flexible forms that will allow the Anthroposophical Society to emerge from its at least partially self-imposed isolation and to communicate its spiritual assets in a great variety of ways. The society's leadership must be supported and its flexibility preserved by an organization of active representatives who feel equally responsible for our work as a whole.

In this appeal we have done no more than outline the Anthroposophical Society's new tasks as we perceive them. We would like to submit these ideas to an assembly of delegates for advice. In view of the extraordinary scope and consequences of the decisions we must make, we are asking the working groups in Germany to send delegates with a warm interest in reconfiguring the Anthroposophical Society to a congress that will take place from February 25 to 28 in Stuttgart. Until that time, we the undersigned will serve as the body responsible for the affairs of the Anthroposophical Society.

Stuttgart, February 13, 1923

Jürgen v. Grone, Dr. Eugen Kolisko, Johanna Mücke,
Emil Leinhas, Dr. Otto Palmer, Dr. Friedrich Rittelmeyer,
Dr. Carl Unger, Wolfgang Wachsmuth

Memorandum to the Committee of the Independent Anthroposophical Society, for Purposes of Orientation

RUDOLF STEINER, MARCH 1923

1. With regard to the external constitution of the Independent Anthroposophical Society, the goal should be compliance with the [old Anthroposophical Society's] draft articles of incorporation. This will preserve the independence of diverse individuals within the society while ensuring that the society is not constantly threatened with dissolution. Anyone who understands the draft articles in the appropriately flexible sense will find everything necessary in them.
2. The first necessary step is to identify all those who are already members of the Anthroposophical Society and whom the committee believes to be coming from a perspective that would justifiably result in the separation of the society as a whole into two groups. Mere dissatisfaction with the old leadership is not enough; participants must be actively oriented toward an Anthroposophical goal that the old leadership was presumably unable to achieve.
3. Members so identified will effectively constitute the Independent Anthroposophical Society. Drawing from this membership, representatives acknowledged by the committee should then be appointed. Representatives should have an active interest in introducing Anthroposophy into modern culture. In addition to members of the old society, these representatives may also include new members, but in the case of the latter, it is important to ensure that they have adopted the positive aspects of Anthroposophy as the fundamental direction of their own lives. Individuals whose social interests are general and lack a significant Anthroposophical element should not be appointed as representatives, even if they have been admitted

to the society with the expectation that they will grow into real Anthroposophists.

4. To a certain extent, involvement with the Anthroposophical worldview *should* be a deciding factor in admission to membership. Initially, however, broadmindedness must prevail with regard to admission into the general Independent Anthroposophical Society. More rigorous standards should be applied only in the formation of more close-knit working groups.
5. The Independent Anthroposophical Society is intended to become an instrument for disseminating Anthroposophy. *It* must give birth to lecture activity, institutes, and the other work of dissemination.
6. The Independent Anthroposophical Society at large is distinct from the communities to be formed within it. The latter (whether exoteric or esoteric) must bring together individuals who sense that they belong together and choose to experience spirit in common. In addition to such groups, it is quite possible that branch activity will develop in the sense of the draft articles of incorporation. It is also possible, however, that members of the Independent Anthroposophical Society will join branches of the Anthroposophical Society and work together with their members.
7. The work of the communities of choice that develop within the society will be self-contained and aimed at the spiritual advancement of their own members. When doing outreach work, the members of such communities function as representatives of the Independent Anthroposophical Society at large. Of course, such communities may also develop outer activity of their own, but it remains desirable for their individual members to appear as representatives of the Independent Anthroposophical Society at large. This proviso need not be imposed by a bureaucratic administration but can remain a matter of individual consciousness.
8. The two committees (that of the Anthroposophical Society and that of the Independent Anthroposophical Society) should establish representative bodies co-responsible for the common affairs of the Anthroposophical Society as a whole.

9. All of the institutions of the Anthroposophical Society as a whole must be encompassed by the interests of the two societies. It would be good to establish a central location for administering the affairs of the society as a whole on behalf of the two committees (via their representative bodies). The separation of the society into two groups should certainly not lead to any Anthroposophical institution—especially a preexisting one—to be seen as involving one group to the exclusion of the other. A portion of both societies' income from dues (the proportion to be determined by the Committees) should be credited to a central treasury to finance the administration of matters involving the society as a whole.
10. It should be understood that the two groups came about only because of very clear differences of opinion among the members and that both groups wanted *the same* Anthroposophy but wanted to experience it in different ways. If correctly understood, the relative separation of these different opinions will not lead to divisiveness but to a harmony that would not have been possible without the separation.
11. The Independent Anthroposophical Society should make no attempt to undo the *historical* forces governing the development of the Anthroposophical Society. Those who want independence must leave the independence of others untouched. The presence of imperfections in the old Anthroposophical Society must fuel not continued feuding but the formation of an Independent Anthroposophical Society that avoids these imperfections, at least in the opinion of the relevant individuals.
12. All of the prerequisites are in place to guarantee that young people, in particular, feel comfortable in the Independent Anthroposophical Society. Its working communities, as independent groups of individuals who understand one another, will form the basis for ensuring that no one in the Independent Anthroposophical Society at large feels constrained in his or her freedom.

[Rudolf Steiner]

Report on the Dornach Youth Address of March 17, 1924

FRED POEPPIG

No transcripts exist of the two addresses to young people given in Dornach on March 17, 1924, and in Stuttgart on April 11, 1924. We include here a report on the Dornach gathering by Fred Poeppig, taken from Chapter 11 ("Old Young People") of his book *Schicksalswege zu Rudolf Steiner* [Destiny paths to Rudolf Steiner] (2nd ed., Stuttgart, J. Ch. Mellinger, 1955).

We then asked Dr. Steiner to meet with us. Approximately thirty young people, primarily security guards and eurythmists, met one evening in the Schreinerei (carpentry studio) with Dr. Steiner and members of the Executive Council. Dr. Steiner introduced the evening and then asked us to speak. A number of us described how our experiences as young people differed from those of the older members. It was like a public confession. On person, telling about a friend who would have become a criminal if he had not found his way to Anthroposophy, demonstrated how that friend used to pound on the table, saying, "If life has no other meaning, we'll smash everything to pieces!" Becoming a priest of the Christian Community gave his considerable will forces a positive outlet. After several people had spoken in a similar vein, Rudolf Steiner came forward. Instead of stepping up to the podium, he leaned against the lectern as he talked casually about his own youth:

"When I was as young, as you are now, young people's experiences were in some respects similar to what you describe. Even then there were young men who enjoyed chasing the girls and students who were dissatisfied with what was going on in the universities. But there is one thing we did not see back then that shows how times have changed. In my day you would never have seen serious students like you committing themselves to guarding some old barn—which is what this Schreinerei actually is. The fact that you are here reveals something of the change in contemporary culture and in your own lives. That you are here guarding our property is a clear indication that you are dissatisfied with what you find elsewhere.

What was *not* the same when I was young was that modern spiritual science did not yet exist. As a consequence, many of my student friends fell apart later in life. They could not cope with life because they found no answers to their profound inner questions. This is different today. Today we have a spiritual science that can provide concrete answers to such questions. Ultimately, are you not here because you expect to find what you cannot find in our general culture?

But how did this spiritual science come about? At this point, dear friends, I want to tell you about a very external aspect of my life without which spiritual science would never have been possible. You can also read about this in the chapters of my autobiography that are now appearing in *Das Goetheanum* [The Goetheanum news].† Just think about what would have happened if I had accepted a public position as a teacher or university instructor instead of doing freelance work. Spiritual science or Anthroposophy would never have happened. It was able to develop only because I chose not to enter any of the existing professions.

As our spiritual-scientific work continued, it became obvious that the lectures I had to give—which are rather remote from the rest of contemporary culture—did not fit into the context of existing public lecture halls. They were out of place there; those spaces simply did not match the content of the lectures. So what had to happen? We had to create the right space, a worthy venue for these spiritual-scientific lectures and related artistic presentations. *So that is why we built the Goetheanum!* We had to build because no suitable space existed for the events spiritual science was meant to foster.

You see, my young friends, *you must do something similar!* Each one of you, wherever you find yourselves in life, must act to make the right thing happen!"

Then he added, "I wish the man one of you described—the one who always pounded his fist on the table—could have been here. That is what it all depends on—those initial acts of will. You have all described very interesting aspects of your life, but that will not get us any further. Much of what we hear today from the mouths of young people is actually just the old, tired soul content of the times, so we get the impression that young people talk just like old folks. There's something old about young people's words that covers up their deeper impulses instead of revealing them. As a result, we are often stuck in the same old rut. *What do you actually want to do here on Earth?* That is what you must keep in mind. You can become conscious of your youthfulness only if you focus on what you have to *do* differently from today's old people."

Reports by Various Participants on the Stuttgart Address of April 11, 1924

Rudolf Steiner mentions the Stuttgart meeting in his report "Educational Conference at the Stuttgart Waldorf School" in the newsletter *What Is Happening in the Anthroposophical Society* of April 29, 1924 (No. 15): "Our young Anthroposophists held a youth meeting to discuss the significance of Anthroposophy for the aspirations of modern young people. It was evident in the faces of these young friends that their feeling of youthfulness coincides with their feeling for Anthroposophy. I look back on this part of the education conference with profound satisfaction."

In his essay "Impressions of the Stuttgart Education Conference," which appeared in the newsletter of April 27, 1924 (No. 16), Ernst Lehrs writes, "The special youth meeting with Dr. Steiner in the packed hall of the building on Landhausstrasse was organized by the Independent Anthroposophical Society for conference participants, but instead of being one meeting among many, it became part of the conference itself. Dr. Steiner himself spoke at this meeting, and for the first time the public call went out to young people: 'Kali Yuga is over. This lives as an active force in your souls!'"

The Stuttgart meeting is also mentioned in a letter to the members of the Independent Anthroposophical Society by Ernst Lehrs, Maria Röschl, and Wilhelm Rath (newsletter of April 27, 1924): "Rudolf Steiner called upon young people to become conscious that it is not enough to wait for the spirit to descend. Rather, it is inherent in our being to struggle to break through to the spirit through our own efforts. 'My dear friends,' he cried, 'this takes three things—courage, more courage, and still more courage!' Spirit, however, needs no programs. It is unique in that once it is active somewhere, things begin developing by themselves and continue to do so. The Youth Section at the Goetheanum intends to serve spiritually striving young people out of this living spirit. Consequently, it makes no sense to ask about the section's program. How much the section means to young people will depend on these individuals themselves. If young people know enough to ask about spirit, Anthroposophy can provide the youthful wisdom they need to be co-active in world renewal."

Rudolf Steiner's Breslau Youth Addresses of June 1924

KURT VON WISTINGHAUSEN

In the last year of his life Rudolf Steiner had an encounter with Anthroposophically aspiring young people that changed many of their lives. The meeting took place in Silesia, in connection with the Agricultural Course at Koberwitz, near Breslau.

On June 6, 1924, on the Friday evening before Whitsunday, a small group of guests were standing in the vestibule of Koberwitz Manor. We were in a festive mood as we awaited Rudolf Steiner's arrival. Count Keyserlingk picked him up at the main railway station in Breslau after his long trip. It was already getting dark when the car finally drove up. When Rudolf Steiner stepped out, we were all shocked by how unwell he looked. Although it was summer, he wore a winter coat, and the strap of his heavy briefcase cut deep into the dark fabric. My first impulse as the youngest one there was to leap forward to take the heavy briefcase from him, but a slight gesture clearly indicated that he had to keep it on his person. The rules of bourgeois courtesy and helpfulness did not apply here. As we learned later, the fat briefcase was full of membership cards, reissued after the Christmas Conference. Rudolf Steiner had signed each one personally, his glance resting on each name.

The next morning, we asked Rudolf Steiner to meet with us in Breslau during the Agricultural Course. He agreed immediately and expressed interest in our work with young people who, for the most part, were not yet members of the Anthroposophical Society.

The first meeting took place on June 9 in a music hall in the center of Breslau that had been made available to the Christian Community. The members of the Executive Council who had made the trip to Silesia attended, as did several other older members. A second, somewhat smaller gathering took place a few days later in a school auditorium with almost no older Anthroposophists present. Shortly after the Agricultural Course ended, an even smaller group of young participants met at Koberwitz to spend a blessed time with Rudolf Steiner and our hosts.

There is no record of the second youth meeting, presumed to have taken place on June 11. This is probably due to the fact that at the end of the first meeting, Steiner expressed his pleasure that "no one is taking notes today." We young organizers were forced to confess that Mrs. Lili Kolisko was indeed sitting in the background writing down what he said. Laughing heartily, Steiner gave his approval, but the seriousness with which he expressed his original, general intention never "to permit printing of things that are best communicated from person to person" deterred the participants from recording his words in shorthand at their next meeting.

Especially among young people, Steiner made a point of avoiding convention and allowing only the purely human element to work. "Speak frankly.... I'm sure the Dornach Executive Council will listen attentively to what you have you say. We have much to learn from you as we develop the Youth Section, and so we will attempt to relate to you as sons, not fathers." (In his words of welcome, the young chairman had chosen to address Steiner not as a "grandfather" to us young folks but as someone who could teach us how to be young in the right way. Days earlier, in a large gathering of members, Steiner had been welcomed as the "father" of the Anthroposophical Movement and had affably refused the title. "But fathers are old, or at least no longer very young.... In Dornach, I encouraged the young people to speak clearly and concisely, and a number of them stood up and spoke very sincerely. Then it was my turn to speak, and at the end of the meeting, someone who knows me well told me that I sounded like the youngest of the young. That is what can happen today: First you are addressed as the old father and then as the youngest of the young.... But climbing up and down the ladder of age like this offers opportunities to see what is moving the hearts and minds of people of different ages."

The camaraderie with which Rudolf Steiner spoke to us was only an introduction to what was to come. We would not have dared to consider the spiritual basis of the connection between the spiritual stream he represented and the generation born after the turn of the century. Now he was talking directly about us: "You see, before we descend into physical, earthly existence, our experiences in the spiritual world are much richer in content and much more powerful than what we experience on the Earth. I do not mean to undervalue earthly life—without it, freedom could never develop. Nonetheless, life between death and birth is much grander. Souls that descend to the Earth—the souls living in you, my friends—have perceived a tremendously important spiritual movement that runs its course behind physical existence. In the context of the Anthroposophical Society I have called this the Michael Movement.... Here, however, these souls had to find their place within a human race that actually excludes the individual or transforms the individual into a mask.... The Anthroposophical Movement attempts to look up from the Earth to the Michael Movement. Young people bring to the Earth recollections of the Michael Movement from pre-earthly existence. This is the karmic connection between our two groups."

With these words about Michael events in the spiritual world, Rudolf Steiner introduced a theme that ran throughout not only the Breslau youth meetings but also the entire activity of his last years. The mission and the serious problems of the younger generation appeared in an unanticipated new, great light. A new Michaelic age had dawned in 1879. With the turn of the century, the Dark Age (Kali Yuga) came to an end. "In essence, now that Kali Yuga has ended, the subconscious depths of young souls are crying out for spirit." May the movement aspire to "the renewal of the constitution of the human soul" on the Earth.

In the question-and-answer session, which took considerable time on June 9, the burning issue of choosing the right, spiritually appropriate career came up. After dealing with the subject in terms of the Michael idea, Rudolf Steiner spoke decisively about the deadening effect of conventional careers and about the need to look outside one's work to find a way to the source of energy that shapes our lives. In this context, he talked about the great Michael festivals he hoped to see happen in the future, saying that he would absolutely prevent them from happening as long as the Anthroposophical Movement was not strong enough to celebrate them worthily. "Celebrated with due dignity, such festivals will trigger great impulses in humankind." As Steiner spoke of these future "festivals of hope and expectation," he gazed over our heads as if into a great distance, with a steely look in his eyes that seemed to us to reflect the world he was perceiving directly. Raising his voice, he told us that in celebrating these festivals, "the image of Michael with his guiding eyes and hands and his spiritual armor must stand before us." It was a fatefully impressive moment.

His talk ended on an equally unexpected note: Steiner described his book *How to Know Higher Worlds* as a "Wandervogel book." He said that like most of his books, he had written it lying in bed, so his critics were wrong in saying that it had been composed on a typewriter. On the contrary, its writing definitely included nature. Hiking by itself is not important; what is important is to see with the heart.

A related question was asked at the second gathering, devoted entirely to questions and answers: There are two ways of experiencing nature—one when you go out singing and talking and experience primarily yourself and each other and the other when you go out alone and attempt to read the shapes and lines of natural phenomena like letters in a script. Which way is the right one? Steiner emphasized the importance of the question, and in connection with Nietzsche's *The Birth of Tragedy*, he talked about Dionysian and Apollonian modes of experience. The importance of the latter in deepening our understanding of nature on the basis of Anthroposophy emerged clearly and suggested a totally new way of understanding the Wandervogel. Steiner then spoke with great earnestness and tenderness of the nearness of comrades who had died in the World War.

Because of its importance, I will still specifically mention Steiner's answer to one other question during this second youth meeting. A young woman was at odds with her parents because of her participation in the Anthroposophical youth group, and the resulting difficulties were disrupting the peace at home for her many brothers and sisters. She asked whether it would be better in such instances to give up Anthroposophical activities. Steiner responded that after their deaths, her parents would be grateful to her for this exposure to spiritual science. (This is recounted from memory.) For many people, this statement became a source of strength in serious differences of opinion and a guideline for appropriate behavior in the struggle for truth.

The two motifs of the Michael mission and an enspirited understanding of nature came together in a very profound way at the third meeting at Koberwitz on June 17. Young participants in the Agricultural Course had asked Rudolf Steiner for an opportunity to present their questions and views to him, and he had very generously agreed. The session that followed was far more than an address; it was a farewell blessing. Steiner's tone of voice was very serious as he spoke of the nineteenth century's "appeal to nature" and the nightmarish fulfillment of Rousseau's longing in the form of materialism and its derisively laughing demons. "But how can we avoid the circle dance of wild demons that answered this call in the nineteenth century? We must not be overwhelmed by them. The twentieth century must not become materialistic. And so today the voice of karma in the souls of young people calls out, 'If you allow the twentieth century to become as materialistic as the nineteenth, you will lose not only much of your own culture but also much of human civilization in general.'"

Young people are searching for a way of perceiving nature that allows them to experience gods dying the death of transformation "in order to come to life again in the light-filled crystal. If you can transform what is already knowable but appears to dwell exclusively in ideas into real reverence, you are on the right path. Transforming this knowledge into reverence is the best path of all. Meditation means transforming what we know—specifically, what we know about individual concrete things—into reverence. We say we are forging the sword of Michael, but there is more to it than that. In the esoteric portion of the world, the Michael sword we are forging must be placed on an invisible underground altar, where it can be found by receptive souls. This is what we learn as we become familiar with subterranean powers of nature. As young people, you must have the strong, yet modest conviction that you are karmically called upon to seek and find the sword of Michael." Forging the sword of Michael and placing it on an altar—a very strange image, initially! Later, we began to understand how such images enrich our spiritual practice, since the forging is a soul process.

At the end of this unforgettably admonishing address, which was nonetheless radiant with love—there is no other way to put it—Rudolf Steiner made a point that both surprised and moved the participants. As he had done on June 9, he mentioned the word "Wandervogel" as it referred to an early twentieth-century youth movement and gave it an entirely new and deeper meaning. "If you think of it in great images, you will then understand why two words were combined to describe the striving of young people." What these young people were actually looking for was Wotan, the wanderer of ancient times "who surges in the wind and clouds and waves of the Earth organism" and the language of birds, which we learn "by activating Siegfried's power of recollection within ourselves, along with Siegfried's sword, which is simply a prophetic precursor of the sword of Michael." With his sword Siegfried overcame the dragon. He bathed in its blood and tasted it to learn the language of the birds. "We must find the way from wandering to Wotan to Siegfried."

A longing fed by ancient Germanic Mysteries is alive in the young generation that came to the Earth after the turn of the century. This longing, however, must be understood and taken further in order to grasp the Michael Mystery of our time. If it is not, we can reasonably conclude that it will succumb to demons as it degenerates into materialism and calls for an untimely return to the forces of the past. This is what Steiner told us at Whitsun in 1924. Shortly afterward the Youth Section challenged us to look forward to the 1930s in a preview of the growing dangers to which Central Europe later succumbed in its secret urge for grand movements, true leadership, and the "I"-mystery of the blood. Steiner's words, however, remain a legacy to the present and to those born later. What happened in 1924 can be seen as a very first step, barely understood by those involved at the time, toward true Michaelic youthfulness, with Steiner as our simultaneously grave and joyful guide. At the end of the Koberwitz address, Steiner grasped the hand of each participant in his own two hands. Then we accompanied him to the Breslau railroad station and saw him off to Jena, where he was to inaugurate Anthroposophical curative education.

The first youth meeting, described at the beginning of this account, had a brief and unexpected sequel. I was one of the organizers and was also allowed to participate in the Agricultural Course as a guest. The next day, Steiner met me in the entry and stopped me to ask, "Were you satisfied with how it went yesterday?" Greatly surprised by the question, I stammered out thanks on behalf of all the participants. In the same instant, however, I had the impression that now would be an opportunity to ask a question. So I said, "Dr. Steiner, you're writing weekly letters to the members in the newsletter. Couldn't you also give some guidelines for our youth work? We often have no idea how to go about it." Rudolf Steiner thought for a bid and then said, "Yes, that could happen, but not every week, do you think?" "Certainly not, Dr. Steiner. Only as often as you can manage. Maybe once a month or quarterly." "Yes," he replied, "and it would have to be something like Feuchtersleben."[†] "Like who?" I asked, all ignorance. "You haven't heard of Feuchtersleben?" At that point the conversation ended because Steiner was called away. Only later did I learn about the Vienna physician from the first half of the nineteenth century and his *Diet for the Soul*, which was well known in Rudolf Steiner's youth. Owing to Steiner's illness and death, the letters to young people never came about. Nonetheless, he had given us an important tip about the "youth wisdom" he had in mind.

Reports by Various Participants on the Breslau Youth Address of June 11, 1924

It will be very difficult to obtain an objective account of Dr. Steiner's second Breslau address to young people. Each of us remembers something different, depending on our personal perceptions. It would not have occurred to us to take notes at that point. We were deeply impressed not only by Dr. Steiner's comment in that regard but also by his whole approach to the individuals who asked questions and to the current situation in our circle, as well as by *how* he said some things to us.

After the introduction, as I recall, the first question was something like this: "When we go out into nature, I always feel uncomfortable about how noisy we are in enjoying it, and I often wonder whether we humans shouldn't also be giving something back to nature." Dr. Steiner said, "That's a very nice question, a very good or important question," and added that he wanted to come back to the theme of the first meeting about Apollonian and Dionysian approaches. He told us very seriously that young people live one-sidedly in the Dionysian element, and added, "You know, in the end, Nietzsche's Zarathustra goes mad. That is the danger. The Dionysian experience must be complemented by the Apollonian, which also needs to be sought out and cultivated." In retrospect, this answer was quite shattering, because the young friend who asked the question died two years later as a consequence of mental illness. [No further notes are available on Rudolf Steiner's recapitulation of the Dionysian/Apollonian elements.]

The next question was this: "*How to Know Higher Worlds* challenges us to always practice tolerance. How can we rise to this challenge as young people who so often find ourselves in conflict with older people, such as our own parents? We don't practice tolerance in these situations!" Dr. Steiner said, "After their deaths, your parents will be grateful to you, because disagreements with young people have beneficial consequences for old people after death."

The last question dealt with relationships with the dead. As the last one left from my Wandervogel group, I felt compelled to mention that only a small number of us were actually present and called to mind our dear companions and brothers from the Youth Movement, the idealists who went to war. Many of them never returned. My question was this: "What can we do for these comrades? How can we include them in our common work?" Dr. Steiner's response was something like this: "Yes, that's a very serious question. The best ones died, didn't they?" He said that in everything that needs to be done, it is important to also include the dead. He talked about the unused ether bodies of people who die young. "An alert consciousness would develop undreamed-of forces." See also *Der Tod als Lebenswandlung*, [Death as metamorphosis of life] (CW 182).

Dear Sir,

In matters such as yours, it is difficult to give advice. Remaining in your present job for a while would allow you to get on your feet, and you could then switch to something better suited to your inclinations and talents. I cannot share your opinion that it is impossible to feel satisfied in a position such as yours, which can serve as an opportunity for self-education. And if you look at the broader significance of your current job, it can be quite satisfying to realize that you are advancing your own education while doing something to help other people. Many types of work that are not inherently satisfying still need to be performed in service to humanity. Once you have worked at this job long enough to save some money, I am sure you will discover opportunities that interest you more. In these difficult times, it does not seem right to me to use borrowed money to equip yourself for the future. I hope you will not take offense at these frank words. Your father's assessment of the situation seems correct to me, and I speak from experience. I had to support myself at an early age and did so as a private tutor for quite a long time. I must say, I would have found your current job no less pleasant than my own, given the uncertainty of finding something else. I am leaving town today, so I have only time enough to write these few lines to express my opinion.

Sincerely yours,
Dr. Rudolf Steiner
Berlin, July 24, 1916

Sehr geehrter Herr!

Es ist schwierig in solchen Angelegenheiten wie der Ihrigen zu raten. Wenn Sie in der Stellung, in der Sie jetzt sind, einige Zeit verbleiben, so stellen Sie sich auf die eigenen Füße und können dadurch gerade später so umsatteln, wie es Ihren Neigungen und Talenten entspricht. Dass man sich in einer solchen Stellung durchaus unbefriedigt fühlen müsse: diese Meinung kann ich nicht teilen. Gerade auf der Basis einer solchen Stellung kann man sich weiter bilden. Wenn Sie die gegenwärtige Stellung in ihrer weiteren Bedeutung nehmen, so können Sie sagen, Sie tun nicht bloss etwas zu Ihrer Ausbildung, sondern verrichten etwas, was anderen Menschen zu Gute kommt. Und gerade dieses giebt ein schönes Bewusstsein. Gar manche Arbeit befriedigt nicht unmittelbar durch ihren Inhalt; allein im Dienste der Menschheit will sie getan sein. Haben Sie sich in dieser Stellung später einiges erspart, dann werden Sie bei den Zeiten, die da kommen, wohl sicher Gelegenheit finden, in Bahnen einzulaufen, die Ihnen liegen. Jetzt in diesen schweren Zeiten scheint es mir nicht richtig, auf aufgenommene Gelder hin, sich für die Zukunft vorzubereiten. Ich hoffe, dass Sie mir dies offene Wort nicht übel nehmen werden. Mir scheint die Empfindung, die Ihr Herr Vater von der Sache hat, doch das richtige zu treffen. Ich darf aus der Erfahrung heraus urteilen. Ich selbst war früh auf die eigenen Füße gestellt; und wenn ich auch durch lange Zeit als Hauslehrer dies habe zu erreichen gesucht, so darf ich sagen, dass mir damals Ihre gegenwärtige Stellung nicht weniger angenehm gewesen wäre als eine solche, wie die meinige war, bei der schließlich doch stets die Sorge bleibt, ob man zeitig wieder etwas finden werde.

Ich muss heute abreisen; daher kann ich nur mein Urteil in diese wenigen Zeilen zusammenfassen.

Mit herzl. Gruss

Berlin 24. Juli 1916.

Dr. Rudolf Steiner

Recollected Images of Two Lectures by Rudolf Steiner on Painting, Given during the Youth Course in Stuttgart on October, 13-15, 1922

MARIA STRAKOSCH-GIESLER

During the Youth Course that Rudolf Steiner gave in Stuttgart from October 3 to 15, 1922, he spoke about painting in two special lectures. Many young people who attended this course were looking for tips on choosing their life's profession, and some had a general interest in education. Steiner kept this fact in mind during his presentations and gave many indications relevant to education. Many of the people who are now Waldorf teachers and heads of curative-educational institutes participated in the Youth Course. Steiner's intention during this course was to awaken a sense of the artistic in his listeners, and so he chose to talk about painting and the world of colors. During these two special lectures he gave not only valuable indications but also actual examples, painting as he spoke.

At that time Der Kommende Tag, the company founded to promote spiritual and economic values, supported a scientific research institute in Stuttgart. In one of its laboratories, a knowledgeable chemist was developing plant pigments based on Rudolf Steiner's suggestions and had already produced more or less usable paints. A short time later Der Kommende Tag was forced to abandon the great work planned for this research institute for economic reasons.

When Steiner lectured on painting during the Youth Course, he asked for samples of these plant-based paints so that he could try them out and see how usable they were as artist's paints. I had been involved with these painting attempts and the production of some of the pigments, so it fell to me to obtain these supplies for Rudolf Steiner.

I.
October 13, 1922

During the first lecture Dr. Steiner did some painting himself to show us examples. His paintings were executed with a wonderful sense of color and delicate but fully conscious strokes. He explained the images to his interested and astonished audience as he painted. What follows is an attempt to approximate his words, though the basis for this effort leaves much to be desired. No one, myself included, took official notes during these lectures. For the most part the only notes available, taken by various young people, are difficult to decipher because the note takers themselves usually did not understand what they were writing. The result is a tangled thicket of thoughts. Another source is our recollections, which were supported by lively discussions on color issues with the young people who came to my studio on the grounds of the Waldorf School after the lectures. After the Youth Course ended, a number of these young friends remained in Stuttgart, and we got together in my studio and attempted to work out Rudolf Steiner's indications together. Trying to get to the center of the problems independently is perhaps the best reinforcement for memory. As a result, Steiner's indications and guidelines were not lost but found a place in our practical efforts.

It is becoming ever more apparent, however, that for new workers in the many institutions within the Anthroposophical Movement, it is not easy to find access to the world of color with its healing potential that promises so much for the future. This is why I will attempt here to reproduce some aspects of these lectures, in part from various notes and in part from my own experience, which gradually developed out of my recollections of Steiner's words. Here and there in these sketches are words and sentences—often only half sentences—that Rudolf Steiner actually spoke. To identify them, these passages are printed in *italics.*

On October 13, in the first of the lectures on painting given during the Youth Course, Steiner spoke first about art in general, saying that "Kunst" [art] comes from the word "Können" [to be able to do something]. In the world of sensory perceptions, where people learn to see colors, color is initially dead and needs to be *ensouled.* When the activity necessary for doing this dies in the artist, art dies too. A color—yellow, for example—cannot simply be seen outwardly and then applied to paper.

In front of Steiner stood an easel with a nice white piece of paper ready for him to paint on. He said, "The *'point of departure'* for painting is the surface. What is a surface? Our willing cannot express itself on a surface because it is three-dimensional. *Will works in three dimensions; feeling expresses itself in two dimensions. A surface is two-dimensional; from a surface, I can experience nothing more than the world of feelings within me. Thoughts cannot be painted at all, because thoughts have only one dimension."*

Then Steiner commented that in this case the surface is white. *"Colors die in white."* By this he meant when they are painted next to white on a surface, because later he said, *"Through white, we enter all the colors as if through a gate.* In our efforts to understand this statement, we experience that pure white must be overcome when we paint. It must become light. The white is overlaid ever so delicately by yellow and thus becomes ensouled. Color, if experienced in the right way, should ensoul everything."

Then Steiner began to paint, saying, *"I'm going to paint some rather subdued blue. I must be able to experience a dull blue surface; the color must be entirely within me. Perhaps I can bring something out of this dull blue, but if it is to come out, the blue experience must be transferred to something."*

As he said these words, he used the plant pigments to paint a subdued blue to the right and left of the center of the surface, in rich tones corresponding to the blue [in the center]. These patches of color became like a large gesture surrounding the center of paper. The blue of the night sky still rested within it, yet it was slightly lightened by a different color. The blue experience was already transitioning to something different. *"I want to paint something that is approaching me,"* he said. *"I have something on the surface that wants to work out of the surface."* So he began to paint the empty center of the paper with radiant forms of shining yellow. These plant pigments, especially the yellow, seemed to shine from within, and so the effect Steiner produced was deeply moving and inwardly transformative. Unfortunately, the plant pigments soon faded and lost their luminous quality.

When he had painted this much, Steiner said, *"That's much too restless; I can help it only by adding a support down below."* He then painted the Earth's surface in rose-red tones. Then he said, *"Out of blue, lightened in the center by reddish and yellowish, which exert their influence all around and are supported from below—that is how we experience a sunrise through color.* I must experience this constantly, not only when I paint. In painting it all depends on bringing everything out of the color. If at all possible, drawing should be avoided. In painting, drawing means telling lies. It means not living out of the color."

Then Steiner turned to a second easel covered with white paper and began to paint again. He said, *"Out of blackish blue, I want to experience something like a cosmic hole boring itself into the color. The hole can be somewhat reddish. Now I'm playing a bit with the strong blue; I'm giving it a support, which can have something of a different color. The result is a moon mood. Through your own experience of color, your heart opens to the colors of nature. Physicists observe only the world's corpse. But what shimmers and hovers and plays above things—that has a future. Color is the child of the cosmos."*

A moonrise had come about in the center of the white page. To the right, Steiner then did a different, totally unrelated exercise, another attempt to show the young people something of the nature of color. He did this by drawing a profile of a head, calling it *"the first element of a face in profile: blue-yellow."* Then he said, *"The yellow wants to form fringes* (nose, eyes, mouth, chin). *The blue recedes."* In a round, restful shape, like hair, the blue enclosed the parts of the face that were given form in a mobile "fringe" of yellow. Here Steiner emphasized the movements of the colors in a most impressive way: Yellow attempts to radiate from the inside out. Blue, which recedes and shuts itself off, is darker on the outside but becomes lighter inside.

In a face with a down-turned forehead, two colors—red and yellow—are again juxtaposed. The red advances toward us in the forehead, which is inclined forward. The yellow lies farther back, in the lower part of the face, receding in comparison with the red. *"You must recall the creative element inherent in the world of color. You yourselves become creators when you play with color, but you must retain the necessary modesty. If I want to paint something devilish, I will have to start with cinnabar red—and then paint a gentle, tender blue. Red always tends to advance, and anything devilish is always ready to pounce on me. If I paint an angel, who allows us only to look at it (the gentlest of all activity), I can paint it only in the most delicate blue, the gentlest of colors."*

II.
October 15, 1922

During this second lecture Rudolf Steiner did not paint anymore. His two previously painted sheets—sunrise and moon ambiance—provided plenty of stimulation for ongoing work. In this second lecture he attempted to address and awaken his listeners' artistic sensibilities. First, he said a few words about plant pigments and the importance of finding the right paint base. In the laboratory in Stuttgart where the plant pigments were produced, he had grappled with this problem extensively and was very satisfied with the result—a milky-looking paint base made up of eight different resins and etheric oils.

Rudolf Steiner had given three lectures in Dornach on the nature of color in May of 1921. In the last of these lectures he specified factors to consider in representing the three kingdoms of nature—mineral, plant, and animal—on the basis of the nature of color. In this lecture on October 15, 1922, he briefly mentioned the mineral and animal kingdoms and the human form, indicating the need to find a different approach to each of these natural kingdoms. He dealt with the nature of plants in greater detail and showed how colors in plants develop in the flowers in particular. We must approach lifeless objects very differently from plants.

In the case of a plant we must experience its earthly and sun-related aspects and seek out the effects of sunlight on it. The plant's primary thrust is upward as it strives toward the point of bearing fruit. This upward direction comes from the previous year and represents all of the plant's most useful aspects. Color, along with the plant's great beauty, spirals around the upward-directed stalk in the form of leaves and flowers. It comes from the current year.

The indications that follow are in Rudolf Steiner's own words: *"We cannot develop concepts about natural beauty. Every bit of nature is a revolt against aestheticism. Nature is beautiful when it entwines the useless and the useful. Painters must be able to experience how the flower gives itself its color. In artistic composition, painting from a model is totally impossible. Sensitive artists must learn from nature, the great artist. Today it is difficult for our souls to grow into the ability to design freely and creatively, but the world of color is inherently creative, and we must find our way into it actively and thoroughly."*

Above all, then, we must again learn to sense how a blue spot recedes into the depths while a red spot advances toward us. The surface, the life element of sentience in its two-dimensionality, catches and holds the life element of color. Blue approaches the surface from behind, as it were, while red and yellow seem to approach it from in front.

We must experience color as perspective. Central perspective is dead; it is related to intellectuality. In color perspective we must learn that colors on the cold side of the spectrum recede, while warm colors come forward. Color must be caught on paper, so to speak. In school, color perspective can be introduced like this: *"First you paint a round blue spot with yellow all around it. Then you attempt to awaken the children's awareness that the blue recedes and the yellow moves forward. The blue acts like a hole. Then you paint a red spot surrounded by blue-green. The red appears to protrude."*

Steiner then pointed out the need to work out of one's material, taking sculpture as an example: *"If you're working in wood, it's like scratching out all of the hollows, but if you're working in marble, it's as if everything—the nose, for example—has to be superimposed."* Then he mentioned that the question of framing is inherently inartistic. Putting gold frames around paintings is the last remnant of the golden backgrounds of the old masters, who—if they possessed spiritual sight—saw objects and human figures emerging from bright gold.

Again Steiner attempted to awaken artistic sensibility and the right receptivity to art in his listeners, especially in observing the visual arts. He took Dürer's famous etching *Melencolia* (Melancholy) as an example, showing that Dürer's intention was not to depict melancholy (which means black-colored) but to allow this blackness to be overcome by light. The picture shows how light shapes space. It is an exercise in light and darkness, a study of light's mysteries in the mineral, plant, animal, and human kingdoms. Steiner then said, *"Sentimental people will ask whether Dürer didn't sense something different and more profound, because our age no longer wants to perceive true artistry. We really must experience it in its pure form, even in painting. Form must emerge from color!"*

Thus Dürer was attempting to study the manifestations of light. At this point, allow me to insert Steiner's personal comments about Dürer's etching when he gave me the assignment of transposing it into colors. His first assignment was to investigate how many shades of light and darkness Dürer used in the polyhedron (center left in the etching). He said that all of the shades that appear in the entire picture are concentrated in this geometric form. On closer study of a reproduction that really shows all the fine distinctions, I discovered twelve different shades, ranging from the brightest light to the deepest black.

When I told Steiner this, he nodded in agreement. *"Next, translate the entire etching into color, but pay attention to the two light sources in the picture. One falls on it from outside and illuminates the objects, while the other emerges from the picture itself."* As he spoke, he gently touched the image with his delicate, expressive hands, his left hand resting lightly on the sphere at the feet of the angelic figure. This sphere is illuminated from outside. He placed his other hand on the light breaking mightily out of the clouds over the sea and the land. A rainbow arches over this source of light; from it flees a dark bat bearing a streamer inscribed with the word *Melencolia*. The sphere and its surroundings are illuminated by the sun shining on them from outside. The effects of this light will take shape in yellowish shades. In contrast, the element of light that breaks forth over land and sea will appear in the color of peach-blossom. For darkness, blue and purple will be the main colors used where the yellowish light is active, but in the case of the peach-blossom all of the rainbow colors will be used.

After that, Steiner again spoke in greater detail about the nature of color. We must experience color perspective artistically. Spatial perspective actually does not enter space. We must also learn to live with the material. Goethe's color theory is a treasure trove with regard to color perspective, especially the chapter on the sensory-moral effects of colors. Our heads cannot grasp it, but our fingers can, and we paint with our hands, not our heads! Steiner then gave very valuable indications on how the nature of color manifests in the human being. His explanation went something like this: Through color we must really experience the inner aspect of the human being. This is possible when we experience the color of the person's face.

We cannot experience the inner aspect of animals through color, even if their fur is removed. But when we paint the human face, we will attempt to penetrate its color, and we will see the colors of the astral body all around it. The human face resembles nothing else in the natural world. It is the human being's most human aspect. The human body's most valuable feature is not the brain but the color of the face, which is an external manifestation of the person's inner aspect. Because the human head reveals its truth to the outside, it is cosmic and cannot be found anywhere else.

Legs are formed from outside, out of the Earth's gravity. Legs are inserted into the human body by the Earth. Someone with a very clear experience of the brain becomes a geometrician. We become mathematicians by experiencing our limbs right down into the skeletal system. A talent for mathematics does not come from the nervous system; it is simply reflected in the brain. In us, the human nude is transformed into an experiencing in the color.

Nowadays living in color has been lost. Painting with incarnadine or peach-blossom is no longer deeply experienced. Raphael and his contemporaries could not yet abandon human forms. Raphael expressed the color of the human being in how he dressed people—Mary and Joseph in blue and red, female and male. In da Vinci's *Bacchus and John the Baptist*, in the Louvre in Paris, we can observe how all color coming from outside bounces off John, while in the figure of Bacchus all color comes from within.

Painting must come from the hands. We must recognize the artist's personality in the brushstrokes. In the most amorphous fleck of color, we must see the hand [at work] and be able to tell whether the artist painted that bit of red from left to right or vice versa. "Painting should be done with moving, fluid color from pots, not with solid paints taken from the palette." This final indication, given by Steiner in one of his three lectures on the nature of color, is necessary to understand his statements about brushstrokes.

A Special Note from the German Editor

The addresses compiled in this volume were commonly called the Youth Addresses. The addresses of March 20 and September 8, 1921; June 9 and 17, 1924; and July 20, 1924 were duplicated and distributed as early as 1949 as working material for those involved in Anthroposophical youth work. The first printed edition, which included five additional addresses, appeared in 1957. Subsequently, one more address was added to complete all of Steiner's talks to young adults for which notes survive.

In reproducing these texts, we must emphasize that almost without exception there are gaps in the existing transcripts, and most of the notations are aphoristic. The transcript for the March 20, 1920, lecture is comprised of notes written down at a later time and have been supplemented with participants' recollections. These special circumstances should be taken into account by the reader.

Werner Teichert did much of the preliminary work of preparing these addresses for publication. With great effort, he compiled scattered texts found in the possession of various people who had participated in Anthroposophical youth meetings. Editing the Youth Addresses was just one of the tasks he left unfinished at his early death in 1955. It was Mrs. Steiner who decided to publish these addresses.

* * *

From the preface to the German edition

Geistige Wirkenskräfte im Zusammenleben von alter und junger Generation [Spiritual forces active in the living together of old and young generations} was the title Marie Steiner gave to the lectures Rudolf Steiner presented in Stuttgart in October 1922 and first published privately as the *Pädagogischer Jugendkurs* [Pedagogical youth course]. Mrs. Steiner had worked over these lectures in Dornach in

1947 in preparation for a new edition, which did not appear until 1953. Although Rudolf Steiner repeatedly made his young audiences aware of educational principles, the new title is more descriptive of the content of this thirteen-lecture cycle. That generation was not yet conscious of it, but the question "How can we find the *spirit*?" was the driving force behind the times and led to what was commonly called the Youth Movement. In reality, as Steiner emphasized, the spiritually active forces that produced this movement were manifesting in this form for the first time. These events influenced a variety of different issues in numerous contexts. University students, too, were affected by the struggles that characterized the second decade of the twentieth century. But Steiner was the first to bring clarity to the many forms that resulted from the difficulties of young people. These connections of destiny lay beneath the surface of daily consciousness, but were active nonetheless as impulses pressing to assume form.

At the very first event in the newly built Goetheanum, in the fall of 1920, Steiner gave an address to the students assembled in Dornach and continued on the same theme in the spring of 1921 in Stuttgart. Ultimately, he gave a total of fifteen addresses to young adults. The first group of five began during the first Higher Education Course in 1920 in Dornach and ended at the public conference "Cultural Prospects of the Anthroposophical Movement" in Stuttgart in 1921. The following year, the October lectures of the Youth Course took place, taking previous addresses as their point of departure. At Christmas 1922 Steiner announced a lecture cycle, "The Moment of Emergence of Natural Science in World History and Its Subsequent Development" [published in English as *The Origins of Natural Science* (CW 326)]. The invitation was issued by the association of scientific researchers at the Goetheanum and by the branch of the Anthroposophical Society. The lectures were open to "every member of the Anthroposophical Society and individuals with an unbiased interest in our movement," and a number of young adults were in attendance. Steiner addressed them specifically on January 6, 1923, after the loss of the first Goetheanum. This address was entitled "The Cognitive Task of Academic Youth." In 1942 Marie Steiner compiled this address and four others from early January 1923 into a brochure entitled "Die Not nach dem Christus. Die Aufgabe der akademischen Jugend. Die Herz-Erkenntnis des Menschen" [The need for Christ. The task of the academic youth. The heart-knowledge of the human being]. For our first edition of Rudolf Steiner's complete addresses to young people, we chose the title of his address of January 6 but left out the qualifier "academic," in view of the content of Steiner's subsequent presentations in 1923 and (primarily) 1924.

The high point of 1923 was Steiner's founding of the General Anthroposophical Society at Christmas. Within the Independent School of Spiritual Science, Steiner called into being a Section for the Spiritual Striving of Youth. In a series of essays he drafted the idea of this workplace for young adults and the goals it would attempt to realize. These essays are organically related to the addresses of 1923 and to Steiner's subsequent meetings with young adults in Breslau (Upper Silesia), Koberwitz (Poland), and Arnheim (Holland) in 1924.

Heavy demand for the out-of-print version led us to issue this new edition as a volume in Rudolf Steiner's Gesamtausgabe [(GA), or Collected Works (CW)]. It retains the same title but appears as GA 217a, a supplement to GA 217, the *Pädagogischer Jugendkurs* [Available in English as *Becoming the Archangel Michael's Companions* (CW 217)]. The addresses given between 1920 and 1924 will also appear in chronological order in the respective volumes of the Gesamtausgabe.

* * *

A list of all the youth addresses given by Rudolf Steiner:

October 1, 1920, Dornach
October 16, 1920, Dornach
March 20, 1921, Stuttgart
April 9, 1921, Dornach
September 8, 1921, Stuttgart
March 10, 1922, Berlin
January 6, 1923, Dornach
February 8, 1923, Stuttgart

February 14, 1923, Stuttgart
March 17, 1924, Dornach
April 11, 1924, Stuttgart
June 9, 1924, Breslau
June 11, 1924, Breslau
June 17, 1924, Koberwitz
July 20, 1924, Anheim

EDITORIAL AND REFERENCE NOTES

Page xii, "seeking young people, who were coming toward it in increasing numbers "
In Germany, the Youth Movement, in the form of the Wandervogel movement went back to the beginning of the century. The first Wandervogel group was founded in Berlin in 1901. But earlier, there had been Jung Wien (1890s) and the Jugendstil. And it is perhaps important to remember that this comes at the same point as the Scout movement and Catholic youth movements. After World War I, the Wandervogel movement reorganized itself along more clearly political lines. The death of millions of people in World War I, the challenges of reconstruction, and a sense that the older generation had failed to prevent the catastrophe (whether one defined the catastrophe as war itself or as military defeat) combined to give a new impulse to the youth movements everywhere. (See also note for p. 42.)

Page 1, "'Exclude no one; include everyone who wants to work with you'"
This was a widespread feeling on all sides of the political spectrum throughout Europe in 1920. It was a year of turmoil, between the effects of the First World War and its settlement, the Russian Revolution and Civil War, the troubled birth of the Weimar Republic following defeat and an attempted Revolution. While there was a great deal of pessimism, a sense that World War I had represented a major failure for Western society, there also existed a sense of fluidity, a sense that it was essential (and possible) to overcome artificial barriers between groups and individuals.

Page 3, "Address on ... Academic Youth"
This address to students took place during the first Anthroposophical Higher-Education Course, which was held from September 26 to October 16, 1920, at the Independent School of Spiritual Science at the Goetheanum in Dornach. The course was organized by the Verein Goetheanismus (Goetheanism Association) and the Bund für anthroposophische Hochschularbeit [Alliance for Anthroposophical work in higher education]. Dr. Roman Boos, who also composed the text of the invitation, was responsible for practical arrangements.

Page 3, "'Appeal to Academic Youth'"
This appeal was issued by the Bund für anthroposophische Hochschularbeit [Alliance for Anthroposophical work in higher education], is included in the Appendix of this volume.

Page 3, "establishment of a cultural council"
This call for the establishment of a cultural council was issued at Whitsun 1919 by the working committee of the Bund für Dreigliederung des sozialen Organismus (Alliance for Threefolding the Body Social) in Stuttgart. It is

reprinted in Hans Kühn's *Dreigliederungszeit: Rudolf Steiners Kampf für die Gesellschaftsordnung der Zukunft* [Time of the efforts for a threefold social order: Rudolf Steiner's fight for the future of society], Dornach, 1978. Among the many signatures, a few names stand out: Thomas Mann, who lived in Munich at that time, and the conductor Fritz Bush of Stuttgart. The comprehensive appeal closes with the following words:

> The foregoing leads to the following basic demands, which can be met by a threefold body social: 1. Education must be freed from any state oversight. Primary schools shall be established exclusively on the basis of pedagogical perspectives; their administrators shall include only individuals active in the autonomous administration of cultural life. 2. The system of state certification of secondary and vocational-technical schools must be abolished. 3. The autonomy of institutions of higher learning must be guaranteed.
>
> We hereby submit these issues for public discussion. We turn to all those who take culture (in the broadest sense) deeply to heart, but most especially to the representatives of science, art, and education; to parents; and last but not least to students of institutions of higher learning. We also turn to Germans living in other countries, for whom the unhealthy mingling of cultural activity with political and economic interests has always been especially painful. We are calling on everyone willing to work together on the emancipation of cultural activity to unite in a community whose task will be the reorganization of the education system in line with the principles outlined above. This community will be an independent association of individuals active in diverse sectors of cultural life and imbued with the insight that the emancipation of the spiritual and cultural life is one of life's great necessities. We are filled with the hope that the common work of this association will lay the foundation for organizing an independent and self-reliant spiritual culture.

Page 3, "'Appeal to the German People and Culture'"
Rudolf Steiner's book, *Toward Social Renewal* (CW 23), was published in an initial run of 40,000 copies. The "Appeal to the German People and Culture" appears at the end of that book. It was disseminated by a committee with members in Germany, Austria, and Switzerland. It is reproduced in the Appendix of this volume.

Page 4, "Kant"
Immanuel Kant, 1721–1804.

Page 5, "DuBois-Reymond"
Emil DuBois-Reymond, 1818–1896. Literally, "According to its deed of foundation [Stiftungsurkunde, perhaps "articles of incorporation"], the University

of Berlin, stationed across from the palace, is the intellectual bodyguard of the House of Hohenzollern." From a speech given on August 3, 1870.

Page 5, "published an essay...during his tenure"
To date, this editorial has not been identified.

Page 6, "Oswald Spengler"
Oswald Spengler (1880–1936), philosopher of history and culture. His main work, *The Decline of the West,* caused a worldwide stir when it first appeared and was soon translated in all European languages.

Page 8, "Gravina"
Domenico Benedetto Gravina, born in 1807 in Palermo, was a writer on art and abbot of the Benedictine monastery of Monreale. Steiner is perhaps exaggerating his case: Gravina wrote and illustrated the first extensive study of the mosaics of Monreale Cathedral. This was the largest intact ensemble of mosaics, illustrating the twelfth-century meeting of Arab, Byzantine and Norman artistic styles in a traditional Romanesque frame. They have been described as "a perfect blend of the best that the Christian and Muslim worlds of the twelfth century had to offer."

Page 8, "Wilhelm Scherer"
Wilhelm Scherer (1841–1886), linguist and literary scholar, author of the classic *Survey of German Literature from the Origins to the Age of Goethe,* was a Goethe-specialist and one of the founders of the Weimar Goethe Archive.

Page 11, "suffering from brain decadence"
It is easy to imagine the distress this statement would have caused at a time when eugenics was in full flower. Eugenics' two-pronged approach to the improvement of humanity aimed at identifying the ablest and healthiest people and keeping out of the reproductive path the least able, to preserve from 'degeneracy' the quality of the human stock. This overlapped with concerns about environmental influences that might cause ill health, early death, insanity, and ultimately defective (degenerate) offspring. It was generally assumed that the biggest problem was to be found among the urban poor, who were both more exposed to pollution or toxic substances and leading more chaotic/toxic lives. Members of the upper class were not immune to degeneracy, in their case caused by soft living and sexual over-stimulation—and in the case of the aristocracy by interbreeding. Steiner's statement however escalated the issue by speaking of across-the-board "brain degeneracy" in regard to the middle class.

Page 11, "waste products of ... scholarship"
This idea that we are working with the waste products of an earlier time (or less dramatically that we are in an age of "epigones" is one which the young Steiner was already sensitive to in his early twenties.

Page 12, "proletarian masses will have to be the 'audience' for a long time to come."
The original Waldorf School was specifically intended for children of all social classes. It was founded by decision of the workers' council of the Waldorf-Astoria factory. Rudolf Steiner felt very strongly that the quick exit of working class children as the school became a school for the children of well-endowed Anthroposophists was due to insufficient attention to his initial suggestions on the proper way to teach in the Lower School (Volksschule).

Page 12, "expert in the field of Oriental and Assyrian studies"
To date this scholar has not been positively identified.

Page 13, "professor of botany who was also an ardent Theosophist"
Otto Penzig, 1856–1929 was professor of botany at the University of Genoa and author of a major work on abnormalities in plants.

Page 13, "Hölderlin"
Friedrich Hölderlin, 1770–1843.

Page 14, "Mr. Thomas"
Calvin Thomas (1854–1919), professor of German language and literature at Columbia University in New York. He published a biography of Goethe in 1917. *Schmidt:* Erich Schmidt, 1853–1913, literary historian and director of the Goethe archives in Weimar from 1885 to 1886; a student of Wilhelm Scherer (see note for p. 8).

Page 15, "Bölsche"
Wilhelm Bölsche, 1861–1939, a scientific writer and social commentator, was one of the central figures of the countercultural center of the Friedrichshagen Poets' Circle. He was a co-founder of the German Monist Association and a member of the Society for Race Hygiene. All his writings concerned science, but science in his case was the central language of modernity, and its metaphors the proper ones for all aspects of culture. His book on love life in nature was a roaring success. He popularized the knowledge of his time, with a particular focus on Darwin and Haeckel and their offshoots.

Page 15, "topics that need to be addressed today"
On the strength of this suggestion, a few Waldorf teachers and lecturers established Independent Anthroposophical Higher-Education Courses in Stuttgart. These courses were affiliated with the first Anthroposophical Higher-Education Course at the Goetheanum in Dornach.

Page 17, "Dr. Stein"
Dr. Walter Johannes Stein, 1891–1957, teacher at the Independent Waldorf School (Stuttgart), was a prolific and controversial writer and lecturer on subjects

of karmic history. He was a close associate of Ita Wegman, particularly interested in research on karma, He was encouraged by Steiner and Ita Wegman in the insights he had in his own past incarnations in 1924, which eventually led to his first book, on ninth-century world history and the Holy Grail. He moved to England in 1933 in the wake of the conflicts within the Anthroposophical Movement, hoping to work on threefold social organizing with Dunlop.

Page 17, "and then taking a hike."
Not entirely accurate: auditing, or treating classes like public lectures was in fact a fairly widespread practice, albeit one unlikely to make you the teacher's pet student and potential 'heir'.

Page 17, "World School Association"
The World School Association mentioned by Rudolf Steiner did not come about at that time. It was not imagined as an association of already existing Waldorf schools but rather as an international organization, active throughout the civilized world, that would promote and support independent cultural activity and finance institutions—especially the founding of new independent schools and colleges—that would form the basis of a cultural life independent of state facilities. After Rudolf Steiner's death, another attempt was made to establish such an association, but it also met with no success, due in great part to deeply conflicting priorities and personal rivalries within the Anthroposophical Society's Executive Council. The reason why the World Association became a sore point in the Society, contributing to the traumatic breaks of the 1930s, was the perception that any funds going to the World School Association would be diverted from finishing the Goetheanum. This was in particular Marie Steiner's fear, and the fact that Ita Wegmann's Dutch friends were connected with wealthy potential donors did not make things easier. But the conflict about financial priorities had already emerged before Rudolf Steiner's death, distressingly so (cf. Christian Lindenberg's biography of Steiner).

Page 20, "Question-and-Answer Session"
Participants in the Independent Anthroposophical Higher-Education Courses in Stuttgart had asked Rudolf Steiner to give an address on the Youth Movement. This gathering took place on Palm Sunday during the semester break courses following the first semester of the Independent Higher-Education Courses. During the semester break, Steiner gave a course of eight lectures, *Naturbeobachtung, Mathematik, wissenschaftliches Experiment und Erkenntnisergebnisse vom Gesichtspunkt der Anthroposophie* (GA 324).

Page 20, "reversal that took place"
The end of Kali Yuga. Cf. also Rudolf Steiner's lecture of June 11, 1922, entitled "Anthroposophy as an Attempt to Christianize the World." This lecture, addressed to members of the Anthroposophical Society during the Vienna West-East Conference on June 11, 1922, is reprinted in CW 211, *The Sun Mystery*

and the Mystery of Death and Resurrection, which contains twelve lectures given in various cities in 1922. The lecture of June 11 was attended by a number of young friends who asked Steiner to give a course for young adults, which then took place in Stuttgart in the late fall of 1922.

Page 22, "Friedrich Nietzsche"
Friedrich Nietzsche (1844–1900). See Rudolf Steiner's *Friedrich Nietzsche, Fighter against His Time* (CW 5) and his essays on Nietzsche in *Gesammelte Aufsätze zur Kultur- und Zeitgeschichte 1887 bis 1901* (GA 31).

Page 24, "Kurella's body-soul"
Probably a reference to Alfred Kurella, (1895-1975) At the turn of the century, the Silesian phrenologist and psychiatrist Hans Kurella (1858-1916) had written on the bodily (somatic) foundations of psychological life and in particular on the biological basis of gender; he also translated into German the works of the criminologist Lombroso and of the English sexologist Havelock Ellis. His son Alfred continued the family tradition of psychosomatic sexology, with a series of books on sexual hygiene and sexual identity (e.g. *The Sexual Questions of Youth–1919*, about sexual issues in the Wandervogel movement). He later became a bureaucrat of the cultural wing of the Komintern and a writer on Communist sexuality and morality. He was exiled to Central Asia at one point, eventually returning to Germany, where he held office in the DDR cultural services. There doesn't seem to have been a book titled Body-Soul, but the unified body-soul concept was of course central to his writings.

Page 25, "fewer men than women on the Earth"
In actuality, the opposite seems to be the case at the beginning of the twenty-first century.

Page 26, "Schiller's treatise 'On Naïve and Sentimental Poetry'"
Written in 1794–1795.

Page 28, "world association ... for Anthroposophy"
See Rudolf Steiner's account in the concluding words to the fourth evening debate of April 8, 1921, *Die befruchtende Wirkung der Anthroposophie auf die Fachwissenschaften* (GA 76).

Page 30, "Professor Römer"
Oskar Römer (1866–1952) was professor of dentistry, first in Strasbourg/Alsace and then, from 1918 to1934, in Leipzig, at the University of Leipzig (full professor, 1920; dean of the medical faculty, 1925; president, 1928).

Page 30, "Dr. Unger"
Carl Unger, Ph.D. (1878–1929), engineer, was the head of a mechanical engineering business. Member of the board of the first Anthroposophical Society in

1913. Member of the board of Futurum—see below. Assassinated by Nazis in 1929.

Page 30, "Der Kommende Tag ... and Futurum"
In October 1919, Rudolf Steiner had called for the creation of business ventures in the spirit of threefolding, to help support the work of the Goetheanum. The result was the creation Der Kommende Tag AG investment company in Stuttgart(1920-25), and Futurum AG in Dornach (1920-24). The Kommende Tag was a consortium of business ventures including mail-order book sales, two printing presses, machine manufacturing, chemical factory, building contractors, cardboard and packaging manufacture, flour mill, lumber mill, medical clinics and spas, research institutes, and the Waldorf Astoria cigarette company. Poor management conspired with the disastrous economic environment to put the ventures in difficulty. By 1921, Kommende Tag went into reorganization. Some of the ventures involved were saved, but the bulk of the corporation was liquidated. In Switzerland, while Futurum disappeared, two of its components survived, a knitting factory and a pharmaceutical company—International Laboratories Arlesheim, which would eventually evolve into Weleda.

Page 31, "Professor Fuchs"
In Vol. 5, No. 2, of the Stuttgart weekly *Threefold Social Organism* (August 1920), in an essay entitled "A Few Words on the Attack by Professor Fuchs," Rudolf Steiner wrote: "If we are to take any researcher seriously, we must expect him to have some feeling for objective facts. Anyone presented with an anatomical specimen preparation that speaks against some absurd claim is taken seriously as a scientist only if he looks at the specimen and considers it in relationship to other facts. Dr. Fuchs heard that my baptismal certificate had been presented in Stuttgart to refute the idiotic assertion that I am Jewish, and his response—like that of so many others who are unscrupulously disseminating this lie—was that there are Jews who have been baptized. In fact, however, my baptismal certificate contains information that speaks emphatically against the possibility of my being Jewish and makes it quite apparent that any statement to that effect is sheer nonsense. It goes without saying that I myself place no value on my ancestry in this regard. My only concern is the audacious falsehood of the statement. For me, then, anyone who talks about facts, even in passing, the way Professor Fuchs talks about my presumed Judaism is no scholar." Reprinted in *The Renewal of the Social Organism* (CW 24).

Page 32, "Mr. von Gleich invented a character named Winter"
See Rudolf Steiner's closing speech at the fourth evening debate in *Die befruchtende Wirkung der Anthroposophie auf die Fachwissenschaften* (GA 76).

Page 32, "Count Keyserling"
Count Hermann von Keyserling, 1880–1946. Social commentator and diarist, connected through his mother to the Bismarck family, without any direct political

influence, but very influential in a 'social butterfly' kind of way. He literally knew everybody, and talked to everybody, although his personal convictions—which he didn't conceal—were pacifist, and leaning to the left. His diaries during the years of Hitler's ascent were especially insightful and increasingly pessimistic.

Page 32, "Haeckel's views"
In his *Philosophy als Kunst* [Philosophy as art] (published in Darmstadt, 1920)], Keyserling wrote of Rudolf Steiner, "In any case, it is symbolic of his being that his intellectual career takes Haeckel as its starting point in certain respects." In Stuttgart (November 16, 1920), Steiner spoke about his connection to Haeckel in a public lecture entitled "The Truth of Spiritual Science and the Practical Demands of Life in the Present" in *Konferenzen mit den Lehrern der Freien Waldorf Schule 1919 bis 1924*, Volume 2 (GA 300b). He concluded by saying, "It is not true that I sought any contact with Haeckel. Haeckel spontaneously approached me and my endeavors. I did not run after Haeckel; he came to me—yes, Haeckel himself came to me. Similarly, I did not approach the Theosophical Society; they came to me and requested my services as a lecturer" (in *Threefold Social Organism*, Vol. 2, No. 22). How Haeckel approached Rudolf Steiner is described precisely in *Autobiography* (CW 28). However, his letters to Rosa Mayreder and the Specht family suggest a less indifferent attitude on Steiner's part, partly because he was then trying to position himself for a university teaching post.

Page 32, "published a booklet"
Der Weg zur Vollendung: Mitteilungen der Gesellschaft für freie Philosophie. Schule der Weisheit [The path to perfection: communications of the Society for Independent Philosophy. The School of Wisdom], Issue 1, November 1920.

Page 33, "'Well, If I was incorrect ... Steiner's specific sources'"
Literally, this reads: "I would have been receptive to the correction of a possible error on my part, since I had no time to research Steiner's specific sources ... but instead Steiner flatly accused me of lying."

Page 33, "Roethe"
Gustav Roethe (1859–1926), expert on German studies who also spoke and composed leaflets on nationalistic politics. His *Deutsche Reden* (German Speeches) appeared posthumously in 1927.

Page 34, "Goetheanum"
On October 18, 1917, in a public lecture in Basel (to the great surprise of the Anthroposophists present, who knew the building as the Johannesbau), Rudolf Steiner said, "Based on the sources that brought me to it, Goetheanism is my preferred name for the worldview that emerged as I have just described. Similarly, my preference would be to call the building dedicated to this worldview, which is going up in Dornach, the Goetheanum."

Page 35, "feature pages"
From Elsbeth Ebertin's yearbook, *Ein Blick in die Zukunft* (A Glimpse of the Future), Freiburg/Bremen, 1921, p. 63. See also Rudolf Steiner's Dornach lecture of January 23, 1921, reprinted in *Die Verantwortung des Menschen für die Weltentwickelung durch seinen gesitigen Zusammenhang mit dem Erdplaneten und der Sternwelt* (GA 203), eighteen lectures in Dornach, Stuttgart, and The Hague, in 1921.

Page 35, "'a real spark … end to Dornach's pride and joy.'"
On New Year's Eve 1922/23, the Goetheanum was destroyed by fire.

Page 36, "September 8, 1921"
From August 23 to September 7, 1921, a public conference on the theme "Cultural Prospects of the Anthroposophical Movement" took place at the Gustav Siegle House in Stuttgart. Rudolf Steiner presented the lecture cycle *Anthroposophie, ihre Erkenntniswurzeln und Lebensfrüchte* (GA 78), eight lectures in Stuttgart, in 1921. On September 4 approximately 1,200 members of the Anthroposophical Society gathered to confer on the society's premises, tasks, and goals. Steiner, who had been asked to give advice, ended the gathering with a rather long address. Unfortunately, we cannot reprint it in its entirety here but must limit ourselves to reproducing the three principles Steiner presented:

> "My first piece of advice is to ensure that the remnants of theosophical sensibility—by which I mean the sensibility of the Theosophical Society itself, not theosophical contents—are finally eliminated from our society. The second is to develop institutions in our society that by their very nature allow not only ideal trust—which of course we value highly—but also uninterrupted, animated communication to prevail among our members. And my third piece of advice is to acquire the capacity to approach issues with all due seriousness instead of with modern, worldly superficiality." Steiner then referred to Alfred Heidenreich's words and said, "But we must understand these principles in their totality. If we do, we will also be able to develop a feeling for what is approaching our Anthroposophical movement. During this conference a representative of the Youth Movement spoke to us, and a number of students are with us today! To be approached by members of such movements and groups is epoch-making in the history of our movement. We must make it possible to do everything they rightly expect of the Anthroposophical Society." Rudolf Steiner then spoke of the student movement in terms of "a fruitful continuation of our movement into the future."
>
> Young Anthroposophists had asked Rudolf Steiner for a private meeting, which then took place on September 8 in the society's branch building at Landhausstrasse 70.
>
> In the above-mentioned gathering on September 4, 1921, Alfred Heidenreich had said: "With all due humility, as a young person who

has asked to speak, I would like to share some information with you. We Anthroposophists who have come out of the Youth Movement met in a special session during the conference. We realized that we face specific tasks as intermediaries between the Youth Movement and Anthroposophy. We recognized that it is our duty not only to bring Anthroposophy to the Youth Movement but also to devote our youthful forces to appropriate Anthroposophical activity."

Page 36, "at Easter"
See the question-and-answer session of March 20, 1921 (p. 20ff).

Page 37, "an article on the Youth Movement and Anthroposophy"
A short time later, Dr. Alfred Heidenreich, 1898–1969, who also spoke these words of welcome, wrote a little book entitled *Jugendbewegung und Anthroposophie* (The Youth Movement and Anthroposophy), which was published by Der Kommende Tag AG in Stuttgart. The first edition of 5,000 copies was soon sold out. In September 1922, Dr. Heidenreich participated in the founding of the Christian Community and was immediately drafted into its guiding council as a Lenker. He worked first in Frankfurt/Main, moved to England in 1929, and became an Oberlenker in 1938.

Page 37, "history of the Anthroposophical Movement"
See Rudolf Steiner's *The Anthroposophical Movement* (CW 258), eight lectures in Dornach, 1923.

Page 38, "the Criminals' Table"
The "Criminals' Table" was the reserved-table (Stammtisch) of a group of North German and Scandinavian writers and journalists presided over by Otto Erich Hartleben [at the Berlin all-night tavern Der Stramme Hund on Dorotheenstrasse?].

Page 38, "Otto Erich Hartleben"
Otto Erich Hartleben (1864–1905), poet, dramatist, and short-story writer. He was Steiner's collaborator in the *Magazin für Literatur* [Magazine for literature]. For details of their fraught friendship, see also Steiner's *Autobiography* (GA 28) and *Correspondence and Documents*, Vol. 2, Dornach, 1953.

Page 42, "Wandervogel"
The Wandervogel movement: *(literally, Migrating Bird)* was founded in 1901 by a Berlin school teacher and his high school students. Soon imitated by thousands of adolescents and young adults, it was launching a massive fad that would define German culture for the next 40 years. Groups of adolescents and young adults, at first in single-sex groups, later in mixed groups, would go on long hikes through the countryside, living close to nature, assembled around bonfires to sing folk-songs and dance folk dances. Their focus was on their youth, the connection

with the German Romantic movement and a gentle optimism. During World War I, 15,000 members of the movement were drafted and more than 5,000 died. Under the Weimar Republic, the movement became increasingly targeted and fractured by political ideologues; some of its wings were taken over, first by the nationalist movement, and later by the National-Socialist regime, although its essential appeal remained personal and apolitical, often infused by elements of the Lebensreform movement (see below).

Page 43, "(Lebensgestaltung/ Lebensreform)"
At the turn of the nineteenth and twentieth centuries, the German-speaking world saw the growth of a galaxy of alternative social and aesthetic impulses, loosely connected by the concept of *Lebensreform*, ("lifestyle reform"). That concept—which overlapped with a wide range of political ideologies of the Right and Left—covered all aspects of personal and public life. Without necessarily rejecting political solutions, it rested on the assumption that ultimately the health and happiness of the body social would depend on slow, small-scale reforms in personal and public hygiene, sexuality, nutrition, clothing, housing, education, economic forms.... It had many facets, in a variety of permutations, combined in each person's life to ensure maximum health and happiness. Vegetarianism, physical exercise, natural or whole foods, simple and functional dress and house design, exposure to light and fresh air—including nudism, freedom in education, sexual liberation, dreams of communal living, return to the land and closeness to nature etc., all were responses to the stresses of industrialization and urbanization.

Page 46, "Muck-Lamberty"
Friedrich Muck-Lamberty (1891–1984), musician, dancer, wood craftsman and charismatic preacher. Called by some people "the Thuringian Messiah," he saw himself as a John the Baptist figure preparing the ways for the true German Messiah. In the middle of his teaching, he placed Woman, referring to the Catholics' Virgin Mary as much as to the strong Woman of Germanic tradition. In 1920, he started a "soul revolution," wandering through Franconia and Thuringia with a large "army" of young people, many of them young women. Following this "pied piper" from town to town, they would hold folk-song and dance festivals in public spaces, occasionally welcome in churches. On one occasion, 10,000 people were dancing on the mountainside near Regensburg. During the winter of 1920-21, a core of the band took its winter quarters in the medieval castle of Leuchtenburg devoting themselves among other things to the manufacturing of lathe-turned furniture and toys, and one of several experiments with a barter economy. He called for a German revolution, by which he didn't mean a political upheaval, but a spiritual awakening from "the battle of young against old, living men who will be divine men, and proletarians, who are men for hire, utilitarian men."

Accusations of sexual promiscuity led to lawsuits and dispersal of the followers; but Muck-Lamberty remained active with a smaller following. He kept his distance from the National-Socialist movement and vice-versa. He had settled in Naumburg, his very successful toy manufacture becoming a thriving family business.

Page 46, "Häusser"
Ludwig Christian Häusser (1881-1927) the son of a Pietist Wurttemberg farm family, he was one of a number of charismatic vagrant-visionaries (sometimes known as "*Inflationsheilige:* inflation-saints") operating in Germany during the 1920s. High inflation, high unemployment, widespread homelessness and a chaotic political situation provided the environment for their activities. For a period of a few years in the early 1920s, Häusser's "lectures" offering quick solutions to the economic and political problems of Germany attracted many listeners; the artist Fidus and the writer Gertrud Prellwitz joined briefly his floating commune and he gained enough support to consider a career in politics. Always extreme, his rants became increasingly violent, relying on wild blood imagery. When he died in 1927, he had spent several years as a psychiatric patient, and briefly in jail.

Page 47, "Fidus"
Fidus (pseud. for Hugo Höppener) (1868–1948) was a prolific painter, illustrator and editor. He belonged to the same literary and artistic circles as Steiner during the early Berlin years. A friend of Wilhelm Hübbe-Schleiden, founder of the German Theosophical Society, he illustrated the Theosophical journal *Sphinx*. He was a member of the Theosophical Society for a time. Later, he became successively a member of the Friedrichshagen Literary Circle and the Monte Verità Ascona Community and was associated with Häusser, National Socialism, as well as the East German propaganda services. In all these guises, he was the painter of youth, the lush natural world, and naked bodies inhabiting a sun-flooded old Germany.

Page 47, "Gertrud Prellwitz"
Gertrud Prellwitz (1869–1942) was a poet and essayist. Like Fidus, she was a member of the Theosophical Society for a while. She was best known in later years for her children's books. She shared a household and a populist Christianity with Fidus whose child she bore. (That daughter's marriage would later be held in The Christian Community with Rittelmeyer officiating.) Involved for a while with Muck-Lamberty's movement, she later wrote a rueful reflection on the self-delusional nature of that episode.

Page 48, "Neue Schar"
"Neue Schar" is the name of the band wandering under Muck-Lamberty's leadership (see the note for page 46). The word "Schar" is a reference to the "armies or bands" of Anabaptists at the time of Peasant Wars.

Page 49, "Aristotle...middle route...dissoluteness"
See also Rudolf Steiner's lectures on theosophical morality (Norrköping, May

28–30, 1912) in *Christ and the Human Soul* (CW 155), ten lectures given in Norrköping and Copenhagen, 1912–1914.

Page 49, "Stammler"
Rudolf Stammler (1856–1938), German legal scholar.

Page 49, "Gertrud Prellwitz intervened with her new theories"
Gertrud Prellwitz was involved in a polygamous household with Fidus. In 1921 a book was published by Emil Engelhardt under the title of *Muck und Muckertum. Die höhere freie Liebe; Eine Auseinandersetzung mit Gertrud Prellwitz* [Muck and muckerdom. The higher free love. A debate with Gertrud Prellwitz]. The wording suggests that Engelhardt condemns Muck as well as Prellwitz, perhaps in the name of a higher free love. Muck-Lamberty was known for his multiple sexual liaisons with devoted followers, some of whom later brought suit against him, but were dismissed when he argued convincingly that these had been fully consensual relationships.

Page 52, "Wyneken and Lietz"
Gustav Wyneken (1875–1964) was an educational reformer, free thinker and charismatic leader. From 1900 to 1906, he was a collaborator of Herman Lietz in the early "farm-schools." Founder of the Free School Movement (Freie Schulgemeinde) that founded boarding schools across Germany, he coined two influential terms: The first was *pedagogical eros*, the name given to the erotic attraction and/or love between a teacher and a pupil. The concept, based on Plato's image of the erotic relationship as the ideal conduct for pedagogical relationship was embodied and popularized in Wyneken's Wickersdorf Free School Community in Germany; this was blended with high Germanic philosophical ideas. The second term was *Jugendkultur:* wherever possible, adults should refrain from overtly "leading" youth groups, and older youths should instead lead younger youths. Students were called "companions" and teachers "colleagues." The companions lived in "families" each with a mother or father. One source describes a housemother as "combining the qualities of a very refined and knowledgeable 'Grande Dame' with the ethical standards of a youth group leader." He had a deep influence on the Youth Movement. Although in theory Wyneken's pedagogical eros was not intended to be identified with homosexuality, his involvements with two pupils led to his retirement in the late 1920s.

Hermann Lietz (1868–1919) was a progressive pedagogue and founder of the *Landerziehungsheime für Jungen* (Country Education Schools for Boys). A North German farmer's son, he studied theology, history and German linguistics. His interest in the reform of education was nurtured by a stay in England, at the progressive Abbotsholme, a school for boys, which combined comprehensive individual instruction with physical exercise and practical work. This led to the foundation of the first of several private country boarding schools, followed by a similar establishment for orphans. Although he personally believed in segregating the sexes, the country boarding schools soon became coeducational. As described by one of Lietz's collaborators, "The spiritual point of departure was the human and humanist ideal developed by Goethe in *Wilhelm Meister:* Goethe and Fichte were, in Lietz's eyes, the spiritual sources of the pedagogical movement."

Page 53, "Addresses Given in 1923"
The year 1922 is not represented in this volume, though Rudolf Steiner did address a group of students at a gathering on March 10. René Maikowski (See below) wrote to Steiner on March 22, 1922, thanking him for his presentation, but no transcript of that address exists.

René Maikowski (1900–ca. 1991/92) was a Waldorf school teacher.

Page 56, "in our literature"
See the overview of Rudolf Steiner's complete works in the back of this volume.

Page 59, "lectures on the development of modern science"
See Rudolf Steiner's *The Origin of Natural Science* (CW 326), nine lectures, in Dornach, 1922/23.

Page 63, "Address ... in Preparation for the Delegates' Assembly"
The events of the year 1923, especially those brought about by the burning of the Goetheanum, were documented by Marie Steiner in the book *Rudolf Steiner und die Zukunftsaufgaben der Anthroposophie. Ansprachen und Fragenbeantwortungen. Ein Rückblick auf das Jahr 1923* [Rudolf Steiner and the future tasks of Anthroposophy. Talks and answers to questions. A review of the year 1923], Dornach, 1943. The Stuttgart addresses of February 8 and 14 relate to the attempt to restructure the Anthroposophical Society by a newly formed advisory committee for matters concerning the society.

The delegates' assembly took place from February 25 to 28, in Stuttgart. See Rudolf Steiner's two lectures on the delegates' assembly in *Anthroposophical Community Building* (CW 257), ten lectures in Stuttgart and Dornach, 1923.

Page 63, "draft of a circular"
This circular, from the above-mentioned advisory committee, was sent from Stuttgart to the members of the Anthroposophical Society on February 13, 1923.

Page 64, "his last lecture to the Stuttgart Branch"
See the lecture of February 6, 1923, in *Anthroposophical Community Building* (CW 257), ten lectures in Stuttgart and Dornach, in 1923.

Page 65, "Albert Steffen about the Educational Course at the Goetheanum"
Albert Steffen (1884–1963). "Der Lehrerkurs Dr. Rudolf Steiners im Goethanum 1921" [Dr. Rudolf Steiner's course for teacher at the Goetheanum in 1921],

Dornach/Basel, 1922. See also Steiner's *Soul Economy* (CW 303), sixteen lectures, Dornach, 1921/22.

Page 66, "Pan-German nationalist groups"
This is a reference to the violent hostility aroused among German nationalists by the activities in Northern Silesia of the movement for a Threefold Social Organization. According to the Treaty of Versailles the populations of Upper Silesia were to hold a plebiscite in order to determine the future of the province. Although Prussian-ruled Upper Silesia had become part of the German Empire during the unification of Germany in 1871, it had a substantial Polish and Catholic population (up to 60% in some districts, while urban areas tended to be German-speaking). Pan-German nationalists were campaigning for full integration with Germany. Polish nationalists campaigned for return of these areas to Poland. Rudolf Steiner argued that the future of Silesia, and of the Germans of Silesia did not lie in absorption of Silesia by Germany, nor could it lie in complete absorption by Poland. In either case, it would represent a step backward. The goal should be the preservation and cultivation of the original Silesian identity born from the historical meeting of Prussian, Slavic and Austrian cultures each contributing essential elements. During the campaign preceding the plebiscite, Threefold Movement propaganda in that sense had encountered violent reactions. Steiner and Anthroposophists were labeled traitors to the German nation. In the end, the results of the plebiscite were considered inconclusive and Silesia was divided, with Eastern Upper Silesia attributed to Poland, and Western Upper Silesia annexed to Germany.

Page 66, "people like Leisegang"
Hans Leisegang (1890-1951), philosopher and physicist, was a student of Dilthey and Husserl. He was an assistant professor at the University of Leipzig, teaching Pedagogy and Psychology. A noted opponent, in 1922 he published *Grundlagen der Anthroposophie* [Foundations of Anthroposophy] in which he gave a critique of the writings of Rudolf Steiner.

In 1934 he was jailed, then fired, for "slandering national-socialism." Reinstated after 1945, he taught in East Germany, and, after his exile from the DDR, at the Berlin Free University. His other books included *The Gnostic Gods*—still considered a classic on the subject, *The Occult Revelation, Pistis Sophia,* several books on Plato and late Platonism, a biography of Goethe, etc.

Page 67, "the Movement for Religious Renewal"
See Rudolf Steiner's lecture of December 30, 1922, in *Man and the World of the Stars* (CW 219), twelve lectues, Dornach, 1992.

Page 69, "Become geniuses at being interested!"
Reported by Karin Ruths-Hoffman, who was present at the address.

Page 70, "appeal ... issued to the members of the Anthroposophical Society

in Germany"
See the Appendix.

Page 70, "upcoming delegates' assembly"
See note for page 63.

Page 74, "dog skeleton"
See also Lecture of January 3, 1919, in *Der Goetheanismus, ein Umwandlungsimpulse und Auferstehungsgedanke* [Goetheanism, a metamorphosis impulse and resurrection thought] (GA 188), twelve lectures, Dornach, 1919.

Page 76, *"global economy"*
See also Rudolf Steiner's course in *World Economy* (CW 340), fourteen lectures, Dornach, 1922.

Page 77, "modern architecture must be born out of our own experiences"
See Rudolf Steiner's *Architecture as Synthesis of the Arts* (CW 286).

Page 77, "group sculpture in the Goetheanum"
A reference to the wood sculpture of the Representative of Humanity between Lucifer and Ahriman, now located in its own room in the second Goetheanum.

Page 78, "Dr. von Baravalle's or Caroline von Heydebrand's pamphlet"
Both were teachers at the Independent Waldorf School in Stuttgart.

Dr. Hermann von Baravalle: *Zur Pädagogik der Physik und Mathematik* [To the pegagogy of physics and mathematics], Stuttgart, 1921.

Caroline von Heydebrand: *Gegen Experimentalpsychologie und–pädagogik* [Against experimental psychology and pedagogy], Stuttgart, 1921.

Page 79, "Nietzsche gave a vivid and brilliant account"
In his lectures given in Basel in the first few months of 1872 "Über die Zukunft unserer Bildungsanstalten" [On the future of our educational institutions] (published only after Nietzsche's death).

Page 81, "Essays on the Youth Section … of Spiritual Science"
The essays that follow were also published in *Die Konstitution der Allgemeinen Anthroposophischen Gesellschaft und der Freien Hochschule für Geisteswissenschaft. Der Wiederaufbau des Goetheanum 1924–1925* [The constitution of the General Anthroposophical Society and the free high school for spiritual science. The rebuilding of the Goetheanum 1924–1925], (GA 260a).

Page 83, "Announcing a Section for Youth"
This article appeared in the newsletter *"What is happening in the Anthroposophical Society: News for Members,"* which began publication in 1924.

Page 86, "impossibility of knowing ... especially young souls."
In this connection, it is interesting to read Steiner's early articles about the shortcoming of the German philosophy of his time: again and again, he denounced the timidity of mainstream philosophers. Also, see in his autobiography the chapters devoted to his student friends Joseph Koeck, Emil Schoenaich, and especially Rudolf Ronsperger, For the latter, see also Steiner's Memorial published in 1900 in the *Magazin fur Literatur*. Although the image he gives is one of desolate souls gasping for air, and ultimately wasted lives, he accurately points out in 1924 that earlier in the century, there still was a sense of hope about academic careers, provided one could enter them. Koeck and Ronsperger's tragedy was that they had failed in that respect, for reasons that had to do with the class system. Steiner himself remained confident of his prospects in that regard, and did not give up on that avenue until the early 1900s.

Page 104, "the so-called Dark Age"
Kali Yuga, ca. 3101 B.C.E. to 1899 C.E.

Page 105, *"in the first few months of this year"*
See Fred Poeppig's report on page 161ff.

Page 106, Headmaster Bartsch
Moritz Bartsch (1869–1944) was the central figure of the Anthroposophical Movement in Silesia, remembered for his role in the 1920–21 "Threefolding Campaign" and in the Koberwitz Agricultural Course. As Chairman of the Breslau Public Schools Teachers' Association, he was a respected spokesman for a socially responsible teaching profession. An early interest in Indian philosophy and epistemological questions led to his involvement in Anthroposophy. An early supporter of Waldorf Education, he lectured widely on pedagogy. A member of the Executive Council of the German Anthroposophical Society, he also was, in 1923, one of the founders of the "Independent (Free) Anthroposophical Society." He was chair of the Breslau group of the Anthroposophical Society.

In January 1921, he helped organize and run the "Propaganda-Action" for the threefold social structuring of an autonomous Silesia, as an alternative to annexation by Germany or by Poland, the two options offered by the Entente-run plebiscite. This intense campaign in 16 cities of Upper Silesia (more than 300 talks all over Upper Silesia over a year and a half) attracted much attention but ultimately failed due in part to the fierce opposition by German and Polish nationalists, the Communist Party and the Catholic Church, organization of the "propaganda-action" but also in Bartsch's opinion, due to the absence of Polish translations of the relevant literature. While he hoped to remedy this lack, the hasty organization of the "propaganda-action" made it unfeasible.

Page 106, "the Michael Movement"
See *Karmic Relationships, Vol. III* (CW 237) and *The Michael Movement* (See this also in GA 26 in the German).

Page 107, "empty phrases, conventions, and routines … instead of spirit, law, and economics"
See also *Becoming the Archangel Michael's Companion* (CW 217).

Page 111, "You must either enter a modern profession"
See Rudolf Steiner's letter on page 175.

Page 115, Hermann Bahr
Hermann Bahr (1863–1934) was spokesman for the literary group Young Vienna. Bahr was an active member of the Austrian avant-garde, producing both criticism and Impressionist plays. Bahr's critical essays were important in the definition of new literary categories: he was the first critic to apply the label Modernism to literary works, and was an early analyst of the Expressionist movement. The exceptionally ecumenical reach of his literary interests applied to Western European literary streams, as well as to the literatures of the Eastern European realm, formerly part of the Austrian and Prussian Empires. The relationship with Rudolf Steiner was an ambivalent one: as young men, they frequented some of the same circles. Steiner found his writing too "nervous" (the kind of thing that he liked to read lying down and smoking a cigarette) yet respected him sufficiently to hope to recruit him when he took up the editorship of the *Magazin für Literatur* [Magazine for literature].

Page 116, "That is a very individual issue"
See Rudolf Steiner's letter on page 175.

Page 120, "Koberwitz, June 17, 1924"
From June 7 to 16, 1934, Rudolf Steiner held a series of lectures on agriculture at the estate of Count Carl von Keyserlingk. See *Agriculture* (CW 327) and the report on the Agriculture Course in *Die Konsitution der Allgemeinen Anthroposophischen Gesellschat und der Freien Hochschule für Geisteswissenschaft. Der Wiederbau des Goethanum* (GA 260a).

Page 122, "Saturn … Sun and Moon epochs"
See *Outline of Esoteric Science* (CW 13).

Page 122, "Goethe himself cried out"
In an essay entitled "Nature," first published in the *Tiefurter Journal* in 1782. See also Goethe's scientific writings, edited and with commentary by Rudolf Steiner from Kürschner's *Deutsche National Literatur* series, GA 1a-e, especially *Nature's Open Secret* (CW 1).

Page 124, "our good friend Mr. Ritter"
Dr. Walter Ritter (1892–1960) was responsible for the biodynamic agricultural management of the Köfering estate belonging to Count Lerchenfeld.

Page 132, "Arnheim, July 20, 1924"
See Rudolf Steiner's report on the Anthroposophic teacher's conference in Holland in *Die Konsitution der Allgemeinen Anthroposophischen Gesellschat und der Freien Hochschule für Geisteswissenschaft. Der Wiederbau des Goethanum* (GA 260a).

Page 136, "survey to young people"
Rudolf Steiner's first question was: As a young person today, what do you want? The second was: With regard to the development of your career, what do you imagine the world will be like in 1935?

Page 136, "trinity of fixed phrases, conventions, and routines"
See note to page 107.

Page 137, "as the great goal of our century"
In a lecture to members in Arnheim, July 19, 1924, in *Karmic Relationships,* Vol. VI (CW 240).

Page 139, *"Michelet"*
Jules Michelet (1798–1874) was a French Romantic historian, operating in a time when scholars and professors could be and often were inspirational role models for a wide public. His lectures at the College de France were considered dangerous enough to be banned when he refused to take a loyalty oath to the government of Napoleon III. Due to the romantic and visionary qualities of his imagination; his interest in and deep understanding of the interactions between economic, political and cultural realities; the wide span and long distance of his mind's reach; his sense for both the small details of daily personal lives and the large-scale evolution of humanity; the strength and vividness of a style as unmistakably personal as it is universally minded made his *History of the People* and his monumental *Histoire de France* popular bestsellers throughout Europe for several generations; they also ensured his place as an inspiration, for successive generations of professional historians, who didn't necessarily share all his premises or political stance.

Page 153, "responsibility lies with the actual founders."
Steiner's correspondence with Marie Steiner during these years indicates that in fact he played a very active role in these ventures, being frequently consulted in decision-making. He came to feel keenly the burden of it.

Page 154, "L. Kolisko"
Lili Kolisko (1889–1976). Although her research on the potentizing of substances gave her an important role in the foundation of biodynamic agriculture, she also pioneered the study of nutritional rhythms with her work on the spleen and platelets production.

Page 154, "Hermann von Baravalle"
Hermann von Baravalle (1898–1973), mathematician and physicist, was one of the original teachers at the Stuttgart Waldorf School, and teachers' teacher, famous for his ability to pioneer the work of reuniting science and mathematics with the joy of art.

Page 154, "Heydebrand"
Caroline von Heydebrand (1886-1939) was one of the most beloved teachers at the original Waldorf School in Stuttgart, highly respected by Rudolf Steiner. Her classic *Childhood* was the fruit of her long teaching experience. Her monograph on the uses and misuses of experimental psychology was originally written for a teachers' convention, reprinted as an appendix to Margit Jünemann's biography *Der Winter weicht: Caroline von Heydebrand, Pionierin der Waldorfpädagogik* [Winter gives way: Caroline von Heydebrand, pioneer of Waldorf pedagogy].

Page 156, "Professor Drews"
Arthur Drews (1865–1935). In 1922 Drews had published an essay attacking Anthroposophy: "Metaphysik und Anthroposophie in ihrer Stellung zur Erkenntnis des Übersinnlichen" [Metaphysics and Anthroposophy in relation to knowledge of the supersensensible]. Drews was one of the early twentieth century scholars who devoted their career to demonstrating the non-historical character of Jesus. His *Christ Myth* (1909) was based on Eduard Von Hartmann's ideas on the subconscious creation of the concept of divinity. Later volumes examined the lack of reliable contemporary witnesses from outside early Christianity, the origins of Christianity in older Gnostic myths and wisdom Judaism, the inconsistencies of liberal modern theology, Plotinus and Christianity, etc. His work on the Gospel of Mark argued that it reflected an astro-mythical journey along the zodiac. He also published controversial books attacking Nietzsche and Wagner.

Page 162, "chapters of my autobiography"
Autobiography: Chapters in the Course of My Life: 1861–1907 (CW 28) was originally written in weekly installments for *Das Goetheanum*, beginning with the issue of December 9, 1923, and continuing serially for seventy weeks. The last chapter was published in the issue of April 5, 1925, five days after the author's death.

Page 172, "Feuchtersleben"
Feuchtersleben, Ernst 1806–1849, Vienna, was a physician and writer and the founder of psychosomatic medicine as a systematic discipline. He gave articulate expression to the principle that the human being is a psychophysical totality. Straddling the split between physiology and psychology, Feuchtersleben championed the use of psychotherapy with the mentally diseased (a method he called "second education") and simultaneously insisted that psychosis always entailed disturbed physical function. His *Principles of Medical Psychology* (1845) is considered a key book in the history of psychiatry introducing a new standard

and a new methodology, and a number of terms which came to stay. His *Zur Diätetik der Seele* (1838, translated as *Dietetics of the Soul,* 1852), is a masterpiece of psychological popularization and was one of the great bestsellers of its time, going through 50 editions by the end of the century.

RUDOLF STEINER'S COLLECTED WORKS

The German Edition of Rudolf Steiner's Collected Works (the Gesamtausgabe [GA] published by Rudolf Steiner Verlag, Dornach, Switzerland) presently runs to over 354 titles, organized either by type of work (written or spoken), chronology, audience (public or other), or subject (education, art, etc.). For ease of comparison, the Collected Works in English [CW] follows the German organization exactly. A complete listing of the CWs follows with literal translations of the German titles. Other than in the case of the books published in his lifetime, titles were rarely given by Rudolf Steiner himself, and were often provided by the editors of the German editions. The titles in English are not necessarily the same as the German; and, indeed, over the past seventy-five years have frequently been different, with the same book sometimes appearing under different titles.

For ease of identification and to avoid confusion, we suggest that readers looking for a title should do so by CW number. Because the work of creating the Collected Works of Rudolf Steiner is an ongoing process, with new titles being published every year, we have not indicated in this listing which books are presently available. To find out what titles in the Collected Works are currently in print, please check our website at www.steinerbooks.org, or write to SteinerBooks 610 Main Street, Great Barrington, MA 01230:

Written Work

CW 1	Goethe: Natural-Scientific Writings, Introduction, with Footnotes and Explanations in the text by Rudolf Steiner
CW 2	Outlines of an Epistemology of the Goethean World View, with Special Consideration of Schiller
CW 3	Truth and Science
CW 4	The Philosophy of Freedom
CW 4a	Documents to "The Philosophy of Freedom"
CW 5	Friedrich Nietzsche, A Fighter against His Own Time
CW 6	Goethe's Worldview
CW 6a	Now in CW 30
CW 7	Mysticism at the Dawn of Modern Spiritual Life and Its Relationship with Modern Worldviews
CW 8	Christianity as Mystical Fact and the Mysteries of Antiquity
CW 9	Theosophy: An Introduction into Supersensible World Knowledge and Human Purpose
CW 10	How Does One Attain Knowledge of Higher Worlds?
CW 11	From the Akasha-Chronicle
CW 12	Levels of Higher Knowledge

CW 13	Occult Science in Outline
CW 14	Four Mystery Dramas
CW 15	The Spiritual Guidance of the Individual and Humanity
CW 16	A Way to Human Self-Knowledge: Eight Meditations
CW 17	The Threshold of the Spiritual World. Aphoristic Comments
CW 18	The Riddles of Philosophy in Their History, Presented as an Outline
CW 19	Contained in CW 24
CW 20	The Riddles of the Human Being: Articulated and Unarticulated in the Thinking, Views and Opinions of a Series of German and Austrian Personalities
CW 21	The Riddles of the Soul
CW 22	Goethe's Spiritual Nature And Its Revelation In "Faust" and through the "Fairy Tale of the Snake and the Lily"
CW 23	The Central Points of the Social Question in the Necessities of Life in the Present and the Future
CW 24	Essays Concerning the Threefold Division of the Social Organism and the Period 1915-1921
CW 25	Cosmology, Religion and Philosophy
CW 26	Anthroposophical Leading Thoughts
CW 27	Fundamentals for Expansion of the Art of Healing according to Spiritual-Scientific Insights
CW 28	The Course of My Life
CW 29	Collected Essays on Dramaturgy, 1889-1900
CW 30	Methodical Foundations of Anthroposophy: Collected Essays on Philosophy, Natural Science, Aesthetics and Psychology, 1884-1901
CW 31	Collected Essays on Culture and Current Events, 1887-1901
CW 32	Collected Essays on Literature, 1884-1902
CW 33	Biographies and Biographical Sketches, 1894-1905
CW 34	Lucifer-Gnosis: Foundational Essays on Anthroposophy and Reports from the Periodicals "Lucifer" and "Lucifer-Gnosis," 1903-1908
CW 35	Philosophy and Anthroposophy: Collected Essays, 1904-1923
CW 36	The Goetheanum-Idea in the Middle of the Cultural Crisis of the Present: Collected Essays from the Periodical "Das Goetheanum," 1921-1925
CW 37	Now in CWs 260a and 251
CW 38	Letters, Vol. 1: 1881-1890
CW 39	Letters, Vol. 2: 1890-1925
CW 40	Truth-Wrought Words
CW 40a	Sayings, Poems and Mantras; Supplementary Volume
CW 42	Now in CWs 264-266

CW 43	Stage Adaptations
CW 44	On the Four Mystery Dramas. Sketches, Fragments and Paralipomena on the Four Mystery Dramas
CW 45	Anthroposophy: A Fragment from the Year 1910

Public Lectures

CW 51	On Philosophy, History and Literature
CW 52	Spiritual Teachings Concerning the Soul and Observation of the World
CW 53	The Origin and Goal of the Human Being
CW 54	The Riddles of the World and Anthroposophy
CW 55	Knowledge of the Supersensible in Our Times and Its Meaning for Life Today
CW 56	Knowledge of the Soul and of the Spirit
CW 57	Where and How Does One Find the Spirit?
CW 58	The Metamorphoses of the Soul Life. Paths of Soul Experiences: Part One
CW 59	The Metamorphoses of the Soul Life. Paths of Soul Experiences: Part Two
CW 60	The Answers of Spiritual Science to the Biggest Questions of Existence
CW 61	Human History in the Light of Spiritual Research
CW 62	Results of Spiritual Research
CW 63	Spiritual Science as a Treasure for Life
CW 64	Out of Destiny-Burdened Times
CW 65	Out of Central European Spiritual Life
CW 66	Spirit and Matter, Life and Death
CW 67	The Eternal in the Human Soul. Immortality and Freedom
CW 68	Public lectures in various cities, 1906-1918
CW 69	Public lectures in various cities, 1906-1918
CW 70	Public lectures in various cities, 1906-1918
CW 71	Public lectures in various cities, 1906-1918
CW 72	Freedom – Immortality – Social Life
CW 73	The Supplementing of the Modern Sciences through Anthroposophy
CW 73a	Specialized Fields of Knowledge and Anthroposophy
CW 74	The Philosophy of Thomas Aquinas
CW 75	Public lectures in various cities, 1906-1918
CW 76	The Fructifying Effect of Anthroposophy on Specialized Fields
CW 77a	The Task of Anthroposophy in Relation to Science and Life: The Darmstadt College Course
CW 77b	Art and Anthroposophy. The Goetheanum-Impulse

CW 78	Anthroposophy, Its Roots of Knowledge and Fruits for Life
CW 79	The Reality of the Higher Worlds
CW 80	Public lectures in various cities, 1922
CW 81	Renewal-Impulses for Culture and Science–Berlin College Course
CW 82	So that the Human Being Can Become a Complete Human Being
CW 83	Western and Eastern World-Contrast. Paths to Understanding It through Anthroposophy
CW 84	What Did the Goetheanum Intend and What Should Anthroposophy Do?

Lectures to the Members of the Anthroposophical Society

CW 88	Concerning the Astral World and Devachan
CW 89	Consciousness–Life–Form. Fundamental Principles of a Spiritual-Scientific Cosmology
CW 90	Participant Notes from the Lectures during the Years 1903-1905
CW 91	Participant Notes from the Lectures during the Years 1903-1905
CW 92	The Occult Truths of Ancient Myths and Sagas
CW 93	The Temple Legend and the Golden Legend
CW 93a	Fundamentals of Esotericism
CW 94	Cosmogony. Popular Occultism. The Gospel of John. The Theosophy in the Gospel of John
CW 95	At the Gates of Theosophy
CW 96	Origin-Impulses of Spiritual Science. Christian Esotericism in the Light of New Spirit-Knowledge
CW 97	The Christian Mystery
CW 98	Nature Beings and Spirit Beings – Their Effects in Our Visible World
CW 99	The Theosophy of the Rosicrucians
CW 100	Human Development and Christ-Knowledge
CW 101	Myths and Legends. Occult Signs and Symbols
CW 102	The Working into Human Beings by Spiritual Beings
CW 103	The Gospel of John
CW 104	The Apocalypse of John
CW 104a	From the Picture-Script of the Apocalypse of John
CW 105	Universe, Earth, the Human Being: Their Being and Development, as well as Their Reflection in the Connection between Egyptian Mythology and Modern Culture
CW 106	Egyptian Myths and Mysteries in Relation to the Active Spiritual Forces of the Present
CW 107	Spiritual-Scientific Knowledge of the Human Being
CW 108	Answering the Questions of Life and the World through Anthroposophy

CW 109 The Principle of Spiritual Economy in Connection with the Question of Reincarnation. An Aspect of the Spiritual Guidance of Humanity
CW 110 The Spiritual Hierarchies and Their Reflection in the Physical World. Zodiac, Planets and Cosmos
CW 111 Contained in 109
CW 112 The Gospel of John in Relation to the Three Other Gospels, Especially the Gospel of Luke
CW 113 The Orient in the Light of the Occident. The Children of Lucifer and the Brothers of Christ
CW 114 The Gospel of Luke
CW 115 Anthroposophy – Psychosophy – Pneumatosophy
CW 116 The Christ-Impulse and the Development of "I"- Consciousness
CW 117 The Deeper Secrets of the Development of Humanity in Light of the Gospels
CW 118 The Event of the Christ-Appearance in the Etheric World
CW 119 Macrocosm and Microcosm. The Large World and the Small World. Soul-Questions, Life-Questions, Spirit-Questions
CW 120 The Revelation of Karma
CW 121 The Mission of Individual Folk-Souls in Connection with Germanic-Nordic Mythology
CW 122 The Secrets of the Biblical Creation-Story. The Six-Day Work in the First Book of Moses
CW 123 The Gospel of Matthew
CW 124 Excursus in the Area of the Gospel of Mark
CW 125 Paths and Goals of the Spiritual Human Being. Life Questions in the Light of Spiritual Science
CW 126 Occult History. Esoteric Observations of the Karmic Relationships of Personalities and Events of World History
CW 127 The Mission of the New Spiritual Revelation. The Christ-Event as the Middle-Point of Earth Evolution
CW 128 An Occult Physiology
CW 129 Wonders of the World, Trials of the Soul, and Revelations of the Spirit
CW 130 Esoteric Christianity and the Spiritual Guidance of Humanity
CW 131 From Jesus to Christ
CW 132 Evolution from the View Point of the Truth
CW 133 The Earthly and the Cosmic Human Being
CW 134 The World of the Senses and the World of the Spirit
CW 135 Reincarnation and Karma and their Meaning for the Culture of the Present
CW 136 The Spiritual Beings in Celestial Bodies and the Realms of Nature

CW 137	The Human Being in the Light of Occultism, Theosophy and Philosophy
CW 138	On Initiation. On Eternity and the Passing Moment. On the Light of the Spirit and the Darkness of Life
CW 139	The Gospel of Mark
CW 140	Occult Investigation into the Life between Death and New Birth. The Living Interaction between Life and Death
CW 141	Life between Death and New Birth in Relationship to Cosmic Facts
CW 142	The Bhagavad Gita and the Letters of Paul
CW 143	Experiences of the Supersensible. Three Paths of the Soul to Christ
CW 144	The Mysteries of the East and of Christianity
CW 145	What Significance Does Occult Development of the Human Being Have for His Sheaths–Physical Body, Etheric Body, Astral Body, and Self?
CW 146	The Occult Foundations of the Bhagavad Gita
CW 147	The Secrets of the Threshold
CW 148	Out of Research in the Akasha: The Fifth Gospel
CW 149	Christ and the Spiritual World. Concerning the Search for the Holy Grail
CW 150	The World of the Spirit and Its Extension into Physical Existence; The Influence of the Dead in the World of the Living
CW 151	Human Thought and Cosmic Thought
CW 152	Preliminary Stages to the Mystery of Golgotha
CW 153	The Inner Being of the Human Being and Life Between Death and New Birth
CW 154	How does One Gain an Understanding of the Spiritual World? The Flowing in of Spiritual Impulses from out of the World of the Deceased
CW 155	Christ and the Human Soul. Concerning the Meaning of Life. Theosophical Morality. Anthroposophy and Christianity
CW 156	Occult Reading and Occult Hearing
CW 157	Human Destinies and the Destiny of Peoples
CW 157a	The Formation of Destiny and the Life after Death
CW 158	The Connection Between the Human Being and the Elemental World. Kalevala – Olaf Asteson – The Russian People – The World as the Result of the Influences of Equilibrium
CW 159	The Mystery of Death. The Nature and Significance of Middle Europe and the European Folk Spirits
CW 160	In CW 159
CW 161	Paths of Spiritual Knowledge and the Renewal of the Artistic Worldview
CW 162	Questions of Art and Life in Light of Spiritual Science

CW 163 Coincidence, Necessity and Providence. Imaginative Knowledge and the Processes after Death
CW 164 The Value of Thinking for a Knowledge That Satisfies the Human Being. The Relationship of Spiritual Science to Natural Science
CW 165 The Spiritual Unification of Humanity through the Christ-Impulse
CW 166 Necessity and Freedom in the Events of the World and in Human Action
CW 167 The Present and the Past in the Human Spirit
CW 168 The Connection between the Living and the Dead
CW 169 World-being and Selfhood
CW 170 The Riddle of the Human Being. The Spiritual Background of Human History. Cosmic and Human History, Vol. 1
CW 171 Inner Development-Impulses of Humanity. Goethe and the Crisis of the 19th Century. Cosmic and Human History, Vol. 2
CW 172 The Karma of the Vocation of the Human Being in Connection with Goethe's Life. Cosmic and Human History, Vol. 3
CW 173 Contemporary-Historical Considerations: The Karma of Untruthfulness, Part One. Cosmic and Human History, Vol. 4
CW 174 Contemporary-Historical Considerations: The Karma of Untruthfulness, Part Two. Cosmic and Human History, Vol. 5
CW 174a Middle Europe between East and West. Cosmic and Human History, Vol. 6
CW 174b The Spiritual Background of the First World War. Cosmic and Human History, Vol. 7
CW 175 Building Stones for an Understanding of the Mystery of Golgotha. Cosmic and Human Metamorphoses
CW 176 Truths of Evolution of the Individual and Humanity. The Karma of Materialism
CW 177 The Spiritual Background of the Outer World. The Fall of the Spirits of Darkness. Spiritual Beings and Their Effects, Vol. 1
CW 178 Individual Spiritual Beings and their Influence in the Soul of the Human Being. Spiritual Beings and their Effects, Vol. 2
CW 179 Spiritual Beings and Their Effects. Historical Necessity and Freedom. The Influences on Destiny from out of the World of the Dead. Spiritual Beings and Their Effects, Vol. 3
CW 180 Mystery Truths and Christmas Impulses. Ancient Myths and their Meaning. Spiritual Beings and Their Effects, Vol. 4
CW 181 Earthly Death and Cosmic Life. Anthroposophical Gifts for Life. Necessities of Consciousness for the Present and the Future.
CW 182 Death as Transformation of Life
CW 183 The Science of the Development of the Human Being
CW 184 The Polarity of Duration and Development in Human Life. The Cosmic Pre-History of Humanity

CW 185 Historical Symptomology
CW 185a Historical-Developmental Foundations for Forming a Social Judgment
CW 186 The Fundamental Social Demands of Our Time–In Changed Situations
CW 187 How Can Humanity Find the Christ Again? The Threefold Shadow-Existence of our Time and the New Christ-Light
CW 188 Goetheanism, a Transformation-Impulse and Resurrection-Thought. Science of the Human Being and Science of Sociology
CW 189 The Social Question as a Question of Consciousness. The Spiritual Background of the Social Question, Vol. 1
CW 190 Impulses of the Past and the Future in Social Occurrences. The Spiritual Background of the Social Question, Vol. 2
CW 191 Social Understanding from Spiritual-Scientific Cognition. The Spiritual Background of the Social Question, Vol. 3
CW 192 Spiritual-Scientific Treatment of Social and Pedagogical Questions
CW 193 The Inner Aspect of the Social Riddle. Luciferic Past and Ahrimanic Future
CW 194 The Mission of Michael. The Revelation of the Actual Mysteries of the Human Being
CW 195 Cosmic New Year and the New Year Idea
CW 196 Spiritual and Social Transformations in the Development of Humanity
CW 197 Polarities in the Development of Humanity: West and East Materialism and Mysticism Knowledge and Belief
CW 198 Healing Factors for the Social Organism
CW 199 Spiritual Science as Knowledge of the Foundational Impulses of Social Formation
CW 200 The New Spirituality and the Christ-Experience of the 20th Century
CW 201 The Correspondences Between Microcosm and Macrocosm. The Human Being – A Hieroglyph of the Universe. The Human Being in Relationship with the Cosmos: 1
CW 202 The Bridge between the World-Spirituality and the Physical Aspect of the Human Being. The Search for the New Isis, the Divine Sophia. The Human Being in Relationship with the Cosmos: 2
CW 203 The Responsibility of Human Beings for the Development of the World through their Spiritual Connection with the Planet Earth and the World of the Stars. The Human Being in Relationship with the Cosmos: 3
CW 204 Perspectives of the Development of Humanity. The Materialistic Knowledge-Impulse and the Task of Anthroposophy. The Human Being in Relationship with the Cosmos: 4

CW 205 Human Development, World-Soul, and World-Spirit. Part One: The Human Being as a Being of Body and Soul in Relationship to the World. The Human Being in Relationship with the Cosmos: 5

CW 206 Human Development, World-Soul, and World-Spirit. Part Two: The Human Being as a Spiritual Being in the Process of Historical Development. The Human Being in Relationship with the Cosmos: 6

CW 207 Anthroposophy as Cosmosophy. Part One: Characteristic Features of the Human Being in the Earthly and the Cosmic Realms. The Human Being in Relationship with the Cosmos: 7

CW 208 Anthroposophy as Cosmosophy. Part Two: The Forming of the Human Being as the Result of Cosmic Influence. The Human Being in Relationship with the Cosmos: 8

CW 209 Nordic and Central European Spiritual Impulses. The Festival of the Appearance of Christ. The Human Being in Relationship with the Cosmos: 9

CW 210 Old and New Methods of Initiation. Drama and Poetry in the Change of Consciousness in the Modern Age

CW 211 The Sun Mystery and the Mystery of Death and Resurrection. Exoteric and Esoteric Christianity

CW 212 Human Soul Life and Spiritual Striving in Connection with World and Earth Development

CW 213 Human Questions and World Answers

CW 214 The Mystery of the Trinity: The Human Being in Relationship to the Spiritual World in the Course of Time

CW 215 Philosophy, Cosmology, and Religion in Anthroposophy

CW 216 The Fundamental Impulses of the World-Historical Development of Humanity

CW 217 Spiritually Active Forces in the Coexistence of the Older and Younger Generations. Pedagogical Course for Youth

CW 217a Youth's Cognitive Task

CW 218 Spiritual Connections in the Forming of the Human Organism

CW 219 The Relationship of the World of the Stars to the Human Being, and of the Human Being to the World of the Stars. The Spiritual Communion of Humanity

CW 220 Living Knowledge of Nature. Intellectual Fall and Spiritual Redemption

CW 221 Earth-Knowing and Heaven-Insight

CW 222 The Imparting of Impulses to World-Historical Events through Spiritual Powers

CW 223 The Cycle of the Year as Breathing Process of the Earth and the Four Great Festival-Seasons. Anthroposophy and Human Heart (Gemüt)

CW 224	The Human Soul and its Connection with Divine-Spiritual Individualities. The Internalization of the Festivals of the Year
CW 225	Three Perspectives of Anthroposophy. Cultural Phenomena observed from a Spiritual-Scientific Perspective
CW 226	Human Being, Human Destiny, and World Development
CW 227	Initiation-Knowledge
CW 228	Science of Initiation and Knowledge of the Stars. The Human Being in the Past, the Present, and the Future from the Viewpoint of the Development of Consciousness
CW 229	The Experiencing of the Course of the Year in Four Cosmic Imaginations
CW 230	The Human Being as Harmony of the Creative, Building, and Formative World-Word
CW 231	The Supersensible Human Being, Understood Anthroposophically
CW 232	The Forming of the Mysteries
CW 233	World History Illuminated by Anthroposophy and as the Foundation for Knowledge of the Human Spirit
CW 233a	Mystery Sites of the Middle Ages: Rosicrucianism and the Modern Initiation-Principle. The Festival of Easter as Part of the History of the Mysteries of Humanity
CW 234	Anthroposophy. A Summary after 21 Years
CW 235	Esoteric Observations of Karmic Relationships in 6 Volumes, Vol. 1
CW 236	Esoteric Observations of Karmic Relationships in 6 Volumes, Vol. 2
CW 237	Esoteric Observations of Karmic Relationships in 6 Volumes, Vol. 3: The Karmic Relationships of the Anthroposophical Movement
CW 238	Esoteric Observations of Karmic Relationships in 6 Volumes, Vol. 4: The Spiritual Life of the Present in Relationship to the Anthroposophical Movement
CW 239	Esoteric Observations of Karmic Relationships in 6 Volumes, Vol. 5
CW 240	Esoteric Observations of Karmic Relationships in 6 Volumes, Vol. 6
CW 243	The Consciousness of the Initiate
CW 245	Instructions for an Esoteric Schooling
CW 250	The Building-Up of the Anthroposophical Society. From the Beginning to the Outbreak of the First World War
CW 251	The History of the Goetheanum Building-Association
CW 252	Life in the Anthroposophical Society from the First World War to the Burning of the First Goetheanum
CW 253	The Problems of Living Together in the Anthroposophical Society. On the Dornach Crisis of 1915. With Highlights on Swedenborg's Clairvoyance, the Views of Freudian Psychoanalysts, and the Concept of Love in Relation to Mysticism

CW 254 The Occult Movement in the 19th Century and Its Relationship to World Culture. Significant Points from the Exoteric Cultural Life around the Middle of the 19th Century
CW 255 Rudolf Steiner during the First World War
CW 255a Anthroposophy and the Reformation of Society. On the History of the Threefold Movement
CW 255b Anthroposophy and Its Opponents, 1919-1921
CW 256 How Can the Anthroposophical Movement Be Financed?
CW 256a Futurum, Inc. / International Laboratories, Inc.
CW 256b The Coming Day, Inc.
CW 257 Anthroposophical Community-Building
CW 258 The History of and Conditions for the Anthroposophical Movement in Relationship to the Anthroposophical Society. A Stimulus to Self-Contemplation
CW 259 The Year of Destiny 1923 in the History of the Anthroposophical Society. From the Burning of the Goetheanum to the Christmas Conference
CW 260 The Christmas Conference for the Founding of the General Anthroposophical Society
CW 260a The Constitution of the General Anthroposophical Society and the School for Spiritual Science. The Rebuilding of the Goetheanum
CW 261 Our Dead. Addresses, Words of Remembrance, and Meditative Verses, 1906-1924
CW 262 Rudolf Steiner and Marie Steiner-von Sivers: Correspondence and Documents, 1901-1925
CW 263/1 Rudolf Steiner and Edith Maryon: Correspondence: Letters, Verses, Sketches, 1912-1924
CW 264 On the History and the Contents of the First Section of the Esoteric School from 1904 to 1914. Letters, Newsletters, Documents, Lectures
CW 265 On the History and Out of the Contents of the Ritual-Knowledge Section of the Esoteric School from 1904 to 1914. Documents, and Lectures from the Years 1906 to 1914, as well as on New Approaches to Ritual-Knowledge Work in the Years 1921-1924
CW 266/1 From the Contents of the Esoteric Lessons. Volume 1: 1904-1909. Notes from Memory of Participants. Meditation texts from the notes of Rudolf Steiner
CW 266/2 From the Contents of the Esoteric Lessons. Volume 2: 1910-1912. Notes from Memory of Participants
CW 266/3 From the Contents of the Esoteric Lessons. Volume 3: 1913, 1914 and 1920-1923. Notes from Memory of Participants. Meditation texts from the notes of Rudolf Steiner

CW 267 Soul-Exercises: Vol. 1: Exercises with Word and Image Meditations for the Methodological Development of Higher Powers of Knowledge, 1904-1924
CW 268 Soul-Exercises: Vol. 2: Mantric Verses, 1903-1925
CW 269 Ritual Texts for the Celebration of the Free Christian Religious Instruction. The Collected Verses for Teachers and Students of the Waldorf School
CW 270 Esoteric Instructions for the First Class of the School for Spiritual Science at the Goetheanum 1924, 4 Volumes
CW 271 Art and Knowledge of Art. Foundations of a New Aesthetic
CW 272 Spiritual-Scientific Commentary on Goethe's "Faust" in Two Volumes. Vol. 1: Faust, the Striving Human Being
CW 273 Spiritual-Scientific Commentary on Goethe's "Faust" in Two Volumes. Vol. 2: The Faust-Problem
CW 274 Addresses for the Christmas Plays from the Old Folk Traditions
CW 275 Art in the Light of Mystery-Wisdom
CW 276 The Artistic in Its Mission in the World. The Genius of Language. The World of the Self-Revealing Radiant Appearances – Anthroposophy and Art. Anthroposophy and Poetry
CW 277 Eurythmy. The Revelation of the Speaking Soul
CW 277a The Origin and Development of Eurythmy
CW 278 Eurythmy as Visible Song
CW 279 Eurythmy as Visible Speech
CW 280 The Method and Nature of Speech Formation
CW 281 The Art of Recitation and Declamation
CW 282 Speech Formation and Dramatic Art
CW 283 The Nature of Things Musical and the Experience of Tone in the Human Being
CW284/285 Images of Occult Seals and Pillars. The Munich Congress of Whitsun 1907 and Its Consequences
CW 286 Paths to a New Style of Architecture. "And the Building Becomes Human"
CW 287 The Building at Dornach as a Symbol of Historical Becoming and an Artistic Transformation Impulse
CW 288 Style-Forms in the Living Organic
CW 289 The Building-Idea of the Goetheanum: Lectures with Slides from the Years 1920-1921
CW 290 The Building-Idea of the Goetheanum: Lectures with Slides from the Years 1920-1921
CW 291 The Nature of Colors
CW 291a Knowledge of Colors. Supplementary Volume to "The Nature of Colors"
CW 292 Art History as Image of Inner Spiritual Impulses

CW 293	General Knowledge of the Human Being as the Foundation of Pedagogy
CW 294	The Art of Education, Methodology and Didactics
CW 295	The Art of Education: Seminar Discussions and Lectures on Lesson Planning
CW 296	The Question of Education as a Social Question
CW 297	The Idea and Practice of the Waldorf School
CW 297a	Education for Life: Self-Education and the Practice of Pedagogy
CW 298	Rudolf Steiner in the Waldorf School
CW 299	Spiritual-Scientific Observations on Speech
CW 300a	Conferences with the Teachers of the Free Waldorf School in Stuttgart, 1919 to 1924, in 3 Volumes, Vol. 1
CW 300b	Conferences with the Teachers of the Free Waldorf School in Stuttgart, 1919 to 1924, in 3 Volumes, Vol. 2
CW 300c	Conferences with the Teachers of the Free Waldorf School in Stuttgart, 1919 to 1924, in 3 Volumes, Vol. 3
CW 301	The Renewal of the Pedagogical-Didactical Art through Spiritual Science
CW 302	Knowledge of the Human Being and the Forming of Class Lessons
CW 302a	Education and Teaching out of a Knowledge of the Human Being
CW 303	The Healthy Development of the Human Being
CW 304	Methods of Education and Teaching Based on Anthroposophy
CW 304a	Anthroposophical Knowledge of the Human Being and Pedagogy
CW 305	The Soul-Spiritual Foundational Forces of the Art of Education. Spiritual Values in Education and Social Life
CW 306	Pedagogical Praxis from the Viewpoint of a Spiritual-Scientific Knowledge of the Human Being. The Education of the Child and Young Human Beings
CW 307	The Spiritual Life of the Present and Education
CW 308	The Method of Teaching and the Life-Requirements for Teaching
CW 309	Anthroposophical Pedagogy and Its Prerequisites
CW 310	The Pedagogical Value of a Knowledge of the Human Being and the Cultural Value of Pedagogy
CW 311	The Art of Education Out of an Understanding of the Being of Humanity
CW 312	Spiritual Science and Medicine
CW 313	Spiritual-Scientific Viewpoints on Therapy
CW 314	Physiology and Therapy Based on Spiritual Science
CW 315	Curative Eurythmy
CW 316	Meditative Observations and Instructions for a Deepening of the Art of Healing
CW 317	The Curative Education Course
CW 318	The Working Together of Doctors and Pastors

CW 319 Anthroposophical Knowledge of the Human Being and Medicine
CW 320 Spiritual-Scientific Impulses for the Development of Physics 1: The First Natural-Scientific Course: Light, Color, Tone, Mass, Electricity, Magnetism
CW 321 Spiritual-Scientific Impulses for the Development of Physics 2: The Second Natural-Scientific Course: Warmth at the Border of Positive and Negative Materiality
CW 322 The Borders of the Knowledge of Nature
CW 323 The Relationship of the various Natural-Scientific Fields to Astronomy
CW 324 Nature Observation, Mathematics, and Scientific Experimentation and Results from the Viewpoint of Anthroposophy
CW 324a The Fourth Dimension in Mathematics and Reality
CW 325 Natural Science and the World-Historical Development of Humanity since Ancient Times
CW 326 The Moment of the Coming Into Being of Natural Science in World History and Its Development Since Then
CW 327 Spiritual-Scientific Foundations for Success in Farming. The Agricultural Course
CW 328 The Social Question
CW 329 The Liberation of the Human Being as the Foundation for a New Social Form
CW 330 The Renewal of the Social Organism
CW 331 Work-Council and Socialization
CW 332 The Alliance for Threefolding and the Total Reform of Society. The Council on Culture and the Liberation of the Spiritual Life
CW 332a The Social Future
CW 333 Freedom of Thought and Social Forces
CW 334 From the Unified State to the Threefold Social Organism
CW 335 The Crisis of the Present and the Path to Healthy Thinking
CW 336 The Great Questions of the Times and Anthroposophical Spiritual Knowledge
CW 337a Social Ideas, Social Reality, Social Practice, Vol. 1: Question-and- Answer Evenings and Study Evenings of the Alliance for the Threefold Social Organism in Stuttgart, 1919-1920
CW 337b Social Ideas, Social Realities, Social Practice, Vol. 2: Discussion Evenings of the Swiss Alliance for the Threefold Social Organism
CW 338 How Does One Work on Behalf of the Impulse for the Threefold Social Organism?
CW 339 Anthroposophy, Threefold Social Organism, and the Art of Public Speaking
CW 340 The National-Economics Course. The Tasks of a New Science of Economics, Volume 1

CW 341	The National-Economics Seminar. The Tasks of a New Science of Economics, Volume 2
CW 342	Lectures and Courses on Christian Religious Work, Vol. 1: Anthroposophical Foundations for a Renewed Christian Religious Working
CW 343	Lectures and Courses on Christian Religious Work, Vol. 2: Spiritual Knowledge – Religious Feeling – Cultic Doing
CW 344	Lectures and Courses on Christian Religious Work, Vol. 3: Lectures at the Founding of the Christian Community
CW 345	Lectures and Courses on Christian Religious Work, Vol. 4: Concerning the Nature of the Working Word
CW 346	Lectures and Courses on Christian Religious Work, Vol. 5: The Apocalypse and the Working of the Priest
CW 347	The Knowledge of the Nature of the Human Being According to Body, Soul and Spirit. On Earlier Conditions of the Earth
CW 348	On Health and Illness. Foundations of a Spiritual-Scientific Doctrine of the Senses
CW 349	On the Life of Human Being and of the Earth. On the Nature of Christianity
CW 350	Rhythms in the Cosmos and in the Human Being. How Does One Come To See the Spiritual World?
CW 351	The Human Being and the World. The Influence of the Spirit in Nature. On the Nature of Bees
CW 352	Nature and the Human Being Observed Spiritual-Scientifically
CW 353	The History of Humanity and the World-Views of the Folk Cultures
CW 354	The Creation of the World and the Human Being. Life on Earth and the Influence of the Stars

SIGNIFICANT EVENTS IN THE LIFE OF RUDOLF STEINER

1829: June 23: birth of Johann Steiner (1829-1910)—Rudolf Steiner's father—in Geras, Lower Austria.

1834: May 8: birth of Franciska Blie (1834-1918)—Rudolf Steiner's mother—in Horn, Lower Austria. "My father and mother were both children of the glorious Lower Austrian forest district north of the Danube."

1860: May 16: marriage of Johann Steiner and Franciska Blie.

1861: February 25: birth of *Rudolf Joseph Lorenz Steiner* in Kraljevec, Croatia, near the border with Hungary, where Johann Steiner works as a telegrapher for the South Austria Railroad. Rudolf Steiner is baptized two days later, February 27, the date usually given as his birthday.

1862: Summer: the family moves to Mödling, Lower Austria.

1863: The family moves to Pottschach, Lower Austria, near the Styrian border, where Johann Steiner becomes stationmaster. "The view stretched to the mountains...majestic peaks in the distance and the sweet charm of nature in the immediate surroundings."

1864: November 15: birth of Rudolf Steiner's sister, Leopoldine (d. November 1, 1927). She will become a seamstress and live with her parents for the rest of her life.

1866: July 28: birth of Rudolf Steiner's deaf-mute brother, Gustav (d. May 1, 1941).

1867: Rudolf Steiner enters the village school. Following a disagreement between his father and the schoolmaster, whose wife falsely accused the boy of causing a commotion, Rudolf Steiner is taken out of school and taught at home.

1868: A critical experience. Unknown to the family, an aunt dies in a distant town. Sitting in the station waiting room, Rudolf Steiner sees her "form," which speaks to him, asking for help. "Beginning with this experience, a new soul life began in the boy, one in which not only the outer trees and mountains spoke to him, but also the worlds that lay behind them. From this moment on, the boy began to live with the spirits of nature...."

1869: The family moves to the peaceful, rural village of Neudorfl, near Wiener-Neustadt in present-day Hungary. Rudolf Steiner attends the village school. Because of the "unorthodoxy" of his writing and spelling, he has to do "extra lessons."

1870: Through a book lent to him by his tutor, he discovers geometry: "To grasp something purely in the spirit brought me inner happiness. I know that I first learned happiness through geometry." The same tutor allows him to draw, while other students still struggle with their reading and writing. "An artistic element" thus enters his education.

1871: Though his parents are not religious, Rudolf Steiner becomes a "church child," a favorite of the priest, who was "an exceptional character." "Up to the age of ten or eleven, among those I came to know, he was far and away the most significant." Among other things, he introduces Steiner to Copernican, heliocentric cosmology. As an altar boy, Rudolf Steiner serves at Masses, funerals, and Corpus Christi processions. At year's end, after an incident in which he escapes a thrashing, his father forbids him to go to church.

1872: Rudolf Steiner transfers to grammar school in Wiener-Neustadt, a five-mile walk from home, which must be done in all weathers.

1873-75: Through his teachers and on his own, Rudolf Steiner has many wonderful experiences with science and mathematics. Outside school, he teaches himself analytic geometry, trigonometry, differential equations, and calculus.

1876: Rudolf Steiner begins tutoring other students. He learns bookbinding from his father. He also teaches himself stenography.

1877: Rudolf Steiner discovers Kant's *Critique of Pure Reason*, which he reads and rereads. He also discovers and reads von Rotteck's *World History*.

1878: He studies extensively in contemporary psychology and philosophy.

1879: Rudolf Steiner graduates from high school with honors. His father is transferred to Inzersdorf, near Vienna. He uses his first visit to Vienna "to purchase a great number of philosophy books"— Kant, Fichte, Schelling, and Hegel, as well as numerous histories of philosophy. His aim: to find a path from the "I" to nature.

October 1879-1883: Rudolf Steiner attends the Technical College in Vienna—to study mathematics, chemistry, physics, mineralogy, botany, zoology, biology, geology, and mechanics—with a scholarship. He also attends lectures in history and literature, while avidly reading philosophy on his own. His two favorite professors are Karl Julius Schröer (German language and literature) and Edmund Reitlinger (physics). He also audits lectures by Robert Zimmerman on aesthetics and Franz Brentano on philosophy. During this year he begins his friendship with Moritz Zitter (1861-1921), who will help support him financially when he is in Berlin.

1880: Rudolf Steiner attends lectures on Schiller and Goethe by Karl Julius Schröer, who becomes his mentor. Also "through a remarkable combination of circumstances," he meets Felix Koguzki, an "herb gatherer" and healer, who could "see deeply into the secrets of nature." Rudolf Steiner will meet and study with this "emissary of the Master" throughout his time in Vienna.

1881: January: "... I didn't sleep a wink. I was busy with philosophical problems until about 12:30 a.m. Then, finally, I threw myself down on my couch. All my striving during the previous year had been to research whether the following statement by Schelling was true or not: *Within everyone dwells a secret, marvelous capacity to draw back from the stream of time—out of the self clothed in all that comes to us from outside—into our innermost being and there, in the immutable form of the Eternal, to look into ourselves.* I believe, and I am still quite certain of it, that I discovered this capacity in myself; I had long had an inkling of it. Now the whole of idealist philosophy stood before me in modified form. What's a sleepless night compared to that!"

Rudolf Steiner begins communicating with leading thinkers of the day, who send him books in return, which he reads eagerly.

July: "I am not one of those who dives into the day like an animal in human form. I pursue a quite specific goal, an idealistic aim—knowledge of the truth! This cannot be done offhandedly. It requires the greatest striving in the world, free of all egotism, and equally of all resignation."

August: Steiner puts down on paper for the first time thoughts for a "Philosophy of Freedom." "The striving for the absolute: this human yearning is freedom." He also seeks to outline a "peasant philosophy," describing what the worldview of a "peasant"—one who lives close to the earth and the old ways—really is.

1881-1882: Felix Koguzki, the herb gatherer, reveals himself to be the envoy of another, higher initiatory personality, who instructs Rudolf Steiner to penetrate Fichte's philosophy and to master modern scientific thinking as a preparation for right entry into the spirit. This "Master" also teaches him the double (evolutionary and involutionary) nature of time.

1882: Through the offices of Karl Julius Schröer, Rudolf Steiner is asked by Joseph Kurschner to edit Goethe's scientific works for the *Deutschen National-Literatur* edition. He writes "A Possible Critique of Atomistic Concepts" and sends it to Friedrich Theodore Vischer.

1883: Rudolf Steiner completes his college studies and begins work on the Goethe project.

1884: First volume of Goethe's *Scientific Writings* (CW 1) appears (March). He lectures on Goethe and Lessing, and Goethe's approach to science. In July, he enters the household of Ladislaus and Pauline Specht as tutor to the four Specht boys. He will live there until 1890. At this time, he meets Josef Breuer (1842-1925), the coauthor with Sigmund Freud of *Studies in Hysteria*, who is the Specht family doctor.

1885: While continuing to edit Goethe's writings, Rudolf Steiner reads deeply in contemporary philosophy (Edouard von Hartmann, Johannes Volkelt, and Richard Wahle, among others).

1886: May: Rudolf Steiner sends Kurschner the manuscript of *Outlines of Goethe's Theory of Knowledge* (CW 2), which appears in October, and which he sends out widely. He also meets the poet Marie Eugenie Delle Grazie and writes "Nature and Our Ideals" for her. He attends her salon, where he meets many priests, theologians, and philosophers, who will become his friends. Meanwhile, the director of the Goethe Archive in Weimar requests his collaboration with the *Sophien* edition of Goethe's works, particularly the writings on color.

1887: At the beginning of the year, Rudolf Steiner is very sick. As the year progresses and his health improves, he becomes increasingly "a man of letters," lecturing, writing essays, and taking part in Austrian cultural life. In August-September, the second volume of Goethe's *Scientific Writings* appears.

1888: January-July: Rudolf Steiner assumes editorship of the "German Weekly" (*Deutsche Wochenschrift*). He begins lecturing more intensively, giving, for example, a lecture titled "Goethe as Father of a New Aesthetics." He meets and becomes soul friends with Friedrich Eckstein (1861-1939), a vegetarian, philosopher of symbolism, alchemist, and musician, who will introduce him to various spiritual currents (including Theosophy) and with whom he will meditate and interpret esoteric and alchemical texts.

1889: Rudolf Steiner first reads Nietzsche (*Beyond Good and Evil*). He encounters Theosophy again and learns of Madame Blavatsky in the Theosophical circle around Marie Lang (1858-1934). Here he also meets well-known figures of Austrian life, as well as esoteric figures like the occultist Franz Hartman and Karl Leinigen-Billigen (translator of C.G. Harrison's *The Transcendental Universe*.) During this period, Steiner first reads A.P. Sinnett's *Esoteric Buddhism* and Mabel Collins's *Light on the Path*. He also begins traveling, visiting Budapest, Weimar, and Berlin (where he meets philosopher Edouard von Hartman).

1890: Rudolf Steiner finishes volume 3 of Goethe's scientific writings. He begins his doctoral dissertation, which will become *Truth and Science* (CW 3). He also meets the poet and feminist Rosa Mayreder (1858-1938), with whom he can exchange his most intimate thoughts. In September, Rudolf Steiner moves to Weimar to work in the Goethe-Schiller Archive.

1891: Volume 3 of the Kurschner edition of Goethe appears. Meanwhile, Rudolf Steiner edits Goethe's studies in mineralogy and scientific writings for the *Sophien* edition. He meets Ludwig Laistner of the Cotta Publishing Company, who asks for a book on the basic question of metaphysics. From this will result, ultimately, *The Philosophy of Freedom* (CW 4), which will be published not by Cotta but by Emil Felber. In October, Rudolf Steiner takes the oral exam for a doctorate in philosophy, mathematics, and mechanics at Rostock University, receiving his doctorate on the twenty-sixth. In November, he gives his first lecture on Goethe's "Fairy Tale" in Vienna.

1892: Rudolf Steiner continues work at the Goethe-Schiller Archive and on his *Philosophy of Freedom*. *Truth and Science*, his doctoral dissertation, is published. Steiner undertakes to write introductions to books on Schopenhauer and Jean Paul for Cotta. At year's end, he finds lodging with Anna Eunike, née Schulz (1853-1911), a widow with four daughters and a son. He also develops a friendship with Otto Erich Hartleben (1864-1905) with whom he shares literary interests.

1893: Rudolf Steiner begins his habit of producing many reviews and articles. In March, he gives a lecture titled "Hypnotism, with Reference to Spiritism." In September, volume 4 of the Kurschner edition is completed. In November, *The Philosophy of Freedom* appears. This year, too, he meets John Henry Mackay (1864-1933), the anarchist, and Max Stirner, a scholar and biographer.

1894: Rudolf Steiner meets Elisabeth Förster Nietzsche, the philosopher's sister, and begins to read Nietzsche in earnest, beginning with the as yet unpublished *Antichrist*. He also meets Ernst Haeckel (1834-1919). In the fall, he begins to write *Nietzsche, A Fighter against His Time* (CW 5).

1895: May, *Nietzsche, A Fighter against His Time* appears.

1896: January 22: Rudolf Steiner sees Friedrich Nietzsche for the first and only time. Moves between the Nietzsche and the Goethe-Schiller Archives, where he completes his work before year's end. He falls out with Elisabeth Förster Nietzsche, thus ending his association with the Nietzsche Archive.

1897: Rudolf Steiner finishes the manuscript of *Goethe's Worldview* (CW 6). He moves to Berlin with Anna Eunike and begins editorship of the *Magazin fur Literatur*. From now on, Steiner will write countless reviews, literary and philosophical articles, and so on. He begins lecturing at the "Free Literary Society." In September, he attends the Zionist Congress in Basel. He sides with Dreyfus in the Dreyfus affair.

1898: Rudolf Steiner is very active as an editor in the political, artistic, and theatrical life of Berlin. He becomes friendly with John Henry Mackay and poet Ludwig Jacobowski (1868-1900). He joins Jacobowski's circle of writers, artists, and scientists—"The Coming Ones" (*Die Kommenden*)—and contributes lectures to the group until 1903. He also lectures at the "League for College Pedagogy." He writes an article for Goethe's sesquicentennial, "Goethe's Secret Revelation," on the "Fairy Tale of the Green Snake and the Beautiful Lily."

1888-89: "This was a trying time for my soul as I looked at Christianity. . . . I was able to progress only by contemplating, by means of spiritual perception, the evolution of Christianity . . . . Conscious knowledge of real Christianity began to dawn in me around the turn of the century. This seed continued to develop. My soul trial occurred shortly before the beginning of the twentieth century. It was decisive for my soul's development that I stood spiritually before the Mystery of Golgotha in a deep and solemn celebration of knowledge."

1899: Rudolf Steiner begins teaching and giving lectures and lecture cycles at the Workers' College, founded by Wilhelm Liebknecht (1826-1900). He will continue to do so until 1904. Writes: *Literature and Spiritual Life in the Nineteenth Century; Individualism in Philosophy*; *Haeckel and His Opponents; Poetry in the Present;* and begins what will become (fifteen years later). *The Riddles of Philosophy* (CW 18). He also meets many artists and writers, including Käthe Kollwitz, Stefan

Zweig, and Rainer Maria Rilke. On October 31, he marries Anna Eunike.

1900: "I thought that the turn of the century must bring humanity a new light. It seemed to me that the separation of human thinking and willing from the spirit had peaked. A turn or reversal of direction in human evolution seemed to me a necessity." Rudolf Steiner finishes *World and Life Views in the Nineteenth Century* (the second part of what will become *The Riddles of Philosophy*) and dedicates it to Ernst Haeckel. It is published in March. He continues lecturing at *Die Kommenden*, whose leadership he assumes after the death of Jacobowski. Also, he gives the Gutenberg Jubilee lecture before 7,000 typesetters and printers. In September, Rudolf Steiner is invited by Count and Countess Brockdorff to lecture in the Theosophical Library. His first lecture is on Nietzsche. His second lecture is titled "Goethe's Secret Revelation." October 6, he begins a lecture cycle on the mystics that will become *Mystics after Modernism* (CW 7). November-December: "Marie von Sivers appears in the audience...." Also in November, Steiner gives his first lecture at the Giordano Bruno Bund (where he will continue to lecture until May, 1905). He speaks on Bruno and modern Rome, focusing on the importance of the philosophy of Thomas Aquinas as monism.

1901: In continual financial straits, Rudolf Steiner's early friends Moritz Zitter and Rosa Mayreder help support him. In October, he begins the lecture cycle *Christianity as Mystical Fact* (CW 8) at the Theosophical Library. In November, he gives his first "Theosophical lecture" on Goethe's "Fairy Tale" in Hamburg at the invitation of Wilhelm Hubbe-Schleiden. He also attends a tea to celebrate the founding of the Theosophical Society at Count and Countess Brockdorff's. He gives a lecture cycle, "From Buddha to Christ," for the circle of the *Kommenden*. November 17, Marie von Sivers asks Rudolf Steiner if Theosophy does not need a Western-Christian spiritual movement (to complement Theosophy's Eastern emphasis). "The question was posed. Now, following spiritual laws, I could begin to give an answer...." In December, Rudolf Steiner writes his first article for a Theosophical publication. At year's end, the Brockdorffs and possibly Wilhelm Hubbe-Schleiden ask Rudolf Steiner to join the Theosophical Society and undertake the leadership of the German section. Rudolf Steiner agrees, on the condition that Marie von Sivers (then in Italy) work with him.

1902: Beginning in January, Rudolf Steiner attends the opening of the Workers' School in Spandau with Rosa Luxemberg (1870-1919). January 17, Rudolf Steiner joins the Theosophical Society. In April, he is asked to become general secretary of the German Section of the Theosophical Society, and works on preparations for its founding. In July, he visits London for a Theosophical congress. He meets Bertram

Keightly, G.R.S. Mead, A.P. Sinnett, and Annie Besant, among others. In September, *Christianity as Mystical Fact* appears. In October, Rudolf Steiner gives his first public lecture on Theosophy ("Monism and Theosophy") to about three hundred people at the Giordano Bruno Bund. On October 19-21, the German Section of the Theosophical Society has its first meeting; Rudolf Steiner is the general secretary, and Annie Besant attends. Steiner lectures on practical karma studies. On October 23, Annie Besant inducts Rudolf Steiner into the Esoteric School of the Theosophical Society. On October 25, Steiner begins a weekly series of lectures: "The Field of Theosophy." During this year, Rudolf Steiner also first meets Ita Wegman (1876-1943), who will become his close collaborator in his final years.

1903: Rudolf Steiner holds about 300 lectures and seminars. In May, the first issue of the periodical *Luzifer* appears. In June, Rudolf Steiner visits London for the first meeting of the Federation of the European Sections of the Theosophical Society, where he meets Colonel Olcott. He begins to write *Theosophy* (CW 9).

1904: Rudolf Steiner continues lecturing at the Workers' College and elsewhere (about 90 lectures), while lecturing intensively all over Germany among Theosophists (about a 140 lectures). In February, he meets Carl Unger (1878-1929), who will become a member of the board of the Anthroposophical Society (1913). In March, he meets Michael Bauer (1871-1929), a Christian mystic, who will also be on the board. In May, *Theosophy* appears, with the dedication: "To the spirit of Giordano Bruno." Rudolf Steiner and Marie von Sivers visit London for meetings with Annie Besant. June: Rudolf Steiner and Marie von Sivers attend the meeting of the Federation of European Sections of the Theosophical Society in Amsterdam. In July, Steiner begins the articles in *Luzifer-Gnosis* that will become *How to Know Higher Worlds* (CW 10) and *Cosmic Memory* (CW 11). In September, Annie Besant visits Germany. In December, Steiner lectures on Freemasonry. He mentions the High Grade Masonry derived from John Yarker and represented by Theodore Reuss and Karl Kellner as a blank slate "into which a good image could be placed."

1905: This year, Steiner ends his non-Theosophical lecturing activity. Supported by Marie von Sivers, his Theosophical lecturing—both in public and in the Theosophical Society—increases significantly: "The German Theosophical Movement is of exceptional importance." Steiner recommends reading, among others, Fichte, Jacob Boehme, and Angelus Silesius. He begins to introduce Christian themes into Theosophy. He also begins to work with doctors (Felix Peipers and Ludwig Noll). In July, he is in London for the Federation of European Sections, where he attends a lecture by Annie Besant: "I have seldom seen Mrs. Besant speak in so inward and heartfelt a manner...." "Through Mrs. Besant I have found the way to H.P. Blavatsky."

September to October, he gives a course of thirty-one lectures for a small group of esoteric students. In October, the annual meeting of the German Section of the Theosophical Society, which still remains very small, takes place. Rudolf Steiner reports membership has risen from 121 to 377 members. In November, seeking to establish esoteric "continuity," Rudolf Steiner and Marie von Sivers participate in a "Memphis-Misraim" Masonic ceremony. They pay forty-five marks for membership. "Yesterday, you saw how little remains of former esoteric institutions." "We are dealing only with a 'framework'... for the present, nothing lies behind it. The occult powers have completely withdrawn."

1906: Expansion of Theosophical work. Rudolf Steiner gives about 245 lectures, only 44 of which take place in Berlin. Cycles are given in Paris, Leipzig, Stuttgart, and Munich. Esoteric work also intensifies. Rudolf Steiner begins writing *An Outline of Esoteric Science* (CW 13). In January, Rudolf Steiner receives permission (a patent) from the Great Orient of the Scottish A & A Thirty-Three Degree Rite of the Order of the Ancient Freemasons of the Memphis-Misraim Rite to direct a chapter under the name "Mystica Aeterna." This will become the "Cognitive Cultic Section" (also called "Misraim Service") of the Esoteric School. (See: *From the History and Contents of the Cognitive Cultic Section* (CW 264). During this time, Steiner also meets Albert Schweitzer. In May, he is in Paris, where he visits Edouard Schuré. Many Russians attend his lectures (including Konstantin Balmont, Dimitri Mereszkovski, Zinaida Hippius, and Maximilian Woloshin). He attends the General Meeting of the European Federation of the Theosophical Society, at which Col. Olcott is present for the last time. He spends the year's end in Venice and Rome, where he writes and works on his translation of H.P. Blavatsky's *Key to Theosophy*.

1907: Further expansion of the German Theosophical Movement according to the Rosicrucian directive to "introduce spirit into the world"—in education, in social questions, in art, and in science. In February, Col. Olcott dies in Adyar. Before he dies, Olcott indicates that "the Masters" wish Annie Besant to succeed him: much politicking ensues. Rudolf Steiner supports Besant's candidacy. April-May: preparations for the Congress of the Federation of European Sections of the Theosophical Society—the great, watershed Whitsun "Munich Congress," attended by Annie Besant and others. Steiner decides to separate Eastern and Western (Christian-Rosicrucian) esoteric schools. He takes his esoteric school out of the Theosophical Society (Besant and Rudolf Steiner are "in harmony" on this). Steiner makes his first lecture tours to Austria and Hungary. That summer, he is in Italy. In September, he visits Edouard Schuré, who will write the introduction to the French edition of *Christianity as Mystical Fact* in Barr, Alsace. Rudolf Steiner writes the autobiographical statement known as the "Barr Document." In *Luzifer–Gnosis*, "The Education of the Child" appears.

1908: The movement grows (membership: 1150). Lecturing expands. Steiner makes his first extended lecture tour to Holland and Scandinavia, as well as visits to Naples and Sicily. Themes: St. John's Gospel, the Apocalypse, Egypt, science, philosophy, and logic. *Luzifer-Gnosis* ceases publication. In Berlin, Marie von Sivers (with Johanna Mücke (1864-1949) forms the *Philosophisch-Theosophisch* (after 1915 *Philosophisch-Anthroposophisch*) *Verlag* to publish Steiner's work. Steiner gives lecture cycles titled *The Gospel of St. John* (CW 103) and *The Apocalypse* (104).

1909: *An Outline of Esoteric Science* appears. Lecturing and travel continues. Rudolf Steiner's spiritual research expands to include the polarity of Lucifer and Ahriman; the work of great individualities in history; the Maitreya Buddha and the Bodhisattvas; spiritual economy (CW 109); the work of the spiritual hierarchies in heaven and on Earth (CW 110). He also deepens and intensifies his research into the Gospels, giving lectures on the Gospel of St. Luke (CW 114) with the first mention of two Jesus children. Meets and becomes friends with Christian Morgenstern (1871-1914). In April, he lays the foundation stone for the Malsch model—the building that will lead to the first Goetheanum. In May, the International Congress of the Federation of European Sections of the Theosophical Society takes place in Budapest. Rudolf Steiner receives the Subba Row medal for *How to Know Higher Worlds*. During this time, Charles W. Leadbeater discovers Jiddu Krishnamurti (1895-1986) and proclaims him the future "world teacher," the bearer of the Maitreya Buddha and the "reappearing Christ." In October, Steiner delivers seminal lectures on "anthroposophy," which he will try, unsuccessfully, to rework over the next years into the unfinished work, *Anthroposophy (A Fragment)* (CW 45).

1910: New themes: *The Reappearance of Christ in the Etheric* (CW 118); *The Fifth Gospel; The Mission of Folk Souls* (CW 121); *Occult History* (CW 126); the evolving development of etheric cognitive capacities. Rudolf Steiner continues his Gospel research with *The Gospel of St. Matthew* (CW 123). In January, his father dies. In April, he takes a month-long trip to Italy, including Rome, Monte Cassino, and Sicily. He also visits Scandinavia again. July-August, he writes the first mystery drama, *The Portal of Initiation* (CW 14). In November, he gives "psychosophy" lectures. In December, he submits "On the Psychological Foundations and Epistemological Framework of Theosophy" to the International Philosophical Congress in Bologna.

1911: The crisis in the Theosophical Society deepens. In January, "The Order of the Rising Sun," which will soon become "The Order of the Star in the East," is founded for the coming world teacher, Krishnamurti. At the same time, Marie von Sivers, Rudolf Steiner's coworker, falls ill. Fewer lectures are given, but important new ground is broken. In Prague, in March, Steiner meets Franz Kafka (1883-1924) and Hugo Bergmann (1883-1975). In April, he delivers his paper to the

Philosophical Congress. He writes the second mystery drama, *The Soul's Probation* (CW 14). Also, while Marie von Sivers is convalescing, Rudolf Steiner begins work on *Calendar 1912/1913*, which will contain the "Calendar of the Soul" meditations. On March 19, Anna (Eunike) Steiner dies. In September, Rudolf Steiner visits Einsiedeln, birthplace of Paracelsus. In December, Friedrich Rittelmeyer, future founder of the Christian Community, meets Rudolf Steiner. The *Johannes-Bauverein*, the "building committee," which would lead to the first Goetheanum (first planned for Munich), is also founded, and a preliminary committee for the founding of an independent association is created that, in the following year, will become the Anthroposophical Society. Important lecture cycles include *Occult Physiology* (CW 128); *Wonders of the World* (CW 129); *From Jesus to Christ* (CW 131). Other themes: esoteric Christianity; Christian Rosenkreutz; the spiritual guidance of humanity; the sense world and the world of the spirit.

1912: Despite the ongoing, now increasing crisis in the Theosophical Society, much is accomplished: *Calendar 1912/1913* is published; eurythmy is created; both the third mystery drama, *The Guardian of the Threshold* (CW 14) and *A Way of Self-Knowledge* (CW 16) are written. New (or renewed) themes included life between death and rebirth and karma and reincarnation. Other lecture cycles: *Spiritual Beings in the Heavenly Bodies and the Kingdoms of Nature* (CW 136); *The Human Being in the Light of Occultism, Theosophy, and Philosophy* (CW 137); *The Gospel of St. Mark* (CW 139); and *The Bhagavad Gita and the Epistles of Paul* (CW 142). On May 8, Rudolf Steiner celebrates White Lotus Day, H.P. Blavatsky's death day, which he had faithfully observed for the past decade, for the last time. In August, Rudolf Steiner suggests the "independent association" be called the "Anthroposophical Society." In September, the first eurythmy course takes place. In October, Rudolf Steiner declines recognition of a Theosophical Society lodge dedicated to the Star of the East and decides to expel all Theosophical Society members belonging to the order. Also, with Marie von Sivers, he first visits Dornach, near Basel, Switzerland, and they stand on the hill where the Goetheanum will be. In November, a Theosophical Society lodge is opened by direct mandate from Adyar (Annie Besant). In December, a meeting of the German section occurs at which it is decided that belonging to the Order of the Star of the East is incompatible with membership in the Theosophical Society. December 28: informal founding of the Anthroposophical Society in Berlin.

1913: Expulsion of the German section from the Theosophical Society. February 2-3: Foundation meeting of the Anthroposophical Society. Board members include: Marie von Sivers, Michael Bauer, and Carl Unger. September 20: Laying of the foundation stone for the *Johannes Bau* (Goetheanum) in Dornach. Building begins immediately. The third mystery drama, *The Soul's Awakening* (CW 14), is completed.

Also: *The Threshold of the Spiritual World* (CW 147). Lecture cycles include: *The Bhagavad Gita and the Epistles of Paul* and *The Esoteric Meaning of the Bhagavad Gita* (CW 146), which the Russian philosopher Nikolai Berdyaev attends; *The Mysteries of the East and of Christianity* (CW 144); *The Effects of Esoteric Development* (CW 145); and *The Fifth Gospel* (CW 148). In May, Rudolf Steiner is in London and Paris, where anthroposophical work continues.

1914: Building continues on the *Johannes Bau* (Goetheanum) in Dornach, with artists and coworkers from seventeen nations. The general assembly of the Anthroposophical Society takes place. In May, Rudolf Steiner visits Paris, as well as Chartres Cathedral. June 28: assassination in Sarajevo ("Now the catastrophe has happened!"). August 1: War is declared. Rudolf Steiner returns to Germany from Dornach—he will travel back and forth. He writes the last chapter of *The Riddles of Philosophy.* Lecture cycles include: *Human and Cosmic Thought* (CW 151); *Inner Being of Humanity between Death and a New Birth* (CW 153); *Occult Reading and Occult Hearing* (CW 156). December 24: marriage of Rudolf Steiner and Marie von Sivers.

1915: Building continues. Life after death becomes a major theme, also art. Writes: *Thoughts during a Time of War* (CW 24). Lectures include: *The Secret of Death* (CW 159); *The Uniting of Humanity through the Christ Impulse* (CW 165).

1916: Rudolf Steiner begins work with Edith Maryon (1872-1924) on the sculpture "The Representative of Humanity" ("The Group"—Christ, Lucifer, and Ahriman). He also works with the alchemist Alexander von Bernus on the quarterly *Das Reich.* He writes *The Riddle of Humanity* (CW 20). Lectures include: *Necessity and Freedom in World History and Human Action* (CW 166); *Past and Present in the Human Spirit* (CW 167); *The Karma of Vocation* (CW 172); *The Karma of Untruthfulness* (CW 173).

1917: Russian Revolution. The U.S. enters the war. Building continues. Rudolf Steiner delineates the idea of the "threefold nature of the human being" (in a public lecture March 15) and the "threefold nature of the social organism" (hammered out in May-June with the help of Otto von Lerchenfeld and Ludwig Polzer-Hoditz in the form of two documents titled *Memoranda*, which were distributed in high places). August-September: Rudolf Steiner writes *The Riddles of the Soul* (CW 20). Also: commentary on "The Chemical Wedding of Christian Rosenkreutz" for Alexander Bernus (*Das Reich*). Lectures include: *The Karma of Materialism* (CW 176); *The Spiritual Background of the Outer World: The Fall of the Spirits of Darkness* (CW 177).

1918: March 18: peace treaty of Brest-Litovsk—"Now everything will truly enter chaos! What is needed is cultural renewal." June: Rudolf Steiner visits Karlstein (Grail) Castle outside Prague. Lecture cycle: *From Symptom to Reality in Modern History* (CW 185). In mid-November,

Emil Molt, of the Waldorf-Astoria Cigarette Company, has the idea of founding a school for his workers' children.

1919: Focus on the threefold social organism: tireless travel, countless lectures, meetings, and publications. At the same time, a new public stage of Anthroposophy emerges as cultural renewal begins. The coming years will see initiatives in pedagogy, medicine, pharmacology, and agriculture. January 27: threefold meeting: " We must first of all, with the money we have, found free schools that can bring people what they need." February: first public eurythmy performance in Zurich. Also: "Appeal to the German People" (CW 24), circulated March 6 as a newspaper insert. In April, *Toward Social Renewal* (CW 23)—"perhaps the most widely read of all books on politics appearing since the war"—appears. Rudolf Steiner is asked to undertake the "direction and leadership" of the school founded by the Waldorf-Astoria Company. Rudolf Steiner begins to talk about the "renewal" of education. May 30: a building is selected and purchased for the future Waldorf School. August-September, Rudolf Steiner gives a lecture course for Waldorf teachers, *The Foundations of Human Experience (Study of Man)* (CW 293). September 7: Opening of the first Waldorf School. December (into January): first science course, the *Light Course* (CW 320).

1920: The Waldorf School flourishes. New threefold initiatives. Founding of limited companies *Der Kommenden Tag* and *Futurum A.G.* to infuse spiritual values into the economic realm. Rudolf Steiner also focuses on the sciences. Lectures: *Introducing Anthroposophical Medicine* (CW 312); *The Warmth Course* (CW 321); *The Boundaries of Natural Science* (CW 322); *The Redemption of Thinking* (CW 74). February: Johannes Werner Klein—later a cofounder of the Christian Community—asks Rudolf Steiner about the possibility of a "religious renewal," a "Johannine church." In March, Rudolf Steiner gives the first course for doctors and medical students. In April, a divinity student asks Rudolf Steiner a second time about the possibility of religious renewal. September 27-October 16: anthroposophical "university course." December: lectures titled *The Search for the New Isis* (CW 202).

1921: Rudolf Steiner continues his intensive work on cultural renewal, including the uphill battle for the threefold social order. "University" arts, scientific, theological, and medical courses include: *The Astronomy Course* (CW 323); *Observation, Mathematics, and Scientific Experiment* (CW 324); the *Second Medical Course* (CW 313); *Color*. In June and September-October, Rudolf Steiner also gives the first two "priests' courses" (CW 342 and 343). The "youth movement" gains momentum. Magazines are founded: *Die Drei* (January), and—under the editorship of Albert Steffen (1884-1963)—the weekly, *Das Goetheanum* (August). In February-March, Rudolf Steiner takes his first trip outside Germany since the war (Holland). On April 7, Steiner receives a letter regarding "religious renewal," and May 22-23, he agrees to address the question in a practical way. In June, the Klinical-Therapeutic Institute opens in Arlesheim under the direction of Dr. Ita Wegman. In August, the Chemical-Pharmaceutical Laboratory opens in Arlesheim (Oskar Schmiedel and Ita Wegman, directors). The Clinical Therapeutic Institute is inaugurated in Stuttgart (Dr. Ludwig Noll, director); also the Research Laboratory in Dornach (Ehrenfried Pfeiffer and Gunther Wachsmuth, directors). In November-December, Rudolf Steiner visits Norway.

1922: The first half of the year involves very active public lecturing (thousands attend); in the second half, Rudolf Steiner begins to withdraw and turn toward the Society—"The Society is asleep." It is "too weak" to do what is asked of it. The businesses—*Die Kommenden Tag* and *Futura A.G.*—fail. In January, with the help of an agent, Steiner undertakes a twelve-city German tour, accompanied by eurythmy performances. In two weeks he speaks to more than 2,000 people. In April, he gives a "university course" in The Hague. He also visits England. In June, he is in Vienna for the East-West Congress. In August-September, he is back in England for the Oxford Conference on Education. Returning to Dornach, he gives the lectures *Philosophy, Cosmology, and Religion* (CW 215), and gives the third priest's course (CW 344). On September 16, The Christian Community is founded. In October-November, Steiner is in Holland and England. He also speaks to the youth: *The Youth Course* (CW 217). In December, Steiner gives lectures titled *The Origins of Natural Science* (CW 326), and *Humanity and the World of Stars: The Spiritual Communion of Humanity* (CW 219). December 31: Fire at the Goetheanum, which is destroyed.

1923: Despite the fire, Rudolf Steiner continues his work unabated. A very hard year. Internal dispersion, dissension, and apathy abound. There is conflict—between old and new visions—within the society. A wake-up call is needed, and Rudolf Steiner responds with renewed lecturing vitality. His focus: the spiritual context of human life; initiation science; the course of the year; and community building. As a foundation for an artistic school, he creates a series of pastel sketches. Lecture cycles: *The Anthroposophical Movement; Initiation Science* (CW 227) (in England at the Penmaenmawr Summer School); *The Four Seasons and the Archangels* (CW 229); *Harmony of the Creative Word* (CW 230); *The Supersensible Human* (CW 231), given in Holland for the founding of the Dutch society. On November 10, in response to the failed Hitler-Ludendorf putsch in Munich, Steiner closes his Berlin residence and moves the *Philosophisch-Anthroposophisch Verlag* (Press) to Dornach. On December 9, Steiner begins the serialization of his *Autobiography: The Course of My Life* (CW 28) in *Das Goetheanum*. It will continue to appear weekly, without a break, until his death. Late December-early January: Rudolf Steiner refounds the Anthroposophical Society (about 12,000 members internationally) and takes over its leadership. The new board members are: Marie Steiner, Ita Wegman, Albert Steffen, Elizabeth Vreede, and Guenther Wachsmuth. (See *The Christmas Meeting for the Founding of the General Anthroposophical Society* (CW 260). Accompanying lectures: *Mystery Knowledge and Mystery Centers* (CW 232); *World History in the Light of Anthroposophy* (CW 233). December 25: the Foundation Stone is laid (in the hearts of members) in the form of the "Foundation Stone Meditation."

1924: January 1: having founded the Anthroposophical Society and taken over its leadership, Rudolf Steiner has the task of "reforming" it. The process begins with a weekly newssheet ("What's Happening in the Anthroposophical Society") in which Rudolf Steiner's "Letters to Members" and "Anthroposophical Leading Thoughts" appear (CW 26). The next step is the creation of a new esoteric class, the "first class" of the "University of Spiritual Science" (which was to have been followed, had Rudolf Steiner lived longer, by two more advanced classes). Then comes a new language for Anthroposophy—practical, phenomenological, and direct; and Rudolf Steiner creates the model for the second Goetheanum. He begins the series of extensive "karma" lectures (CW 235-40); and finally, responding to needs, he creates two new initiatives: biodynamic agriculture and curative education. After the middle of the year, rumors begin to circulate regarding Steiner's health. Lectures: January-February, *Anthroposophy* (CW 234); February: *Tone Eurythmy* (CW 278); June: *The Agriculture Course* (CW 327); June-July: Speech [?] Eurythmy (CW 279); *Curative Education* (CW 317); August: (England, "Second International Summer School"), *Initiation Consciousness: True and False Paths in Spiritual Investigation* (CW 243); September: *Pastoral Medicine* (CW 318). On September 26, for the first time, Rudolf Steiner cancels a lecture. On September 28, he gives his last lecture. On September 29, he withdraws to his studio in the carpenter's shop; now he is definitively ill. Cared for by Ita Wegman, he continues working, however, and writing the weekly installments of his *Autobiography* and *Letters to the Members/Leading Thoughts* (CW 26).

1925: Rudolf Steiner, while continuing to work, continues to weaken. He finishes *Extending Practical Medicine* (CW 27) with Ita Wegman.
On March 30, around ten in the morning, Rudolf Steiner dies.

INDEX